ROOMS WITHOUT
DOORS

ROOMS WITHOUT
DOORS

A HISTORICAL GLIMPSE
INTO THE FAMILY OF
ELIZABETH BARRETT BROWNING

RON
BONNICK

Rev. date: 08/27/2015

To order additional copies of this book, contact:
Xlibris
1-888-795-4274
www.Xlibris.com
Orders@Xlibris.com
695780

Contents

DEDICATION

This book is dedicated to my grandfather Peter Bonnick of Round Hill and Stanmore districts in the parish of St. Elizabeth. He is the first one to give me insight into the great Barrett family, and he is one of the funniest storytellers of his time, 1875–1960.

INTRODUCTION

It was not very long after my children arrived in the United States that the book *Roots*, written by Alex Haley went on the market. A movie was made called *Roots*, and I watched every chapter of it, and when it was concluded, I said to myself, "How can I do the same thing with my ancestors?" Sometime after this, two of my children came home from school and said that their homework involved the tracing of their ancestral lineage to the farthest point. This set off my intellectual machine into forward drive. I knew all my ancestors back to the fourth generation, but with their requests, I wanted to go much further. I knew that my great-grandmother's maiden name was Barrett, and I always like to read poems by Elizabeth Barrett Browning, so I went to my library and looked her up but did not get anywhere, so I told them of all my great-grandparents down to them from four different angles. This satisfied the school for the homework assignment, but it did not satisfy my ego. The following week, I went to Strand Book Store on Broadway, in New York City, where my friend Mr. Bass was quite helpful. He sent me to an aged collection of books, and after one hour's search, I found a book that contained the diary of Elizabeth Barrett Browning for the years 1830–31. I paid for it, and went back to work at the bank where I worked for many years. Before I left that bank I made sure to look at certain dates and occurrences, and bingo, I came to December 1831 during the slave rebellion in Jamaica under the leadership of Samuel Sharpe, now one of Jamaica's national heroes. When I read that her father's estate was not destroyed, I almost went ballistic. I did not know that her father was a Jamaican, born on the hillside overlooking the city of Montego Bay in the parish of St. James. My grandfather always said to me that all the Barrett family are one, and that most of them lived in St. James and Trelawny parishes. Those in St. Elizabeth always go to visit the other families all over the island because they always like to keep in touch from the days of slavery down to the present time. Putting everything in perspective, it was an eye-opener to me.

What was so important in Elizabeth's diary, was the fact that her father had estates in several parishes such as St. James, Trelawny, and Westmoreland but his major estate was in the parish of Cambridge. There is no parish named Cambridge at present in the island of Jamaica, and so it has been for over 140 years. This author had to rock his memory back to sixty-two years when he was in the second grade at Newcombe Valley Elementary School. The teacher was giving a history lesson on the Morant Bay Rebellion, which took place in the parish of St. Thomas in 1865. Her name was Ina Wilson, the wife of a Methodist pastor, who was also manager of the school, and in 1943, when she gave the lecture, the school was still housed in the church building. She said that the rebellion took place twenty-seven years after slavery was abolished in Jamaica, and the poor people petitioned the governor, Sir John Eyre, for land. The white folks had all the arable land in Jamaica, and the freed slaves had none. They were supported in the House of Assembly by one George William Gordon who requested land for the poor people. A preacher named Paul Bogle took up the call for St. Thomas parish, while Gordon took it up islandwide. Gordon was the mulatto son of a Scottish planter and a black woman, and Bogle was the son of slaves.

When the rebellion broke out, Bogle headed the group, and they marched on the courthouse in Morant Bay asking for land to cultivate. Riot broke out, and some white people were killed by stones and machetes. The governor called out the militia and sent them in battle against some stone-throwing Negroes with machetes. He also summoned a British battleship in the port of Kingston to go to Morant Bay, and at the same time, he court-martialed Gordon and had him arrested. The trial was short, and without any evidence, he was found guilty and hanged within minutes after the fraudulent trial onboard the battleship. At the same time, the battleship turned its cannons on the people in Morant Bay at the instructions of the governor, and hundreds of black people, including women and children, were killed. The German custos of the parish was also killed by the rioters, and it is stated that eighteen white people were also killed. The name of the custos was Baron Von Kettleholdt.

The report of the killings angered Queen Victoria so much that she recalled the governor in disgrace and stripped him of his titles. Since most of the people who died were poor black people, and she knew that she was descended from the black Moorish King John of Portugal, which caused her to be very sympathetic to black people. She also welcomed the Emancipation Bill passed in the House of Commons in 1834 to free all black slaves throughout the British Empire. In the place of Sir John Eyre, that notorious barbarian bastard, she sent Sir John Peter Grant to replace him.

It was the work of Sir John Peter Grant, who came to Jamaica in 1866 as governor, that explains why there is no parish of Cambridge in Jamaica. I am now quoting as far as can be remembered from Ina Wilson about Sir John Peter Grant. She said, "Sir John Peter Grant came to Jamaica in 1866, succeeding Sir John Eyre, who was recalled by Queen Victoria because of his actions during the Morant Bay rebellion in 1865. His best known works were: he extended the railway lines from Spanish Town to Old Harbor, and he reduced the twenty-two parishes to fourteen."

This is the statement the author remembered that made him give up on finding a parish of Cambridge. It is now understood that Cambridge parish was located in and around the place in St. James called Cambridge, where a railway station exists. When Elizabeth made it aware that her father owned estates in Jamaica, a new impetus was given to the author to locate the ancient Barrett family and to expose who they were. The questions now were who are the Barretts? Where did they originate? And how did they get to Jamaica?

After going through several books and documents at the College of Arms, located at Queen Victoria Street in London, and the island record office in Spanish Town, Jamaica, it was discovered that the family of Barrett was descended from the Vikings who marauded and plundered the west of Europe southward from Norway and Denmark. Most of them came from Norway. Some were picked up in Denmark and Holland and they were in part buccaneers who did not return to their homelands. They wanted warmer climates to settle down, so they went to England and France, and there they settled for a while. In the year 911, King Francis of France signed a treaty with the Vikings, giving them land called "Land of the Northmen" if they would not attack the capital of France. The Vikings agreed not to attack Paris, so they remained in France from that time onward. Some one hundred years after, that part of France became known as Normandy. From these amalgam of Vikings, the name "Barrett" appeared in a high position with William, Duke of Normandy, who became King of England in 1066, after the Battle of Hastings, when King Harold was defeated.

Just prior to this battle it is said that William boasted in the following quote, "I am William, Duke of Normandy, grandnephew of Emma. The crown of England is mine. I demand it. I will take it by force. I have at my command sixty thousand men, a vast flotilla of boats nearby; the blessing of the pope is given me, I shall make my land flourish along the English coast. So help me God." With this boast, he was showing that he was related to Queen Emma of England who died and did not leave an heir to the throne. It seemed that a grandnephew was too far off to claim the throne, but William had other ideas.

When he attacked Britain with his forces, there was among them, a man by the name Ensign Barrett. The author tried to find the meaning of the word *ensign* and all he could come up with was a person of the rank of second lieutenant. However, further study showed that this was the first name by which he went. No matter which is right, the name was Ensign Barrett, and he was the first Barrett to live on English soil. He must have been very important to William, as after the battle and William the Conqueror was crowned King of England he gave to Ensign Barrett as a dowry the county of Cornwall. No one knew then where the boundaries of Cornwall were but Ensign Barrett settled at a place called Tregarne in Cornwall, and most of the modern Barretts traced their ancestry back to this place and to this man, even though no one heard of another famous Barrett until 1649. Nearly six hundred years had elapsed before anyone heard anything of another significant Barrett. Maybe the whole family for all those centuries was nothing more than inconsequential farmers who did nothing of note.

When the English Civil War broke out in the seventeenth century, and the parliament and King Charles I were at war against each other, there emerged a great leader of the parliament named Oliver Cromwell who was bent on overthrowing the monarchy. Some historians said it was to prevent King Charles from reestablishing Catholic rule in England, which was overthrown by Henry VIII and his daughter Elizabeth I. Some say it was the House of Commons who wanted supremacy over the king but this author says it was both of these reasons. Based upon the evidence, proven and otherwise, it could clearly be seen that the civil war was caused by these two foremost reasons, and several other insignificant ones.

Cromwell established what came to be called his "Red Coat" army, and Hersey Barrett Sr. became a lieutenant in this army. This is where Barrett importance became pronounced. When the war ended in 1649, with the capture of King Charles, a court martial was set up to try the king for treason. The significant names in this court martial for the island of Jamaica were Bradshaw (chairman), Blagrove, Wayte, and Harrison. These families came to Jamaica in 1655 with the expedition of Adm. William Penn (the father of William Penn, the founder of Pennsylvania) and General Robert Venables. They were fleeing England because they thought that Prince Charles, who was under the protective custody of King Philip of Spain, would one day return to England as king. They were right. In 1660, the restoration of the monarchy took place and Prince Charles was crowned as King Charles II.

Now when the court martial found the king guilty of treason, he was sentenced to death, but no one was brave enough to execute him. This is where fame or infamy came to the Barrett family. Lt. Hersey Barrett came forward and he wielded the axe that separated King Charles' head from his body. From that time onward, all the court martial judges and Hersey Barrett were called *regicides*. This is the term used for killing the king, and some who took part fled the country, most of them to Jamaica, West Indies.

Most of the Barretts settled in the city of Port Royal, but Hersey Senior settled in Spanish Town. He lost a large portion of his family when the great earthquake struck in 1692, but this did not deter him from his main objective of becoming rich from the land. After his stay in Spanish Town, he left behind his name on a street that still bears his name in 2007. He went to the parish of St. Ann, where he established properties in the vicinity of Moneague Lake and named the property Albion, which at the time of writing was still owned by a Barrett. Albion is located near the small town of Alderton. He went on to the place that was to become St. James parish, and also acquired land there. Trelawny did not come into existence until his great-grandson told the governor where to set its border when it was cut from the parishes of St. Ann and St. James in 1773. Hersey also had land in Vere called Withywood Paradise Estate, and a large portion of what is now Monymusk were properties owned by the Barretts. The reason why Hersey Senior is so involved here is because he was the ancestor of the people who were later to become involved in the house that had two rooms without doors.

Now, Hersey had two sons. One named Hersey Junior, and the other was Samuel. Samuel, the second son, was the one favored by this father because he had the pioneering spirit just like his father. Hersey Junior was like a playboy, and did not see the importance of running from property to property. When he saw his father showing much more favor to Samuel, he changed his name from Barrett to Barritt. This last name continued until 1819 when all the family with that name changed it back to Barrett. As I will now say, the Barrett family was a close-knit one, and what hurts one hurts the other, but when they are fighting among themselves, strangers should keep out. There were many legal fights among the Barretts, at least one of which will be borne out in this book. While Samuel went to Withywood, Hersey remained in Spanish Town. Their father Hersey Senior was now dead and had left most of his properties to Samuel, who married Margery Green of Vere parish and had a son named Samuel Junior.

The Port Royal earthquake of 1692 devastated the island, but the Barretts in Withywood, Vere, were not affected personally except in the loss of their family. Many Barretts went under with the earthquake, and up to the present moment Port Royal has not recovered and will not recover because more than two-thirds of the city went under the sea. There are many fantastic stories about this earthquake, which are not appropriate for this book, but the economic and military consequences would be felt in the years afterward.

The French, upon hearing that the richest British city had been destroyed by the earthquake of 1692, began preparing an invasion force under Admiral DuCasse, who was stationed somewhere on the island of St. Dominique (Santo Domingo). In 1694, he invaded Jamaica from his fleet anchored off Rocky Point. Samuel Barrett Sr. was captain of the horse guard in Vere, so he took up the challenge and went into battle. He was ambushed by the French and was killed in battle, leaving Samuel Junior to take over the plantation in Withywood at the age of nineteen years. The French were subsequently defeated, but Samuel decided to pack up and head north. He would later become the father of the northside Barretts from whom most of the famous Barretts were descended. He settled in the parish of St. James and established his famous house at Cinnamon Hill, some three miles beyond Rose Hall Great House. His great house was started in 1722 and was completed in 1734, and later on, his son Edward did extensive expansion and repairs, and it was in one of these expansions where two rooms without doors are located, the reason for which will be explained in an appropriate chapter. Many famous people occupied this house when the last Barrett, John Charles Moulton-Barrett, sold it to get his brother Septimus out of debtor's jail for money he owed to the tavern keepers. He drank himself into poverty just as some of his family are doing today. Young Samuel married Elizabeth Wisdom when she was fourteen years old. She had fifteen children (no twins) and died at age thirty but she would produce a son named Edward who was the progenitor of famous Barretts. He became so rich and so famous that when Jamaica was being cut into three counties he and his father saw to it that one was named Cornwall after the county in England from whence the Barretts came. When the name Edward Barrett of Cinnamon Hill was called, the governors of Jamaica always listened.

Edward Barrett was the son of Samuel Junior, who survived the French invasion of 1694. Of all those fifteen children his mother had, he emerged as the real estate kingpin of the family. As the eighth child, when his father died in 1760, he had acquired much more than his father under conditions similar to the robber barons of the United States. No one on the island of Jamaica had more slaves than he had (as a future chapter will show), and he did everything to remain on top. He was a great builder, and sometime in the 1760s there were two great hurricanes that took the roof of the great house twice. He feared for his family, so he built a hurricane shelter, which they called "Cutwind," to protect his family should another hurricane remove the roof of his house again. He also built another mansion connected to the older one for his extended family.

In relation to his many slaves, he did something to the slaves that put the white slave masters in shock. He promoted a slave to that of overseer or *busha* on the largest of his properties, put him on a horse to ride with a modern saddle to oversee work done on that property. He gave him his own name, Edward Barrett, and white people thought that Edward Barrett of Cinnamon Hill was going crazy. The result at the end of each year proved that, that was the right thing to do. No slaves revolted on Barrett's properties and sugar yield and production went up significantly. He also let his slaves work on the hilly land and produce foodstuff, which they sold, and despite everything, Barrett slaves were permitted to work hard in their field, sell the produce, and were given the opportunity to buy their own freedom.

From the Barrett family came all kinds and classes of people. We have the people who disciplined slaves as if they were demigods. The favorite one was Samuel Barrett of Cinnamon Hill, who beat his slaves into subjection and was one of those from whom some American slave owners copied methods of controlling their slaves. There were many who loved liquor so much, such as Richard Barrett from Greenwood Great House, who was twice the speaker of the House of Assembly in Jamaica, and died from an overdose of alcohol. One of the worst liquor men in the family was Septimus Moulton-Barrett, the brother of Elizabeth Barrett Browning, who drank so much liquor that his brother Charles John Moulton-Barrett had to sell three properties to keep him out of debtor's jail. There were racist Barretts who loved to use the N-word, as well as the words *tar brush, tar drums, tar barrel,* and *African monkey* to describe black people. The author's grandfather, Peter Bonnick, whose mother was Ellen Barrett, also used some of these words, especially in his old days when the superego could not control the subconscious mind. They all came out in a volley.

There were many who were Christian slave owners who made some of their slaves overseers, taught some to read, and were very kind to them. Some were slave traders, and had several ships engaged in the tripartite trade of taking sugar, rum, and indigo to England, then took manufactured goods to Africa in exchange for slaves, then back to Jamaica to sell their human cargo. Edward Barrett of Cinnamon Hill fulfilled all of the above. Since all the families had the same Christian names, they had to be specifically identified. This Edward Barrett is the son of Samuel Barrett of Cinnamon Hill, and is the great-grandfather of Elizabeth Barrett Browning. *Elizabeth* was such a common first name in the family that in her direct lineage she was the seventh from Hersey Barrett Sr., who came to Jamaica in 1655. A vast number of the males in this family loved Negro and mulatto women, especially two sons of Edward Barrett of Cinnamon Hill. Between the two were at least sixteen women of color, ranging from complete Negro to mulatto and quadroon. A mulatto is a cross between white and black. A quadroon is a cross between white and mulatto. There were about sixteen children between them. They were never married. They were in charge of the slave ships. Why I am emphasizing all this is because these two were the direct cause of "rooms without doors."

This family was an intellectual one. It produced governors, generals, and all ranks of the British army were filled by Barretts. They were college professors and school teachers of every rank. Some sided with the abolitionists and some protected them. It was a Barrett who headed the West India delegation to the House of Commons and asked for the freedom of slaves throughout the British Empire. They were also falsely charged with encouraging the Sam Sharpe Rebellion in 1831. And when most of the sugarcane plantations were burned and none of the Barretts' estate was touched, people accused them of collusion so that they could get a higher price for sugar on the London market since they had, as a family, the largest amount of sugarcane in Jamaica. Even though the charges seemed reasonable, it was not true, based on the evidence.

The planters did not like the Barretts even after slavery was abolished. They did something the planters hated. The slaves, in 1838, were paid sixpence per day and were driven from their homes on the properties on which they were slaves. The Barretts, in the days of slavery, allowed their slaves to cultivate the hilly land for themselves, sell the produce, and buy their freedom. After slavery, the slaves were allowed to stay on Barrett properties, where they lived and their salary was doubled to that of one shilling per day. This annoyed the other planters, and many people believed that the speaker of the House of Assembly's liquor was poisoned the night he died. He was Richard Barrett, who headed the delegation to London. There was no post-mortem, so no one is sure of what took place.

The ensuing chapters will detail some of the exploits of the Barretts up to the time those rooms became doorless, and quite a few years afterward. In the opinion of the author, the Barretts are a unique family in the history of the world.

Most of the historicity of the story in this book was taken from two books. The one dealing with the Barretts came from the book *The Family of the Barrett* by Jeannette Marks. Any reference that came from this book and was not properly identified, the author is now giving full credit to her for anything that was not given to her. Most of the historical facts came from this book, so full credit goes to her if in case she was not credited in the foregoing chapters. Also, the facts about Robert Browning came mostly from his cousin Vivienne Browning, from her book *My Browning Family Album*. Any credit that may not have been given in the chapter about Robert Browning, the author is now giving credit to any statement made in the chapter or chapters without the proper credit.

I am now doing so because authors have a way of reading several books and have some lines stuck in their heads and write these without remembering from whence they came, and therefore, the proper credit was not given. So in this case, I am making sure that no such thing occurs. I have been through so many volumes on my family that there could be many things in my head without me knowing from whence they came. So at this time, I am giving credit wherever it is due if I did not give the proper accreditation. However, if there are similarities between what my family told me and that told by any historian, I am sticking to my family's traditions.

CHAPTER 1

The story of "Rooms without Doors" is based upon the personality of Edward Barrett of Cinnamon Hill. He will take up a whole chapter and more by himself. Before we come to him, it will be wise to look backward in time to examine who were these Barretts before him and how they came into prominence. His great-grandfather Hersey Barrett Sr. was a lieutenant in the British Army, and he hailed from the county of Cornwall, England. His family settled in two places in Cornwall known as Saltash and Tregarne.

Before Hersey Barrett and his selected descendants are examined, a look back at where he came from would be encouraging. The earliest record of anyone with the name Barrett was the year 1066. William of Normandy made claim to the English throne, claiming to be the grandnephew of Queen Emma, who ruled as Queen of the Anglo-Saxon with her husband Ethered II (the Unready), 1014–1016. She was the aunt of Robert II (the Devil), Duke of Normandy; and William, Duke of Normandy, is his son. This William defeated King Harold of England in 1066 and became known as "The Conqueror." His claim to the throne of England was based on fraud and brute force. He declared he had sixty thousand men at his command, a vast flotilla of boats, and that the blessing of the pope was given to him in order for him to conquer England. Most of these men of Normandy were descended from the Vikings. They came from Denmark, Norway, and Sweden seeking warmer climes. They occupied a part of France they called "Land of the Northmen." In the year 911 AD, King Francis of France made a treaty with them to stay where they were and not to invade Paris, the capital. He even expanded their boundaries in the name of peace, and this land subsequently became known as Normandy.

Among the sixty thousand men that he had under his command was a man by the name of Ensign Barrett who came to England with him. Because of his prowess, after the Battle of Hastings in 1066, when King

Harold was defeated, William the Conqueror gave Barrett that part of England now known as Cornwall as his dowry. From extensive research, this is the first time in history that we hear of the name Barrett. No one seemed to know where the name originates. The author personally believes that it was a transliteration from some Nordic name. The French spell it *Barrette* with an E at the end; and Latin people have it as *Barretto* and *Barretta*. We do not even know the true meaning of *ensign* as a title. The *Concise Oxford Dictionary* has *ensign* as (1) a badge of honor, (2) standard-bearer (formerly, the lowest commissioned officer on foot). The *Random House College Edition Dictionary* states that "(1) Ensign is a badge of office or authority, (2) The lowest commissioned officer in the U.S. Navy, (3) An officer who, (formerly) carried the flag of a regiment or company in the British Army (4) Equal to a second lieutenant in the U.S. Army. The *Webster New Encyclopedic Dictionary* states that an ensign is an officer rank in the navy and coast guard below lieutenant junior grade. But what was it at the time of the Norman conquest? Be that as it may, we will have to suppose that this man, Ensign Barrett, must have been someone important to William.

The name Barrett did not show up in history again until the outbreak of the English Civil War when it appeared that many Barretts fought on the side of Oliver Cromwell and the parliament on one hand, and King Charles I on the other. This was started in 1642 and ended in 1649 with the capture of the king.

There was a great concern about what should be done to the king. The parliament, under Cromwell, decided that he should be tried for treason. They selected a group that decided what should be done, and the group recommended a court martial that had the power to give the death penalty. Never before in the history of England was there a trial for treason of a reigning monarch. There is also no reference to this in all of Europe. Cromwell, who became lord protector, then empanelled a group who should sit on the court martial. Among the group was Judge Bradshaw, who became the president; Daniel Blagrove; Thomas Wayte; and John Harrison. There were many others but these were the ones who fled to Jamaica with their family in 1655, becoming a part of the expedition of Adm. William Penn and Gen. Robert Venables when Jamaica was taken from the Spaniards.

Just consider this question. Suppose the Spaniards had beaten them and they found no place to capture, would they have gone back to England?

The court martial members became known from that time as *regicides*. They all suspected that Prince Charles, the king's son, who was in protective arrangement in Spain, would one day become King of England should there be a restoration. This was prophetic because by 1660 this Prince Charles was restored and became King Charles II of England. It is ironic to note that this same King Charles gave crown lands on several occasions to Lt. Hersey Barrett while he lived in Jamaica, West Indies. This solicits the question, did the king know that Hersey Barrett, to whom he was assigning crown lands, was the man who chopped off his father's head? No one should have thought that he knew, and if he did not, why not?

It was not only Hersey who fled to Jamaica in 1655. A vast number of his family came with him, including his father, brothers, and sisters, with their families. While Hersey was still a soldier trying to root out the lost vestige of the Spanish Army, his family settled in Port Royal and the Spanish capital of the island, Santiago de la Vega. The island name at that time was the one Columbus gave it in 1694. Despite what other people say, that name was "Santiago," and remained so until the British changed it to Jamaica. Because of the terrain of Jamaica, the British had some difficulty in expelling the Spaniards, even though they had a recent map drawn up by a Portuguese Jew, who was cartographer for many Spanish expeditions to the West Indies. He also settled in Jamaica under the name of DaCosta, and is the progenitor of the family of DaCosta now living in Jamaica. This cartographer had a dispute with the authorities in Spain and he went to Oliver Cromwell of England and sold him several maps of Spanish possessions, including Jamaica, so that Admiral Penn and General Venables knew exactly what places to attack. After they were defeated in Santo Domingo because of the ineptitude of General Venables, they proceeded to Jamaica, which was lightly defended by the Spaniards because it was not owned outright by the Spanish Crown; it was the fiefdom of the Columbus family.

The Barrett family did not only flee to Jamaica, they were trusted by Oliver Cromwell to the extent that many Barretts were asked to go to Ireland to colonize it and so try to pacify Ireland by increasing its population of English immigrants. The Barretts headed many of these colonizing groups and many descendants of the Cornish Barretts are now living in Ireland, but they call themselves Irish. In addition to those who went to Jamaica, many Barretts went all over Europe and other places because their names became synonymous with regicide; that is, the killing of the king.

As Hersey Barrett acquired crown lands, he joined the oncoming invading force from England to get the Spaniards completely off the island. They also decided that they would throw the British off the island also. The last Spanish governor sent to Jamaica was a high-ranking Spanish soldier. He was Gen. Don Cristobal Arnoldo de Yssassi. He put up his last stand against the British under the command of Col. Edward Doyley at the battle of Rio Neuvo, in what is now the parish of St. Mary, at a point three miles east of present-day Ocho Rios. The Spaniards had control of the small bay but the British placed cannons on top of the hill overlooking the bay. And after a few days of battle, the fight was over, and the Spanish general fled with his troops to Cuba, ninety miles away. Thus ended Spanish rule in Jamaica from 1494 to 1661, a period of 167 years. From this time onward, the Barretts had Jamaica for themselves to grow crops, rear animals, and request the king for more crown lands, which were given based on the number of members in the family. His family was not very large. He only had two sons, and each adult family member also had their right, but how Hersey Senior got all that land and the rest of the family did not is because he went about claiming land while the others were city dwellers and tradesmen.

He went to Santa Gloria (St. Ann) and claimed land around Moneague Lake and what is now Alderton where the Barretts still owned a property named Albion in 1938. He acquired much land in St. James, some of which became the parish of Trelawny after 1773. He also established properties in Vere that later became the parish of Clarendon sometime after 1866. These properties were extensive and many Barretts lived there. The family owned Paradise Estate, Withywood, with land around Alley, the capital of Vere, extending several miles to Carlisle Bay, near Rocky Point. Hersey Senior also owned Mile Gully property in the parish of St. Elizabeth until it became Manchester in 1814, when the governor, William, Duke of Manchester, cut a parish named after himself from St. Elizabeth, and in 1817 bought one square mile of the Caledonia Estate, then owned by Scotsman Robert Crawford, to make the capital of Manchester, named after his son, Mandeville. Most of the present-day Monymusk Estate were the properties of the Barretts and the Greens, who intermarried and produced a Barrett-Green combination that was to lead to the importance of both families when some Barretts became very renowned.

Although Hersey Senior was someone like a land grabber, he loved to live in the city, where he had established business, and continued his plantations all over the island. He had labor shortages to the point where he bought and sold slaves, and all the family engaged in that business both from the cities of Port Royal and Santiago de la Vega. After the Spaniards were driven from the country, the Barretts and others took possession of the farms that were run by the Spaniards, and it was because of these farms and plantations that the British were able to survive. They slaughtered the cattle for food, and expanded the sugar plantations for commerce. It was then that slavery played such an important part. The first real modern farm that the Barretts captured was Liguanea, the area now occupied by Kingston and St. Andrew. It was owned by an industrious Spanish Madonna by the name of Señora Joanna Fuentes. She had a vast number of cattle, and since she had no husband, only one nephew who lived with her, anything unworthy could have happened to her by these marauding Englishmen. They did not kill her but allowed her to flee to Cuba with her nephew. They used the farm to help feed the troops who were on the battlefield as well as the civilians who lived at Port Royal and Santiago de la Vega.

It was not only in Liguanea that they found developed farms. Upon exploring the island, they found a massive farm in the southwest measurable in square miles. This was the nucleus of the new parish of St. Elizabeth. The Spaniards called this place Hatos de Pereda after the man who founded it in 1515 and onward. His name was Juan Pereda, and he was commissioned by Governor Francisco de Garay to establish these ranches and farms in order to supply the conquistadors on their way to Latin America. The present name is Pedro Plains, and the entire Santa Cruz Mountain where the elite lived, because the Spaniards said that this place was the healthiest place on earth since there was no stagnant water there to breed the kinds of mosquitoes that carry the malaria and yellow fever viruses. The people worked on the lowlands during daylight hours and fled to the mountains at night since these mosquitoes seemed to only bite after dusk. These ranches produced vegetables all during the year, and it is the only place in the country that produces vegetables during the winter months in economic quantities. Many people are amazed at this, but one need only look at the topography of the Pedro Plains and adjacent areas. They are protected on the east by the Santa Cruz Mountain, on the north by the Nassau Mountain, on the northwest by the Dolphin Head Mountain; and these mountain ranges protect the area from the north wind that comes down from North America, across Cuba, then on to the northern areas of Jamaica. When people call other parts of the island "The Garden Parish," one only has to look at which part of the island produces green vegetables between the months of November and February. Only south St. Elizabeth.

The Barretts not only survived hardships from the climate for which they were not accustomed, they also suffered from the buccaneers who plundered anything from anyplace and brought the goods to Port Royal, where they sold them to the highest bidders. Many of the Barretts were at Port Royal and they traded freely with these pirates. The city became so wicked, it was considered the worst on earth. The pirates were at one time under the command of Sir Henry Morgan, who was so fierce, the British fleet in the West Indies could not handle him, so the government knighted him for stealing, then appointed him governor of the island. There was nothing the Barretts could do except to befriend him. America's J. P. Morgan has in his ancestral lineage the name of Sir Henry Morgan, buccaneer and governor of Jamaica. Think about this!

As Port Royal prospered in goods and wicked deeds, so did the Barretts prosper with their businesses and plantations until the Creator of heaven and earth decided that Port Royal should account for all it was doing. So on one June day, 1692, the greatest earthquake in the West Indies took place. Two-thirds of the city went under the sea. Thousands of lives were lost, and the Barretts suffered their greatest calamity ever. A large portion of the family went under with the city, and much of the finance that came from Port Royal to help develop the farms of the Barretts dried up. Most of the British families in Jamaica at that time lost someone important to them at Port Royal. Even though the earthquake rocked the entire island, it seemed that the center was under Port Royal.

This earthquake weakened the defense of the island and the French fleet stationed at Santa Domingo began preparing to invade, which they did unsuccessfully in 1694, but the Barretts suffered a major loss in this invasion, and this is why a reference is recorded here.

Before Hersey Senior died, there was a rift developing in his immediate family. His two sons, Hersey Junior and Samuel, were growing up to be adolescents. The rift was not caused by any one of them but by the father who showed his preference of one over the other. Samuel was just like his father with his pioneering spirit, but Hersey Junior liked city dwelling. He preferred to remain in Spanish Town doing business, and Samuel loved the farm like his father did, and was by his father's side going through the countryside and staking claims to properties all over the island.

As far as it goes, the will of Hersey Senior is not available for us to see how the properties were divided at the time of his death but what is available is the result of what happened. Hersey Junior changed his name by spelling it differently. He spelt Hersey H-E-A-R-C-Y, and he spelt Barrett B-A-R-R-I-T-T. This brought about a name change in the family, and it was not reconciled during the lifetime of Hersey Junior. It took over 132 years from the death of Hersey Senior in 1685 until 1817 for all the Barretts who changed their names to return it to the original. Many historians, including this one, believed that it was the power and influence and wealth of Edward Barrett of Cinnamon Hill that was responsible for the return of the Barritts to the original name Barrett.

Whatever took place in the life of this renowned family, most of their riches seemed to have come from sugar on the south coast of Jamaica in the parish of Vere. Sugar and cotton were grown in this region of the country and exported to England, and many English families settled in this parish because most of it was arable, even though mosquitoes as big as B-52 bombers were in great abundance. The Barretts fought them off and became very well off because of the productivity of the land. Hersey Barrett Jr., now operating under the name of Hearcy Barritt, also joined in the sugar plantation business, because he got some portion of Withywood property, and Paradise Estate, which still has the same name and was owned in the 1960s by the McWhinney family, dominated the sugar production for many years. Many of the Barretts' properties then are now a part of Monymusk Estate in the parish of Clarendon. Vere was annexed to Clarendon in 1866 when the governor, Sir John Peter Grant, reduced the twenty-two parishes to fourteen. This statement will be repeated again and again for emphasis, because most Jamaicans do not know that there were twenty-two parishes.

As the Barretts worked and prospered in Vere and St. Catherine parishes, two disasters were about to strike that was to divide the family of the Barretts forever. One section would go to the north coast of Jamaica, the other would remain on the south coast, but all would spread and cover the entire island until there was no parish in which a Barrett did not operate. In fact, between the British occupation in 1655 to the Sam Sharpe slave revolt of 1831, the history of the Barretts was also the history of Jamaica. Nothing was done in Jamaica that a Barrett was not involved in. They were the military men, the planters, the businessmen, and the politicians. It was more so during the lifetime of Edward Barrett of Cinnamon Hill, when most, if not all, governors who came to Jamaica, whenever they visited the north coast, had to call on or sojourn for some time with this Edward Barrett. Much more will be said about him in an ensuing chapter.

The first of the two tragedies to overtake this British family was the destruction of Port Royal in 1692 by a great earthquake. So devastating was it that it changed the geography of Jamaica. Some parts of the city went under the sea, and the peninsula on which Port Royal stood was reduced by two-thirds its area. The Barretts lost over thirty family members and friends, and a portion of their wealth amounting to millions. It was very destructive to their plans, because some of the financing for the plantation came from the profits earned by the businesses that were in Port Royal. Hersey Barrett Senior and his immediate family were in Santiago de la Vega (Spanish Town) at the time of the earthquake and he was on the farm at Liguanea (St. Andrew), which also had terrible tremors. In fact, the whole island felt the shock but its center was somewhere in the vicinity of the city of Port Royal. In those days, there were no machines to measure earthquakes, but based on the damage, many presumed it would have had to be a nine on the Richter scale. Despite all that happened, the Barretts put the pieces back together and continued on their progressive ways of how to make money in a hostile environment. This breed of Englishmen was not only fascinating, they were tough people and had to risk the most dangerous of diseases from the bite of the yellow fever mosquitoes, for which there was no remedy. To add insult to this injury, they were always under the threat of a French invasion. When the French who were stationed in St. Dominique (Santo Domingo) heard that Port Royal was destroyed, they began to prepare an invasion force. They thought that the British did not hear of the destruction when they did, so they could get an invasion force there before the British could come to its rescue. This was not to be, because the French also had their problems on St. Dominique. The invasion took place two years later when Admiral DuCasse landed forces on the island. He did a lot of destruction until he was driven off, and the family of the Barretts suffered another great disaster. A major family member was killed, and again the family suffered both mental and economic disaster because the French destroyed their plantations, stole their cattle, which they did not kill for food, and went back to St.

Dominique with their ships loaded with horses and cattle. The only thing that was not destroyed in Vere in 1694 was the will of the Barrett family to go forward.

A brief look at Port Royal at this time is necessary to let people know how wicked the city was, and a brief history prior to the arrival of the Barretts. The city was founded by the Spaniards, who occupied the island of Jamaica for over 160 years. Some people dated the occupation from 1494 to 1661 when the last Spanish governor, Don Cristobal Arnoldo de Yssassi, fled from Runaway Bay in St. Ann after his defeat by Col. Edward Doyley at the battle of Rio Nuevo in St. Mary. Others dated it from the British arrived in 1655. The Spaniards named it Cayo de Carena and used it as a fishing port and had a small fortification there. It must be remembered that Jamaica then was the fiefdom of the Columbus family, so it was not fortified as the other Spanish colonies in the West Indies. The British called it Cagway and built a fort, which they call Fort Charles today. The name Port Royal came into being when the House of Assembly met in 1674 and named it as one of the parishes of Jamaica.

The first major building was the fort established by Maj. Gen. Robert Sedgewick of the Massachussetts Bay Colony, who was asked by Oliver Cromwell to run the civil service of Jamaica and to build defenses for the island. When he completed the fort at Port Royal, he told Cromwell, who named it after himself as Fort Cromwell. But after the restoration it got the name Fort Charles, and it became the nucleus of the city of Port Royal. Great leaders were stationed at Fort Charles, such as admirals Lord Rodney, John Benbow, Edward Vernon, and the greatest of them all, Admiral Horatio, Lord Nelson.

Just prior to these great men, there was a situation in which the then governor, Sir Thomas Modyford, had a major problem. The buccaneers under Henry Morgan were playing havoc among the Spanish traders and slave traders. The traders took gold and produce stolen from the Indians to Spain to enrich their coffers. The slave traders brought slaves from Africa to be sold in the West Indies. Morgan and his men robbed both. He took the goods to Port Royal and sold them to the merchants, many of whom were the Barretts. He also intercepted slave ships and brought them to Port Royal where they were sold at public auction. Many of the purchasers were the Barrett family. With this kind of robbery going on and no one to control it, the then governor, Sir Thomas Modyford, issued documents to Morgan and his robbers that if they would help in the defense of the island they were permitted by him to rob the Spanish and French at will without prosecution. Morgan accepted. And so did the rest of the buccaneers. This dishonest strategy protected Jamaica for years from attacks by both France and Spain. Not until the death of Henry Morgan were the French brave enough to attack, and the Barrett family would suffer tragedy as a result.

The place where the Spaniards had their wealth at that time was Columbia and Panama. If one would take a map of the West Indies and looked south between 77° and 78° longitude, 600 miles, that's Panama, with Columbia slightly east. It is the open Caribbean Sea. Nothing is between Jamaica and these two countries. At that time, the two countries were one until the idea of the Panama Canal, then both countries were divided by military intrigue.

The attacks by Henry Morgan and his pirates were so vicious, had it not been for incessant wars on the continent of Europe, France and Spain would have had to unite and bring an armada to the West Indies to fight these pirates. As Port Royal became the richest city in the west per capita, so did the wickedness increase in proportion. Prostitutes were imported from the poor counties of Britain and Ireland, and these were called indentured servants, but many of them ended up on the streets of Port Royal as women of easy virtue. Homosexuality abounded and the boarding houses profited and prospered from the sale of flesh. Promiscuity and venereal disease were the order of the day, and if one believed in a Supreme Being, then he was looking down from wherever he was in wonder and disdain, and pondering what to do with human beings of the kind that wandered and hustled on the streets of Port Royal.

The word *hustle* has several meanings, but nowadays it covers every act of dishonesty. Everywhere you go at the present moment everyone is hustling. When they pick your pocket, rob you with a gun, they are hustling. Henry Morgan made it so difficult for the Jamaican governor and the British king that their only solution was to make him a part of it. They were both recipients of Henry Morgan's loot, and both were becoming richer because of him, so the governor recommended to the king to make Henry Morgan governor. The king agreed and bestowed upon a thief the title of knighthood, and not only that, he made him governor of Jamaica from 1680 to 1682. Imagine, a British king knighting a pirate for stealing. King Charles II was not the first to do this. He had precedent when Queen Elizabeth I knighted Drake and Raleigh for doing the same things. When people talk about morality, they should look at these actions and cry aloud. It is still happening today. Robbers, if they keep the right company, will always be rewarded for wrongdoing. Were the Barretts a part of this rascality that went on in old Port Royal? There was no direct evidence that they were pirates, but based on how many businesses they had, it is questionable whether they were innocent parties.

There were many Barretts living in Port Royal during the time of the buccaneers. A name that should also be mentioned is that of Edward Tittle, a Jew. This name is just mentioned here because he is an ancestor of Robert Browning, who was to create a great upheaval in the Barrett family when he married Elizabeth, the poetess, later on. The name John Waight was also there with his family. He was the cordwainer of Port Royal, and Edward Tittle of Jewish descent was his chief apprentice. He was one of the many Jews who lived on Jew Street in Port Royal. Edward Tittle survived the earthquake of 1692 but John Waight did not. It was this Edward Title who moved to Half Way Tree in St. Andrew to become the cordwainer of Half Way Tree, and had his business on the opposite side of the same street as the Barretts' general store. This street is now known as Eastwood Park Road in the vicinity of the Jamaica Broadcasting Corporation first location, not far from the junction with Molynes Road. Now, a cordwainer is one who manufactures leather and leather goods, such as boots, shoes, saddles, bags, and reins for horses, also whips. He is not only a shoemaker as many people would like to call him, he is much more than this. The Barretts traded with Edward Tittle on a large scale, and history was very kind to them that a few generations down their descendants would make their names more famous than they were previously.

Some Barretts who lived and worked in Port Royal included Thomas Barrett and his sister Mary, who were great business traders, even with the buccaneers. Also, Elizabeth Barrett Floyer and Anne Barrett Ward. She married Henry Ward, one of the richest persons to be in Port Royal. He had a large family and traded with the buccaneers, whom he secretly disdained but traded with them anyway. His greatest fear was Henry Morgan, the chief, who later became governor of the island from 1680 to 1682. He died in 1688 and did not experience the great earthquake. Anyone who crossed his path would have been destroyed immediately, so Henry Ward kept his cool and survived Morgan, but the great earthquake took all his family and his wealth within a few minutes. Not one of the Barretts mentioned escaped. Those families were totally wiped out. The Barretts opposed the Jews in Port Royal, and Henry Ward, who married Anne Barrett, was one of the most opposed for many years. The earthquake put an end to this but the hatred seemed to have been universal. This author even presumed that this could have been one of the reasons why Edward Moulton Barrett disinherited his daughter, Elizabeth Barrett Browning, in 1846, over 150 years later, because Robert Browning was descended on two sides from the Jewish people. More of this later on. We don't know if this was the case, because something more hateful was involved.

There were so many Barretts scattered all over Jamaica that the setback in Port Royal was only a little dent in the family structure in terms of numbers. They had many more families located in Spanish Town, the capital, and in the parish of Vere around Paradise and Withywood estates, as well as Liguanea, which became Kingston and St. Andrew. Before the great earthquake, old Hersey had died and left his two sons Hersey Junior and Samuel to carry on the Barrett tradition. Hersey stayed on in Spanish Town and Samuel went to Vere. Both brothers had properties in several parishes and both lived sometimes in Vere and sometimes in Spanish Town because of business.

As Port Royal became less important, those who survived and remained had to undergo many more disasters. In 1694, the earthquake destroyed two-thirds of the city. There was some partial rebuilding, and in 1704, a great fire consumed the city. It was again partially rebuilt when a great hurricane in 1772 wiped it out again. The ambitious people started another rebuilding effort and in 1794 another great hurricane struck and destroyed what remained. The people believed that these were curses from God, so they quietly started to cross the channel to Liguanea, a portion of which developed into Kingston parish. And from this exodus from Port Royal the city of Kingston emerged as something better than Port Royal. And with considerable immigration also from Spanish Town, Kingston developed, and the capital of Jamaica was moved to Kingston in 1872.

The people were not freed from the fear of earthquake because they came to Kingston. This city also had its share, and in 1907, it was destroyed by earthquake. There have been hundreds more of smaller magnitude, but since Jamaica is a small island sitting on at least one earthquake fault, there is no more place to run, so the people just stay put. When it is not earthquakes, it is hurricanes, and Edward Barrett of Cinnamon Hill became the first person to build a substantial hurricane shelter called "Cutwind" at his great house to protect his family from the ravages of many hurricanes during the eighteenth century. This hurricane shelter is still intact today after 220 years.

The development of estates by the Barretts continued in Liguanea, St. Catherine, Vere, and Mile Gully in St. Elizabeth. It became Mile Gully, Manchester, from 1814, when the governor, William, Duke of Manchester, cut the new parish from St. Elizabeth. Samuel Barrett, the younger son of old Hersey, married in Vere to one Margery Green, whose father was a planter nearby. They produced a son and named him Samuel Junior. To differentiate all these Samuels is difficult to do, but Samuel, son of Hersey Barrett, the lieutenant who came with the expedition of Penn and Venables in 1655, is also called Samuel of Withywood, and he produced a son called Samuel of Cinnamon Hill.

After the great destruction of Port Royal in 1692, the French and the Spanish fleet in the West Indies decided to invade Jamaica and seize it from the British. Physically and psychologically, Jamaica was devastated, and the people thought it was a curse from God. The French fleet was watching the Spanish fleet, and no one was sure who was going to strike Jamaica first. They all started to plan before the news got to England of the destruction of Port Royal. They got the news by itinerant traders who happened to be in Jamaican ports during the earthquake. As the days went by, the British fleet that was stationed in the eastern Caribbean heard and began watching the French and Spanish fleets to see what they would do.

It took two full years for the French under the command of Admiral DuCasse to invade the south of the island. They docked at Carlisle Bay, near Rocky Point in the parish of Vere, and when the British settlers heard, they sent a message to Spanish Town about the French invasion. Before the military could arrive by horse-drawn carriages from the capital, the settlers concocted a makeshift army with Samuel Barrett of Withywood as the captain of a cavalry group that headed south to attack the enemy. After some skirmishes, Samuel was fatally shot by a French soldier and he did not see the final outcome of the battle, as the French fled when British troops arrived from Spanish Town. So ended the life of Samuel Barrett of Withywood at the Battle of Carlyle Bay in 1694, leaving behind two young sons, Richard and Samuel. Richard was born in 1687 and Samuel in 1689.

When the French retreated, they burned everything in sight and killed hundreds of cattle and pigs to resupply their ships, then headed back to Hispaniola to enjoy their ill-gotten gains. When the Spanish heard that the French invasion failed, they did not bother to invade because they knew that by this time the British had sent reinforcements to the island. Even though the French invasion was a failure, it left a young wife and two boys without a husband and father. The Barretts suffered a great loss but it was this disaster that made way for the most famous Barretts to emerge on the north coast of Jamaica, and to produce Barretts of worldwide significance. The south coast Barretts, even though they were successful planters, did not achieve the fame and notoriety of their north coast counterparts, as the story will unfold.

As the two Barrett sons, Richard and Samuel, grew up to be fatherless teenagers, they found themselves as stepsons because their mother, Margery Green Barrett, remarried to another Vere planter with last name Love. Richard decided to stay on the south coast and Samuel moved north through St. Ann parish, acquiring properties as he went, finally settling in the parish of St. James, where he acquired more properties, most famous among them was Cinnamon Hill, and from that time he was commonly called Samuel of Cinnamon Hill to differentiate him from the other Samuel Barretts who were all over the island.

Some of the properties young Samuel Barrett of Cinnamon Hill acquired were those founded by the old Hersey Barrett of the expedition fame. He had these properties, and some were being cultivated by the Barretts who lived in Spanish Town but were not being properly supervised until a Barrett would permanently reside in these north coast areas. It was left to Samuel of Cinnamon Hill to do just that, and he was considered as the one who made the name Barrett famous.

It seemed that he was not interested in a family until he had plenty of properties and slaves, and then made an impression on the planters in St. James before settling down to create a family. All through his youthful years no one heard of any serious relationships with any woman whom he could marry. He lived a single life until he was over thirty years, and in those days life expectancy was just about forty years for a male. It was rather strange for a man who was not poor to have gone on for so long without having a family. He was an unusual Barrett because no one normally waited so long. But when he did, he made up for the lost opportunity, because as the records go, no Barrett was a more prolific producer of children than this Samuel Barrett.

As one traces the family of Barretts and their connection to other families, the common first names of males and females were after a pattern. Most of the Barrett family only used about seven names for their children and they went from generation to generation with Thomas, Edward, and Samuel as the most prevalent for the males, and Elizabeth for the females. It is of significant note that when Elizabeth Barrett Browning was a teenager there were at least seven living females in her immediate family with the name of Elizabeth. There seemed to have been such a love for this name that the family could not do without an existing Elizabeth. As the story goes further into a glimpse of Barrett history, the reader will find the name Elizabeth, Edward, Thomas, and Samuel most intriguing. As we look at the next chapter, the story of Samuel Barrett of Cinnamon Hill will teach us something rather amazing.

CHAPTER 2

Samuel Barrett of Cinnamon Hill

Samuel Barrett was a very young man, the grandson of the regicide Lt. Hersey Barrett who came to Jamaica with the expeditionary force of Admiral Penn and General Venables in 1655. His father was the first Samuel Barrett ever to appear on that most beautiful island. This Samuel Barrett will be commonly called by the name of the place he developed, Cinnamon Hill, because there were so many Samuels in the family, both contemporaries as well as future generations, so a title with which to refer to Samuel is very essential throughout this book.

The first Samuel Barrett went to Withywood and Paradise Estates in Vere parish, where he established his farms and married Margery, the daughter of one of the planters, whose name was Edward Green. They produced a son named Samuel, who was born in 1689, four years after their marriage. Tragedy struck this new family in the year 1694. When young Samuel was five years old, the French Admiral DuCasse invaded Jamaica, landing at Carlisle Bay in the parish of Vere, not far from the Barretts' estates. And when the planters took up arms and tried to defend their estates, Samuel, his father, was shot and killed in the battle before help came from Spanish Town and repulsed the enemy. This was a devastating blow to the family, and Margery Green Barrett was left with three young children under the age of seven whom she had to take care of.

It was a very good thing that the early English settlers lived in some form of communal system even though they were capitalists. The district took care of Margery and her children until a Good Samaritan of the Love family married her. Young Sam and his siblings had someone now to help their mother, but this did not play well with him during his teenage years. He was a Barrett, and hearing the name Love being called too frequently, he decided that when he came to manhood the properties on the north coast would be the place to develop his own family away from the stranger who had come into his life. This was the attitude of most of the Barretts in those days, and so it is with their descendants who now live all over the island of Jamaica. The characteristics of the ancient family are still practiced by people who are more than ten generations down the line.

When Samuel was a little over twenty-one and had arrived at maturity, he bade his family farewell and headed north to become the progenitor of a family that was to be the envy of Jamaica for many years. He had no problem finding good properties because his grandfather Hersey had already acquired lands on the north coast. He then settled at a property called Cornwall, some ten miles east of where Rose Hall Great House is located, and this was still in the parish of St. James because there was no Trelawny as yet. Trelawny became a parish after 1773 when Governor William Trelawny wanted a parish named after his family. There was also no Rose Hall Great House as yet, because the great house (still in existence after refurbishing by John Rollins, the former congressman from Delaware, USA) was not yet built, as Rosa Kelly, the daughter of Rev. John Kelly, the rector of St. Elizabeth parish, did not start this building until 1743, and it was completed sometime after 1746 by her second husband George Ash. More will be said about Trelawny and Rose Hall Great House later on. It was difficult for Samuel as a newcomer to establish himself as a leading planter, but he was very ambitious. He had no formal education and was taught by his mother and Mr. Love according to the little they knew since neither had any formal education whatsoever. It must be recognized that in Jamaica at that time there were no schools to educate these Creole children, and education was only for those planters' children who were wealthy enough to send their children back to school in England. The only concern for these planters was how many hogsheads of sugar they could manufacture to send back to England, so the white boys were trained how to handle Negro slaves, and the girls learned to sew and how to entertain guests at the great houses. Some of the white girls were taught by the African women who were expert at sewing clothes back in the homeland. They were not all illiterate people who were brought from Africa. They were literate in their language and culture and taught the white man much about cultivating and irrigating fields to produce yields in time of drought.

As Samuel Barrett looked around and saw rivers and streams flowing through his properties, he utilized his slaves to assist in watering his sugar plantations. He was so successful that he became the envy of other planters nearby, who borrowed from his system and profited greatly. He also developed a method to control his slaves, and this was not the best, humanely speaking. The humaneness in the Barrett family was left to his grandsons and future generations of Barretts. After spending about ten years living at Cornwall Estate, he expanded the house and decided to get married. The question one would ask is why did he wait so long to find a wife? When he left Vere parish, he was over twenty years old, and now he had passed thirty-one. No one knew why, but the Barrett family had a way of not jumping into marriages early. Some did and their father disinherited them. It was not only when they got married too early, but also if they married someone who was considered too poor to marry the Barretts' daughters. This is a situation for which there is no scientific trend in the family, because some did not care much about who their children married, but these were in the minority. Now, Samuel must have been friendly with some other person of the opposite sex but there is no record of this, and also there is no record of his getting help by miscegenation. He had everything that would pass the St. Elizabeth test for getting a man's daughter for a wife. It was the most rigid test in Jamaica. The four points a St. Elizabeth man would ask when a man asked him for his daughter are these:

a. Do you have a house?
b. Land? How many acres?
c. Cattle? How many heads?
d. And lastly, what type of work do you do?

When all these questions were answered satisfactorily, the father would then give consent for a man to marry his daughter, whether she was poor and barefooted did not matter. Samuel had all of the above for sometime before he was brave enough to take a wife. Maybe he was thinking that he was too harsh in the treatment of his slaves, which a woman would consider cruel, and that she might be thinking about too much control over herself, even in those days. No one really knows what was going on in his mind or maybe in his culture. It could also be that his mother Margery Green in Vere parish had some influence upon him because she was still alive up to 1724 and maybe he had to assist her economically because there is no record that Mr. Love, her husband, was anything but poor and the Barretts were not. Be that as it may, nothing happens before the time, so Samuel decided it was time for him to find a wife.

He went to the home of Henry Wisdom, who was a planter at the same time as his grandfather Hersey Barrett, and asked for his daughter, Elizabeth Wisdom, who was just past fourteen years old. This was tantamount to lasciviousness. How could such a grown man ask consent to marry a baby? This was not the Far East where children get married as early as age nine. They were under British culture and custom, and a fourteen-year-old girl was not yet out of elementary school. This was at age fifteen. There were no schools as such in Jamaica at that time, so Elizabeth was taught at home by her parents, who did not know much themselves.

What an audacity! It is supposed he was just waiting on the law for him to go and ask for her. Under the British legal system, then as now, it would have been carnal abuse, which carries the same sentence as rape, to have carnal knowledge of a girl under the age of fourteen years. We have no good record of her date of birth, but it was acceptable in those days for the father to say his child was what age and others would have to agree. Samuel must now be left alone in this consensus and a look at Henry Wisdom as father of Elizabeth to have given away his daughter at such an early age. The presumption was that he saw in Samuel Barrett an upcoming wealthy farmer in the neighborhood. And since Samuel had lands adjoining his property, Henry Wisdom considered giving Elizabeth to Samuel a very good economic idea. Samuel had all the qualities that a St. Elizabeth man would require, and since at that time Englishmen were scarce, he just sank to his lower nature and accepted the request of Samuel lest some other neighbor would grab her. Those were times when you make the best of your opportunities, for if they go, you may not be fortunate enough to get them back. Such were the conditions, and it is presumed that Henry Wisdom made good use of his opportunity at that time.

It is of significant note that from the Barrett side beginning with Elizabeth Wisdom from her marriage to Samuel Barrett, this name was to permeate the family right down to Elizabeth Barrett Browning and beyond. Everywhere in the history of the Barretts, the name Elizabeth is found. And when the Moulton family married another Elizabeth Barrett, it was discovered that several other Elizabeths came from the

Moulton side. This seems to have been a very famous English name for girls.

In 1721, after consent was given, Samuel Barrett of Cornwall Estate married Elizabeth Wisdom of St. James parish on a property adjacent to that of Samuel. She was fourteen and he was thirty-one. With this marriage came the descendants of the Barretts, who would make world history just as old Hersey Barrett did in 1649 when he was the first person in British history to legally chop off the head of a British king. King Charles I will neither remember nor forget that occasion because he died instantly. So from this regicide family one of the greatest poetesses came, and with her shocking marriage to another great poet, some of the best love letters ever written have been preserved for the human race to enjoy.

The first child of this marriage arrived within the first year on the third day of May 1722. Her name was Mary, and she died shortly after she was one year old on the twenty-fourth of July 1723. The second child, Richard, was born on the tenth of July 1723, fourteen days before Mary died. When Richard was seventeen years old, he married Mary Williams, the daughter of Job Williams of St. Ann parish, on the seventeenth of November 1740. Now, what could a seventeen-year-old juvenile do with any meaningful form of marriage? Well, his father Samuel Barrett was an up and coming rich man, so white people in those days gravitated toward hooking up their daughters with any available men whether they were still in the cradle or fully matured. Such was the scarcity of white men in those days.

There was no recorded child of the marriage but in those days it was the custom of men to have children out of wedlock with quadroons or mulattoes who worked as house slaves. Children born under these conditions in Jamaica could not use their father's last names. They went by the last names their mother had, whether real or given. Richard died at the age of thirty-two on the thirty-first of July 1755. Richard is one of the names frequently used by the Barretts.

The third child was named Elizabeth. Here we have again a frequently used Barrett name. She was born on the twenty-second of December 1725, and within fourteen years of her birth, just like her mother Elizabeth Wisdom, she was married to Ezekiel Lawrence on the twenty-second of October 1739. This is another case of a juvenile being married off in a British colony. The parents of daughters seemed to wait just until the daughters got past fourteen years so the current British law of carnal abuse could not have them arrested. No matter what the custom, these actions are juvenile delinquency at its worst. She died on the third of September 1781.

The fourth child of the Barrett-Wisdom connection was Mary, to replace the first Mary who died when she was one year old. This is another famous name of the Barretts. She was born on the twenty-fourth November 1727 and died on the eleventh of March 1810. She was married at age nineteen to Henry Wayte on the nineteenth of May 1746. Here we have the descendants of two of the regicides who came to Jamaica in the year 1655 with the Penn and Venables expedition, and this is not the only time that a Barrett-Wayte marriage would take place. It is of significant note that the people of the regicide who fled to Jamaica always found their descendants marrying one another.

The fifth child was Wisdom Barrett of Spot Valley, St. James. He was born on the twenty-first of January 1729 and died in January 1798, date unknown. He married twice, first to Anne Ellison, date unknown, and produced one child, Samuel Wisdom Barrett of Spot Valley. Samuel is another familiar Barrett first name. Secondly, he married Anna Maria Bowland at St. Marylebone Church on August 11, 1778. This marriage produced two children, Joseph Francis Barrett and Mary (again) Barrett, who married one James Trant of the island of Montserrat. Wisdom Barrett and his two wives lived and died in London, and they were never a friend of Jamaica. He was what later became known as an "absentee landlord." He allowed other members of his family to take care of his estate at Spot Valley, and his son Samuel seemed to have inherited this property, and very little is known of what happened later.

We now have a strange name appearing in the Barrett family. She was the sixth child of Samuel Barrett and Elizabeth Wisdom. Her name was Christian, and this is one of the few times, if more than one, that this name appeared in the Barrett family. It has not been heard of again. This reminds of one lady in the United States of America who was left without a family because her husband died, leaving her with two sons. One became a sailor and the other the vice president of the United States. Both were never heard from again.

Christian was born on the tenth of March 1731 and died on the sixteenth June 1759, and it is unusual that this name is given to a girl. Only men usually have this name; however, she became a woman, and at the age of fifteen she married Jacob Johnson of Westmoreland parish and produced no children. From age fifteen to twenty-eight years, she tried to produce children but failed. This caused her husband great anguish because in those days the more children people have, the more crown lands they would get from the king free of cost. For every child, in those days, the parents could claim several acres of land from the king. That is one of the reasons why children were getting married, for the purpose of producing as many children as possible to make more and more claims for free land given by the crown. Is it any wonder why Samuel Barrett of Cinnamon Hill and his descendants had so much land?

The seventh child was named a familiar name, after his father Samuel. He was born on the twenty-second of March 1733 and died on the twenty-first of August 1749 at the age of sixteen. He was never married because no match could be found for him at that youthful age, but his father had already gotten his portion of crown land on account of his birth. No matter how old a child is, provided he or she was registered properly, the parents can claim crown land on his or her behalf.

We now come to the most memorable and most distinguished of all the Barrett children. He was the eighth child of Samuel and Elizabeth Barrett of Cinnamon Hill. His name was Edward, later to be called Edward Barrett of Cinnamon Hill. He was the one on whom the Barrett mantle fell and his descendants would be the one to put the name Barrett everywhere in the world. He was born on the second of October 1734, and he was the first of Samuel Barrett and Elizabeth Wisdom's children to be born at Cinnamon Hill and to have died there on November 16, 1798.

His father saw that Cornwall House was too small for the large family he envisioned, and he wanted to be above sea level where he could look over a vast expanse of the Caribbean Sea. So he went up above Rose Hall Estate and started his dream house in 1722, completing it in 1734. As of writing, the same house, in a somewhat altered state, is still in existence, and was owned by many famous people, such as John Rollins, the former (now deceased) congressman from the State of Delaware; and singer Johnny Cash, who owned it up until the time of his death and was sold by his heirs sometime after the year 2000. This writer does not know the present owner.

So much is known about Edward Barrett of Cinnamon Hill, a special chapter of this book will be about him and his exploits. He is one whose actions created the title for this book, *Rooms without Doors*. He was so powerful that many places were named by him and because of him. His descendants became so famous that many books were written by them, for them, and of them.

The ninth child, Amelia, was born on December 12, 1736, and died in London, England, sometime in 1822. She was married twice, first to John Wisdom on the twentieth of June 1751 at the age of fifteen. Here again we see the young age of these juveniles when they got married, and the Barrett and Wisdom families were pioneering these early marriages wherever they resided. It was also significant that these families followed the practice of royalty by allowing nearby cousins to marry each other. John Wisdom was a cousin of Amelia. They produced no children. This marriage lasted only about twelve years, and it is not certain when Wisdom died or whether they were divorced. Divorces in those days were rarities, and there is no evidence of one in this case. Her second marriage was to Thomas Pepper Thompson on April 28, 1763, when she was first past twenty-six years of age and lived until she was eighty-six, yet did not add one soul to the Barrett family. She did not perform her biblical duty of multiplying and replenishing the earth. In those days, children were a bounty to their families because for each child that was born a claim could be made for crown land in Jamaica for each child. That's why her father acquired so much land.

Henry Barrett, even though he lived to be twenty, did not add to the Barrett family as far as could be proven, and there is no evidence of his having children by slaves or mistresses. He was born the tenth child on April 4, 1739, and died on August 27, 1759. In those days, yellow fever played havoc on every family in Jamaica, especially when they lived on properties that have swamps. The wetlands were breeding grounds for the yellow fever mosquitoes, especially at nights, and when they bit, it was like the AIDS virus, which pronounced a death sentence on their victims, no matter who or what.

We now come to the eleventh child, whose name was Margery. She was born on December 19, 1746, and died in London at a place made famous by the Barretts called Portman Square, in the month of January 1798. She was married at the age of twenty-two to George Whitehorn Lawrence. She, just as her sister Amelia before her, had no children. She was also one of the wealthiest female Barretts, and her home at Portman Square in London was the place that Jamaican Barretts frequented when they paid a visit to the mother country. She was a woman of the town and she was the Barrett to host extravagant house parties for the bigwigs of London who had a Jamaican connection.

This looks very funny, but we have another Samuel born to replace the first Samuel who died in 1749. Now we have this new Samuel, born to the same parents, on Christmas Day 1749, the same year that the first Samuel died. Samuel Barrett of Cinnamon Hill made it his duty to always have a living Samuel. This one happened to be his twelfth child. He died at Cambridge Estate in Trelawny on the twenty-second of October 1782. He was never married and had no recorded children. It seemed strange that a Barrett at age twenty-three was never married. This did not say he had no children. At that time, when a child is born out of wedlock it could not be registered in the father's name. There were many instances where white men had children by their slaves in order to get more light-complexioned people to work as house slaves. These mulattoes were the ones who created most of the slave rebellions in the western hemisphere because they did not consider themselves to be Africans and should be treated like white people. This statement will be repeated over and over again, because it is very important in the history of African slavery, and the result is still with us today, even though slavery as such had been abolished many years ago.

To end the saga of the Samuel Barrett and Elizabeth Wisdom's proliferation of children, let us look at the last three children who were born. Green, John, and William were their names. No dates of birth or death were recorded because all three were born and died within the same year, and therefore no records were kept.

The aforementioned information about births and deaths was obtained from a genealogical table that Jeannette Marks used in her book *The Family of The Barrett*, originally published in 1938 by the MacMillan Company, New York, and reprinted by the Greenwood Press in 1973, a division of William House-Regency Inc. It appears that this table is flawed and is incorrect. Readers are discouraged from using this table for precise dates of the births of the children of Samuel Barrett and Elizabeth Wisdom. The table has the following recorded on the sheet, "The above pedigree is compiled from notes collected from various sources, in the possession of E.N. GEIJER, Rouge Dragon, College of Arms, London, August 1933." With this authentication, it should be very clear that everything on the document is correct, but this writer has found to the contrary.

The proof of discrepancies is there. Elizabeth Wisdom, daughter of Henry Wisdom, was born on the sixth of May 1707. She died on the seventeenth of November 1737. She had fifteen children throughout her marriage to Samuel Barrett, sometime around 1721. Six of the fifteen children were born after her death, namely (1) Henry, 1739; (2) Margery, 1746; (3) Samuel, 1749; (4) Green; (5) John; (6) William. No dates are given for the last three, only that they died very young, probably within the same year. So this writer will not acknowledge or write anything further about these children. And for the purpose of this new book, *Rooms without Doors*, only Edward Barrett of Cinnamon Hill and his descendants will be written about. Maybe Samuel of Cinnamon Hill had a mistress after Elizabeth's death and he just kept recording the last six as both Elizabeth and his children in order to get more crown land. Children out of wedlock could not be counted in order to get crown land in those days.

The fact that Samuel Barrett of Cinnamon Hill never married again, and that six children came after his wife died at age thirty, can be cleared up if the date of her death was placed at 1757 instead of 1737. This would put her at age fifty, and those children born after 1737 could be her legitimate children. Based upon other evidence known to the writer, it is his concrete belief that the College of Arms made a mistake and the death of Elizabeth Wisdom Barrett is in fact November 17, 1757. The writer also thought that to criticize the College of Arms for something they did in 1933 would not prove anything significant. And since the topic of *Rooms without Doors* is based solely on the life of Edward Barrett of Cinnamon Hill and not historical accuracy about dates, the investigation will be postponed for a future date. It will be too costly and time consuming to investigate this matter for the time being.

During this time of prolific child getting, Samuel was made the custos of St. James parish. The function of a custos was that of chief magistrate of the parish, appearing at trials of minor cases, and in those days, major ones too in which the death penalty could be imposed, even though many of them did not have legal training and in some instances they could barely sign their names. Some got the job because they inherited large estates with large great houses that could accommodate large numbers of guests, including members of the royal family, when they visited a parish. Also, when the governor visited a parish for a few days, the custos of the parish was his host for whatever time the governor chose to stay. There was no remuneration for this, so the custos had to be a rich man; even today, this practice is still going on with a few minor changes. This old British tradition dies hard.

The custos also had administrative duties to do since he was in charge of all the justices of the peace for the parish, and for emphasis, each parish had a custos. They regulated where each justice of the peace would sit during trials in the petty sessions court. They tried non-indictable cases, such as abusive language (called *bad words* in Jamaica), and simple disputes between litigants, such as trespassing and simple assaults. They could also fine people in court for a restricted amount, as well as send people to prison for thirty days.

In Samuel Barrett's day, when slaves rioted, they could give them the death penalty because British law considered a slave as the goods and chattel of the slave master. Not only were slaves goods and chattel under British law, they were also considered such under United States law, and up to now their descendants in some places are being looked upon as inferior beings. This was so in 1787 when the constitution of these great United States was being drafted. The states with the most slaves wanted them to be full persons for the purpose of allocating seats in the House of Representatives, since seats were allocated based on population. The northern states had fewer slaves and they saw where the Southern states, which had a preponderance of slaves, would outvote them in Congress. They came to a compromise in which a slave would be recorded in the constitution as three-fifths of a person. These slaves were more recognized than the Indians, who were considered equal to zero. It was not until the thirteenth, fourteenth, and fifteenth amendments to the constitution that descendants of slaves and freed slaves got back the suspended two-fifths to make them whole again.

When Samuel Barrett of Cinnamon Hill saw that Cornwall Great House was becoming too small for his family, he went up to the hills from whence he could view a great portion of the Caribbean Sea and located an eight-acre plateau where he decided to construct another great house. This plot was a part of property called Cinnamon Hill because of the great number of wild cinnamon that grew there, and the sweet-smelling savor of these trees hypnotized him until he thought he was in wonderland. The exact location of this place is about three miles up the hill from Rose Hall Great House. It is some distance in the direction of northeast from Rose Hall but the two properties had a common fence at some point to the south and west of Rose Hall property.

At the time Samuel started the house in 1722, Cinnamon Hill Estate was about 1,486 acres. The great house was finished in 1734 after building and rebuilding took place, because there were several alterations that took place. It was not as famous as Rose Hall because there were no legendary occupants of Cinnamon Hill as compared to Rose Hall. The legend was only in the actions of Rosa Kelly Palmer and Annie Patterson Palmer (white witch) who existed about sixty years apart. These two women were specific ladies and nothing but their actions were legendary. Some historians claim that they were all fictitious but their records can be authenticated. This will be done in a future chapter on Rose Hall.

The great house on Rose Hall property, which is now a tourist attraction, was built after Cinnamon Hill. It was started by a woman named Rosa Kelly, who married four husbands, three of whom disappeared mysteriously. The fourth one outlived her, and this was the strangest thing that ever happened in those days on the north coast of Jamaica. The word *disappeared* does not exactly mean that, and will be explained later but it is essential here.

Now that Samuel Barrett had completed his house at Cinnamon Hill, the axis of his estates' operation shifted from Cornwall House to the new residence. He lived there until he died in 1760, and his many children became managers for his real estate holdings and plantations. Very few historians at that time would suggest that cattle rearing as in England was a major part of the economy. Hogs and goats were also a great part. They produced sugar, cotton, and dye woods for export to Europe, but the animals were slaughtered to supply the many ships that came into port selling slaves and bringing manufactured goods from Europe. Even Montego Bay got its name from the Spaniards who supplied ships, going to the Spanish Main for loot to bring back to Spain. Lard made from pig fat, which was used for cooking, was called *mantecca* in Spanish, and so the English transliterated the name to Montego Bay.

Samuel Barrett had vast stretches of these lands, which he inherited and bought, and some of these estates are still relevant in Jamaica today. His many estates include Cinnamon Hill, Cornwall, Little River, Cambridge, Oxford, Spring, Goodin Park, Thatchfield, and Retreat Pen. Some of these were in the parishes of St. Ann, St. James, and St. Elizabeth. Trelawny was not yet a parish, and when his son Edward Barrett of Cinnamon Hill took over, some of the properties became estates in the parish of Trelawny. Samuel Barrett dominated the north coast with sugar production and he became one of the wealthiest men around.

Even though his education was miniscule, he sent his children away to London to be educated. Some returned, others did not because they found other things to do in London, which was more hospitable to survival. Many of them thought that the yellow fever mosquito (*Stegomyia fasciata*) and the malaria fever mosquito (*anopheles*) were too great for them, so they would not return to Jamaica. Samuel Barrett thought correctly that educated men could do much better at farming and handling slaves than those who were not. This proved to be true in the life of his son Edward as will be seen in the next chapter. But irrespective of the education status of Samuel Barrett, he had an intellectual foresight that most planters did not have. He set such an example for his son Edward that the latter took it upon himself to extend the Barrett name and properties to a height that could not be rivaled in his day.

The location and importance of this property became a historical drama and research opportunity in the life of this writer. And even though he knew that Cinnamon Hill was either in the parish of St. James or Trelawny, he could not find a living Jamaican from those parishes who knew where it was. When it was suggested that Capt. Charles Cudjoe of the Maroons ran his camp some twenty miles away at a place called Trelawny Town, which now bears the name of Maroon Town, somewhere adjacent to Vaughnsfield in St. James the writer came closer to locating this property. He understood that one Capt. George Goodin Barrett was preparing the north coast militia to put down a suspected Maroon uprising—which did not materialize—and he was fearful that Trelawny Town was in such close proximity to the Barrett properties that any worthwhile encounter with these Maroons would cause great harm to his family. He went all out to find a solution, and there were some forms of compromise that were satisfactory to the Maroons, so they called off their attack, but the relationship between the planters of the north coast and those Maroons would always be volatile.

One could suppose that the women and children were the most fearful, and that was one of the reasons why many planters sent their families back to England for protection. Not only did their families become scared, the planters were also scared and they fled the island too, and this gave great rise to what was then called "absentee landlordism." Many estates had this strange breed overseeing and running properties for which they were not qualified, so they brutalized the slaves much worse than the real owners, and this type of brutality was also handed down to the missionaries, who were training to make life a bit easier for the slaves. Even some major churches were against the missionaries because their churches were stockholders in the slave trade and fought against the Quakers, Baptists, and Presbyterians who were the foremost objectors to slavery. Some planters used brushes made from feathers to tar the bodies of some missionaries, especially on the north coast of Jamaica, and it was from there that the derogatory term "tar brush" came into existence. When brilliant men emerged from unclassified white aristocracy, a check was always made to see if the tar brush passed nearby. This was a term used frequently by members of the Barrett family when someone they thought had Negro blood got too close to the family.

Having said all this, the location was eventually found when robbers held up singer Johnny Cash in the 1970s and the *Daily Gleaner,* Jamaica's then foremost newspaper, ran an editorial on the house and partially gave its location in the hill country above Rose Hall Great House. It was then that it became known where this great house was located, which occasioned a visit from this writer sometime in the future. More will be said of this visit in a later chapter.

Cinnamon Hill not only produced great Barretts, it also produced great Moultons. It was at this house that the greatest postcard picture by a portrait painter was developed. The world had been accustomed to this most famous painting, which has gone worldwide under the name of *Pinkie*. The majority of people who saw these postcards did not know that the painting represented someone born at Cinnamon Hill. Her name was Sarah Moulton, the daughter of Capt. Charles Moulton and Elizabeth Barrett, who lived at Cinnamon Hill. When Sarah was born, she was so beautiful, her grandmother decided she would be a celebrity. At an early age, she was sent to England with her two brothers to attend school, and her grandmother, Judith Goodin Barrett, commissioned the world-renowned portrait painter Sir Thomas Lawrence to paint a picture of her and send it back to Jamaica. As soon as the painting was completed, Sarah Moulton died. Judith would have nothing to do with the painting because of her grief, so she instructed the painter to dispose of it. This painting became known as *Pinkie,* and in the 1970s it was located at the Colis P. Huntington Library in San Mareno,

California. Its value is now in the millions. So Barretts are not only famous in life, they are also famous in death.

Samuel Barrett of Cinnamon Hill eventually became custos of St. James with no formal education, and became one of its astute businessmen without even knowing how to multiply small numbers. Yet he became the leading lay magistrate of the parish of St. James for many years. He acquired more properties than all his contemporaries, and set the paradigm for running a successful slave organization. With all of the above, he was one of the greatest progenitors of any family, especially his own Barrett family, and produced some of the most brilliant descendants for a family since the Norman conquest of Britain in 1066. Who these Barretts were is as fascinating as who they were to become. Every occupation and every aspect of life have descended from these Barretts. A good history of Jamaica needs nothing more than the family history of the Barretts since 1655. They took part in the political, military, business, and educational development of Jamaica as well as England. No wonder Samuel's grandfather Hersey Barrett Sr. was the man who cut off King Charles I's head in 1649.

Chapter 3

Edward Barrett of Cinnamon Hill

The name Edward Barrett of Cinnamon Hill began a tradition in the Barrett family and after a while there was a vast number of people wanting to give their children the name Edward. This man from Cinnamon Hill was to blaze a trail that had been, in his days, unprecedented. He became the founder of a dynasty in one branch of the family that was not seen or heard of before. So great was his influence upon governors and legislators alike that what he wanted for his family and friends he got. Not that they were afraid of him but because he was forceful and intelligent and was very rich. Based upon information that historians have, he was the wealthiest Barrett to have set foot on Jamaican soil.

He was the son of Samuel Barrett and Elizabeth Wisdom, and was born at Cinnamon Hill shortly after the great house was completed. As the first child to have been born there, he became known as the man from Cinnamon Hill, and the title stuck even upon his wife Judith, who was commonly called the lady from Cinnamon Hill. It is to be understood that the reason for giving the place such a name was the abundance of cinnamon trees in the area, which had to be cut down in order to build the great house.

He came into the world on October 2, 1734, and as the eighth child he was nothing special at birth. But shortly after this, he was seen as almost a prodigy. He was sent to England for schooling, and when he returned as an educated man, he knew well how to handle slaves, properties, and business. He joined his father in the operation of his estates, and he, Edward, bought properties and slaves for himself until he started to rival his father in acreage. He used scientific and business technology on his properties, and very soon they were producing to their

maximum. And up until the time of his death, he was still actively trying
to draft a will that took him over four years to complete. When he died
on November 16, 1798, he had left a mangled document of many pages
that could not be deciphered by normal legal brains. His grandson,
Richard Barrett, speaker of the House of Assembly, was one of the most
able lawyers in the West Indies, and he picked the will to pieces and got
more than what the family bargained for. Some had to sell properties to
repay other members of the family who should have gotten more. And
when it was finally settled, over twenty-five years had passed.

With all the intricacies of his will, Edward Barrett set a pattern for
the drafting of wills for a future generation of Barretts, which many of
them emulated. No family member should be left out of any will. But
later on one of his two favorite grandsons who got most of his wealth
decided that whoever of his children married during his lifetime would
be disinherited, and so the pattern changed, and it could be supposed
that many other Barretts disinherited their children.

At twenty-six years of age, Edward married Judith Goodin, the
daughter of William Goodin of Westmoreland parish, on April 30, 1760,
just one month after his father Samuel Barrett died. As it is in our day,
a family is confronted with a triad of birth, death, and marriage, so a
man getting married just one month after his father died was no real
big thing. Who knows, maybe he was waiting for the old man to die so
as not to cause some inconvenience. This was no problem for Edward.
His only rationale was keeping the family business productive.

The couple had five children. The first one was George Goodin
Barrett, who was born on January 23, 1761. He was a member of the
House of Assembly for the parish of St. James for many years, and died
on the eighth of October 1795 after a short lifespan of only thirty-four
years. He was never married and there were no recorded children in
his name, but this is far from the truth. He was a prolific child getter
by people unsavory to his family. Tradition has it that he sired nine
children out of wedlock and their four mothers were slaves working on
some of the Barretts' own properties. These women were not Africans
per se, they were mulattoes and quadroons, daughters of slave mothers
and English fathers. A mulatto is one whose parents are of two distinct
races, especially black and white. A quadroon is a person whose parents
are white and mulatto. Sometimes the difference between white and
quadroon are not distinguishable. Some quadroons are whiter than

some white people. George had so many of these children that it annoyed his father Edward Barrett of Cinnamon Hill so much that his stress level and blood pressure went up very high. Since George was his first son and was much more educated in business than his father was, he became an invaluable assistant to his father on the vast estates Edward had. He had to take the abnormal behavior by Englishmen standard of his firstborn. He wanted him on his properties more than George wanted to be.

George went to England, where he was trained in the then modern university system and graduated with honors. His parents were very proud of him as one of the brilliant minds on the north coast of Jamaica. No one knew the reason why he did not get married, but his great love was for a quadroon named Elissa Peters on the Cornwall Estate of the Barretts and others elsewhere, even outside the Barrett properties. He loved Elissa and her four children as if they were going out of style. His first son by her had the famous Barrett first name of Thomas, and he was named Thomas Peters instead of Barrett. In those days, the child of unwed parents had to take the mother's last name.

The emphasis on Thomas Peters and his mother Elissa Peters in the life of George Goodin Barrett is most profound. It is this Thomas Peters in particular who was left in his father's will with substantial bequest that later caused an earthquake in the Barrett family. So great was the earthquake that some Barretts had to sell properties and surrender their high lifestyle to clear themselves from debtor's jail. Thomas Peters' was the first case in the history of Jamaica where an illegitimate child was left as the major beneficiary of his father's will, and to add insult to injury in the life of a proud English family, this was the ultimate disgrace.

A controversial statement at this time will break the monotony of all this family history. It is a well-known fact that miscegenation—that is, two people from different races cohabiting and producing offspring—was always considered out of place by the English culture. But one thing that was always practiced by Englishmen in the West Indies was that of keeping a mistress that was crossbred, either a mulatto or a quadroon. To most Englishmen in the Caribbean, a crossbreed is much more sexually attractive than a purebred. The posterior of the feminine gender is so situated that it gives elegance to the curvature of the spinal column, and with mammary glands in the uppermost forward position, give the most attractive curves to crossbred feminine structure than those of the purer race. This idea has passed down to all the men in the Caribbean

area, and the beautiful complexion of not too light plus long hair and
sometimes blue, brown, or gray eyes make the ambulatory figures of
these women most attractive. What has this got to do with history?
Well, one will have to ask those old-time Englishmen and present-day
Caribbean men what they think about that statement.

Now George Goodin Barrett went to England for many years,
studying at some of the most prestigious schools and universities where
all the top English girls were. The fact that he came back and only
associated with mulattoes and quadroons said something much more
potent than the foregone statement. One of the rooms that has no door
at Cinnamon Hill was occupied by George Goodin Barrett.

The second child of the marriage was another son named Henry
Barrett, who was born on August 6, 1762, and died at the age of thirty-
two on September 24, 1794. He married at the age of thrity-one to
Barbara Samuels, the daughter of Richard Samuels, on June 20, 1793.
After a short marriage of just over one year, the couple produced one
child named Elizabeth who was born one month after her father died.
As the second son in those days and not as brilliant as the first, he would
always play second fiddle. Henry was not so much of a second fiddle
because Edward Barrett, his father, was very rich. Henry seemed to have
been given equal status in respect of responsibilities since he managed
many of the ships of his father, and it was not disgraceful at that time to
be engaged in the slave trade since the major churches were themselves
engaged in it and were major stockholders in companies whose chief
produce was slaves from Africa. At this point, it should be noted that the
English Crown was a major shareholder in slave exploitation.

There is no record about how Henry's only child Elizabeth fared
from his will. She got married to one William Sterling of Falmouth
and Content on October 20, 1811, and both went to London, where she
died on April 19, 1830. Her grandfather Edward Barrett became more
annoyed since his two sons were lovers of lower-class people, according
to men of the culture of Edward Barrett. Henry also occupied the room
beside his brother George on the second building that was erected
by Edward sometime during the 1760s. This room also has no door
like the one previously. Those two rooms had doors. The funny thing
about everything was that these two young men made wills and both of
them had their father as executor. Henry's will was not a problem, but
George's will was.

In successive years, Edward and Judith produced children. On October 1, 1763, a little girl was born and she was named Elizabeth after her grandmother Elizabeth Wisdom. We now have another Elizabeth to deal with but she was the most important Elizabeth in the family. As she grew up, she became the apple of the eye of her father. It seemed that in her he remembered his mother who had the same name, but again Edward became disappointed in the life of his daughter, who married a misfit by the name of Charles Moulton. It was not her fault because Edward, her father, had something to do with the selection. Charles sold slaves to Edward and he was a ship captain who sometimes, it is said, captained some of Edward Barrett's ships from the port of Falmouth doing roundtrips in the tripartite trade. This tripartite trade consists of taking sugar and rum from Jamaica to England, then picking up manufactured goods for Africa to exchange for slaves, then bring slaves from Africa to be sold in Jamaica. This was a very profitable business, and Edward Barrett of Cinnamon Hill was the foremost trader.

The marriage between Charles Moulton and his daughter took place in August 1781 and produced three children, Edward Barrett-Moulton, Samuel Barrett-Moulton, and Sarah Moulton (Pinkie). Even though Charles Moulton was hardly around after he sired these children, Edward allowed his daughter to stay at Cinnamon Hill, and both Judith and himself worshipped the two sons and one daughter of Elizabeth. When the children came of age, all three were shipped to London to attend school. Elizabeth went some years later. They had no problem with house in London because the Barretts owned most of Portman Square in London, and a great number of the Barretts were living there, including Edward's favorite sister, Margery Barrett-Lawrence. The two boys of Elizabeth Moulton would play a great part in the lives of the Barretts of Cinnamon Hill, and they later owned and operated the estate.

The fourth child was Sarah Goodin, and she died shortly after birth. And this brings us to the fifth and final child of Edward Barrett and Judith Goodin of Westmoreland parish. The reason for writing the names repetitiously is the simple fact that there are too many similar names. Here we come again to another Samuel Goodin Barrett. He was born on February 25, 1765. He died in Spanish Town, Jamaica, on December 7, 1794. It is of significant note that Edward Barrett of Cinnamon Hill outlived three sons and one daughter of his five children;

only Elizabeth Barrett Moulton was alive when he died. He was also the executor of his sons' wills.

Samuel Goodin Barrett married Elizabeth Barrett Wayte, the daughter of Henry Wayte. These two persons were first cousins. Elizabeth Barrett Wayte is the daughter of Mary Barrett and Henry Wayte. Mary is Edward Barrett of Cinnamon Hill's sister. Therefore, Mary Barrett Wayte is the aunt of Samuel Goodin Barrett, and Elizabeth Barrett Wayte is the daughter of Samuel's aunt Mary. This is not the only cousin marriage in the life of the Barretts.

Samuel had four children by his cousin. The first child was also Samuel Barrett; the second, Richard Barrett; the third, Edward Barrett of Portman Square; and the fourth, George Goodin Barrett, captain of the Fourteenth Dragoon Regiment. There is no one book that can tabulate the lives of the Cornwall Barretts from England who settled in Jamaica and sent their descendants back to England. Only one of these Barretts will be further commented upon. Richard here will be mentioned again since he was the major cause of the earthquake that hit the Barrett family most destructively.

We will now turn our attention back to Edward Barrett of Cinnamon Hill. With his ten or more ships engaged in the tripartite trade, and with his two sons George and Henry helping him, he expanded his properties all over St. Ann, St. James, Westmoreland, and St. Elizabeth. He owned the area of Falmouth, which was St. James until 1773 when Governor William Trelawny visited him at Cinnamon Hill and discussed the boundaries of a new parish he was considering to name after himself. Edward let him know that he would like his wharf and 431 lots surrounding it to become Falmouth, the capital of Trelawny. There was no record as far as could be seen about the answer that the governor gave to Edward. However, Falmouth became the capital of Trelawny. We also know that the county of Cornwall was so named by inducement from the Barrett family because they wanted a county named after the one from whence they came. It is also important to note that whenever a new governor came to Jamaica he had to visit the home of at least one Barrett whenever he visited the north coast of Jamaica, and Edward Barrett of Cinnamon Hill hosted most governors who came to Jamaica between 1760 and 1798. It is also important to note that between 1740 and 1840, in the history of Jamaica, there was never a time when a Barrett was not the custos or chief magistrate of one or all of three north coast parishes. Sometime during the 1830s, there were three Barretts simultaneously sitting as custos of the parishes of St. Ann, Trelawny, and St. James. There was Richard Barrett of St. James, Samuel Moulton Barrett of Trelawny, and another Samuel Moulton Barrett of St. Ann. These Barretts dominated the north coast in sugar plantations; Richard Barrett was the speaker several times of the House of Assembly; and there were other Barretts who were members of the House of Assembly for parishes both on the north and south coasts of Jamaica. This was a family that no one could avoid. They were on every side of the island of Jamaica.

This Edward Barrett of Cinnamon Hill was one of the most prosperous slave traders and producers of rum and sugar. His wealth was so vast and his slaves so many that they created his own slave districts and set up division of labor systems that Adam Smith did not know about. He had many slave overseers who were themselves slaves. He also apportioned hilly and forested land to his slaves to work for themselves and to sell their produce to one another and to other white farmers who did not allow their slaves these privileges.

The slaves looked upon Edward Barrett as being a messenger from the Great Spirit. They were also told to sell their produce, and when they had sufficient money, they could buy their freedom from him and still work on the property with the slaves, only they would be rewarded for work done. Both Edward Barrett and the slaves prospered.

When they worked the hilly land for a number of years, Edward would give them grass seed to sow in their old provision ground, then give them new land on which to work. The new land would be forest, and when new provision grounds were made, Edward would fence them and made the old provision grounds where the grass seeds were sown into new pastureland for cattle and horses. By doing these things, Edward Barrett's slaves worked with more dignity and were more loyal to him. When slaves were planning revolts, they could not enter upon Edward Barrett's properties to do so. The slaves would turn upon the organizers of the revolt and drive them away. They were much better off than the rest of the slave population.

As the colonial times went by, it was not very strange to see the emergence of a new type of slaves on Edward Barrett's properties. The first black overseer on record was found on his property, and the first black schoolteacher was also on his property. A great many of the white

folks chided Edward about his treatment of his slaves but he was too rich
and too powerful for anyone to hurt him. Barretts were sometimes in
charge of the north coast militia, and his son George Goodin Barrett
was captain of the cavalry that was to keep order on the north coast.
Edward told them that the better slaves were treated, the more work you
will get out of them. Some believed and joined Edward in prosperity.
Others did not and paved the way for the revolution of 1831, which,
although the destruction was great, did not adversely affect the younger
Barretts' plantations because they followed in the footsteps of their wise
grandfather, Edward Barrett of Cinnamon Hill.

Edward Barrett saw that the old great house was becoming too small
for his family, so he decided to build another extension to this house,
and it is this new extension that has the two rooms without doors. These
were the rooms occupied by George Goodin Barrett and Henry Barrett.
These were Edward's first two children. This portion of the house was
completed sometime around 1768. He now had enough money to do
anything he wanted, so his parties were more frequent. One of the
problems he could not overcome was the frequency of the hurricanes
that blew in every so often and with such fury that they became a threat
to life and property. The other problems were his two sons, George
and Henry. They would not get married to any girls around, but year
after year they produced children who had a touch of the tar brush. He
did not like this but could do nothing to prevent it. These boys were
attracted to the mulatto and quadroon slave girls. This would give him
the reason to create two rooms without doors on his extended house at
Cinnamon Hill. This could only give a mild amount of satisfaction to his
feelings. He, however, devised a plan to fight the hurricanes.

The decision to build a hurricane shelter to protect his family
at Cinnamon Hill was foremost in the mind of Edward Barrett. No
one in the West Indies ever considered such a plan before, and his
understanding of having one was more important than producing sugar
and rum. He was already one of the richest men in the British Empire,
so the protection of his family became of the utmost importance. There
is no evidence of his consulting with his slave builders but one can
conjecture from the building spree he engaged in since the year 1768,
in which many African slaves took part. He had on his many properties
slaves who could build almost anything.

It must be made quite clear that not all slaves were ignorant.
Some were great builders back in Africa, and one must realize that

the University of Timbuktu where Columbus went in the year 1465 to gain knowledge of the world and the ocean currents off the coast of Africa in order for him to make his westward explorations was not staffed by people of European descent. The professors were pure and endemic Africans. These were some of the slaves who were brought to the West Indies by Edward Barrett's slave trading. He had at least ten ships engaged in the slave trade, and his sons George and Henry were the chief operators of the slave business that operated from the port of Falmouth, which was fully owned by Edward Barrett himself.

There were also English builders on the Barretts' estates who would have been consulted in any major building project, but historians of those days, who were always white, would not be expected to give any credit to the black slave builders. No black ever did anything worthwhile in those days, and when they developed inventions, it was always stolen by the white masters. So in the construction of this hurricane shelter called "Cutwind," all the builders, black and white, available to Edward Barrett would be occupied in the construction, but only whites would get the credit. However, by whatever means possible, Edward Barrett set out to build his hurricane shelter.

The precise date of construction was not handed down to posterity, but it is known that it was started sometime after a hurricane hit in 1781. There was also a previous one in 1780, and these two hurricanes severely damaged the roof of his great house and threatened the lives of his family. He decided never again would this happen without a safe place to hide his family during one of these Caribbean monsters. Cutwind, the famous shelter, came into being. It was designed oval in shape and of solid eighteen-inch concrete and steel, with a height of about ten feet, ten feet wide, and twenty-three feet long. These are the approximate measurements. Inches are not included. We know for sure that it was operating in the year 1786.

The oval structure pointing toward the city of Montego Bay and the sea began taking the shape of a ship with its bow pointing toward Montego Bay. Like a ship's bow going some distance backward toward the house, it took the shape of an oval structure. Only an aerial photograph could clearly show what it looks like as a unit, so its shape will have to be left to the imagination. This author tried with his camera when he paid a visit in April 1987 but did not succeed in getting a correct photograph.

There is one thing that could be said about the materials that went into this construction. No concrete as we know it could remain in that

good condition from 1786 to the present time without large cracks in it.
It is presumed that the old African method of mixing cattle dung and
molasses into the concrete mixture would enhance the endurance of
good old concrete, and many people are of this opinion. This author
went inside the Cutwind from the old house where it was attached, and
from his estimation it could hold as many as twenty people in a partially
comfortable manner. This should be enough about the Cutwind, because
in the next twenty years there were more than ten great hurricanes that
hit the island of Jamaica and Edward Barrett must have been happy that
he undertook such a great effort to protect his family. Even after his
death in 1798, the hurricanes came with a vengeance. It is very surprising
that modern-day Jamaicans do not build something better than this
Cutwind of 1786, because hurricanes are still very active.

We now come to the two rooms that were built on the newer part
of the house by Edward Barrett sometime around 1768. These rooms
were occupied by George Goodin Barrett and Henry Barrett, his sons.
These were the two who loved quadroon and mulatto slave women.
These two sons were the ones who helped him most in the slave trade.
Also helping him was Capt. Charles Moulton, who married his beloved
daughter Elizabeth. With their help, Edward became very rich, and the
two sons became rich.

Henry got married in 1793 and had one daughter of this marriage
named Elizabeth. He died in 1794, one year after marrying. George did
not marry. He died in 1795. Both sons had many quadroon and mulatto
children by slave women. Edward Barrett was executor in chief to both
sons' wills. It was George's will that almost ruined the family fortune
of Edward Barrett's grandson Edward Moulton Barrett, who with his
brother, Samuel Moulton Barrett, got most of the estates of Edward
Barrett of Cinnamon Hill. George Goodin Barrett was a barrister-at-law
and he drafted his will to include the freedom of one mistress, Elissa
Peters, a slave, and also made a son of hers, Thomas Peters, as one of
the executors and gave much wealth to him in his will. Thomas Peters
was George Goodin Barrett's first son by Elissa Peters.

The contents of the will of George Goodin Barrett annoyed Edward
Barrett so much that he went ballistic. Even though Henry's will also
had freedom and wealth for his slave mistresses and his quadroon and
mulatto children, it was George's will that blew his mind because it
stated that the seven or more slave children he had should be freed and

sent to England to be educated at cost to his estates, and that they should remain there and never to return to Jamaica because they would be treated much better in England than in Jamaica for they were children of sugar barons. It is of significant note that no matter how black one was in those days, provided that he or she was the child of a sugar planter in Jamaica, that child would be accepted as white. When black children of sugar planters went to England from Jamaica to study, male or female would be grabbed as if going out of style, because people in Britain believed if they marry children of sugar barons it would put them on the highway to the seventh heaven. The word *black* in this context generally meant quadroons and mulattoes.

Bearing all of the last paragraph in mind, Edward Barrett became partially crazy, so he ordered his builders to remove the doors from the rooms of his two sons, Henry and George, and to have them concreted up so that no one could occupy them again. He then told his family when the job was done that, "Never in the history of my family again, will I allow any member to live in rooms that were occupied by Negro lovers. The sight of tar drums annoys me and I hope that this will not happen again." One must always recognize that although people may appear tolerant of a racial situation because it is economically profitable, deep down within their hearts racial hatred is still boiling. This is the rule, but there are exceptions too, and not everyone is truly racially intolerable. This secret of the Barretts was known only to a few in the family and it passed down from generation to generation, and those of the literary class among the Barretts hid it from the outside world. The author, in his investigation, came upon this secret through family members who passed it on, but outsiders are not aware of these traits endemic within such an enlightened family. It is still present within the family. Elizabeth Barrett Browning's father had it and even the author's grandfather of modern times. The words *tar brush*, *tar drums*, and *tar barrels* are words still endemic in the Barrett family, and are used in the description of black people even in modern times, so the behavior of Edward Barrett of Cinnamon Hill still lives on, not only in the family of the Barretts but also the descendants of many Europeans all over the world. The sooner people realize that genetically we are all one, the better it will be for the whole world. The retribution for Edward Barrett's ill-conceived idea was to pass on to later generations, and even his great-granddaughter Elizabeth Barrett Browning felt some of the result because her father was identical in belief commonly accepted by some Europeans that Africans are not equal to them.

There were other things that Edward Barrett did apart from concreting up the doorways of the rooms of his two sons who loved quadroon and mulatto women. He was a great builder and real estate mogul. When William Trelawny came as governor to Jamaica in 1773, he visited Edward Barrett and told him his intention of creating a parish with the name Trelawny. He told him he would like that parish to be located on the north coast and that St. James and St. Ann would have to be adjusted in size to make way for the new parish. Edward was very happy about this, and suggested to him to make the western boundary west of the area his seaport and wharves of the Falmouth beachfront occupied. The governor listened intently to the man of Cinnamon Hill and decided to cut land from St. James, St. Ann, and St. Elizabeth in the south. At that time, the parish of Manchester was not in existence, and this would not be the last time that the largest parish in Jamaica would be cut. So the cockpit region of St. Elizabeth was taken and a goodly portion of St. Ann and to a lesser degree the parishes of St. James and Cambridge, and Trelawny became a reality named after the governor. Edward Barrett was not done with him yet.

He owned 431 lots on the sea coast located on either side of his wharves, and he recommended to the governor to locate the new parish capital on these lots, which he would sell to new developers with his buildings already there as the foremost economic entity in the area. His wharves also played a great part because they were the chief slave trading area on the north coast. He, Edward, owned at least ten ships engaged in the slave trade, and his future son-in-law, Capt. Charles Moulton, also a slave trader, was the father of England's famous poetess Elizabeth Barrett Browning. He did not succeed at first because the governor considered the suggestion as one that would be looked upon as unethical. Martha Brae got the choice over Falmouth as the capital of Trelawny, but Edward Barrett would not stop at anything.

Nature was on his side, and it silted up the Martha Brae River entrance to the sea, and yellow fever joined in and made the town uninhabitable. And by the year 1790, the government of Jamaica was very happy to ask Edward Barrett to sell a portion of his land in Falmouth to make the new capital of Trelawny. The lots were now more valuable and Edward Barrett got a good price for the lots he sold, and in some cases he doubled the prices that he was offering them for in 1773. So after seventeen years, he got better than his wish. Money was now pouring into his coffers at a pace that he could not handle, so he involved two of his sons, George Goodin Barrett and Henry Barrett, to help him spread the Barrett wealth all over the north coast of Jamaica. His daughter Elizabeth helped him in relieving his pockets of some of the vast wealth in the family. Her marriage went on the rocks and she had three children to support.

The marriage of his beloved daughter Elizabeth to Capt. Charles Moulton proved a disaster within a very short period. It was on August 28, 1781, that Edward Barrett gave his daughter to Charles Moulton. This man was no stranger to him. He bought slaves from Charles Moulton and it has been said that Charles captained one of his ships during the slave era, when most of Edward's ships were engaged in the tripartite trade from the West Indies to England with rum and sugar, then to the west coast of Africa with manufactured goods to exchange for slaves, then back to the West Indies with human cargo.

The marriage lasted less than ten years, during which time the couple produced four children, three boys and one girl. The first child was a girl who became world famous after her death. Her name was Sarah, commonly called "Pinkie," and she became the postcard princess of the world after the famous portrait painting by Sir Thomas Lawrence for the lady of Cinnamon Hill, Judith Goodin Barrett, her grandmother. Sarah died before the painting could get back to Cinnamon Hill, so her grandmother told Lawrence to do what he wanted with it. He put it on display, and the Woolworth family became intrigued with Sarah's beauty and used the painting in their postcard industry and had it immortalized. Her portrait would grace millions of Christmas cards and other decorations all over the world. The painting was sold to Colis P. Huntington of California about fifty years ago, and he placed it in his museum at San Moreno in California, where it is believed to be at the present moment.

In 1785, the couple produced a second child, named Edward Barrett Moulton. He will be the subject of the following chapter, so nothing needs to be said about him at this point. In 1787, the second son was born and his name was Samuel Barrett Moulton. The third son was born the following year but he died a few months after birth. His name was George Barrett Moulton. The two remaining sons grew up with Sarah before she died, and were sent to England to be educated, as was the custom of the wealthy planters. These two boys became the idols of Edward Barrett of Cinnamon Hill.

The story of who their real father was became the talk of Cinnamon Hill. Elizabeth rarely saw her husband Charles Moulton after the children's birth. As a ship captain, he was away for several months at a time and he also had business in New York, where it is said he kept at least one mistress, and when he went to London he had others, but the aggravating situations took place in Jamaica. There is no record of Edward Barrett driving him away from Cinnamon Hill, but when he returned to Jamaica from his overseas trips, he did not go to Cinnamon Hill where his wife and children were, he went to the home of one of his mistresses. And to add insult to injury, these mistresses had the tar brush all over or passing nearby.

To repeat what has been said many times before, the word *tar brush* meant that Negroid connection was present. There are records that Charles Moulton had at least five colored children, some of whom were mulattoes and others were quadroons. This is what annoyed the Barretts of Cinnamon Hill to the highest degree. The only part of their family they could tolerate as being black or partially black were their slaves. Even though Sam Barrett whipped his slaves mercilessly, his son Edward and others of his descendants found a way to treat slaves more humanely than the rest of the British slave masters. One point of emphasis here is that the first black overseer and the first black schoolteacher came from the Barretts' estates.

Beginning with Edward Barrett of Cinnamon Hill, slaves were taught to read and practice religion right up to the abolition of slavery. Many planters chided the Barretts for doing this but the Barretts were an independent-minded clan, and they found out that treating the slaves well gained them more loyalty. The Barretts, beginning with Edward, allowed their slaves to work the non-arable land and sold the produce in the slave markets on weekends, then paid down on their freedom. When a certain amount of money was paid, Edward would free them and still allow them to remain on his property and continue to work their hilly provision grounds, and during crop time he would hire the free men to help reap his sugar cane. As a result of this, the slaves on the Barrett properties had an incentive to be of good behavior with a view of also buying their freedom. These were the kinds of black people that Edward

Barrett liked. But when it came to his family engaging in sexual activity with them, he was most angry. Hundreds of years passed and some of his descendants are just like him even in modern times.

Now that Edward was getting on in years, he decided to make a will that will would include children yet unborn. He adopted the two sons of Elizabeth, his daughter, and decided to give them most of his wealth. His average annual profit from 1754 to 1790 was in excess of sixty thousand pounds. In modern-day money, that is millions of dollars, so one can judge the wealth of Edward Barrett of Cinnamon Hill.

The adoption of the two grandsons posed a problem for him in willing them most of his wealth. Under British law in those days, in order to give them part of his property, these boys would have to carry the surname Barrett. They were registered as Edward Barrett Moulton and Samuel Barrett Moulton. What Edward Barrett did was contact a notary public and justice of the peace by the name of John Graham-Clarke of Newcastle-upon-Tyne and gave him the job of changing the names of his two grandsons. It took John about two years to get it done, and when Edward Barrett got the letters with the change of names, he was content to do what he had proposed. First, he sent all of his daughter Elizabeth's children off to England to attend school. Of the three, only one would return to Jamaica. Sarah (Pinkie) Moulton died at age thirteen. Edward Barrett Moulton-Barrett, as he was now named by deed poll, never returned. Samuel Barrett Moulton-Barrett returned and took charge of the estates until he died in 1737, one year before full emancipation of slaves in the British Empire.

The change of names of Edward Barrett's grandsons had an ironic twist. These boys were under the care of the same John Graham-Clarke and he saw to it that they went to school, and their entire wellbeing was under his care and protection. To make a long story short, after the death of Edward Barrett, John Graham-Clarke gave his first daughter, Mary, to Edward Barrett Moulton-Barrett to wed, even though she was a few years older than Edward. She bore him many children, including the first child, Elizabeth Barrett Browning. Strange coincidence. The next chapter will explain.

Edward Barrett of Cinnamon Hill began to draft his will and it took him four years to do so. On several occasions he had to go back, rewrite, alter, amend, and attached codicils to a will that was several pages long. He was also executor of the wills of his two Negro-loving sons, George and Henry. They both left complicated wills and Edward had to separate their wills from his because all three had interlocking claims to some of the properties that became jointly owned.

Henry's will was not that complicated, but George's was. He was the intellectual genius of the then Barrett family, an Oxford University don and a barrister-at-law before he was twenty-one. He made some clauses in his will that gave Edward a hard time. George's quadroon and mulatto children were also included in his will. They were slaves on other people's properties and the will dictated that their freedom should be bought and they should be sent to England to go to school and to remain there forever. Money was provided in the will to do all of these, and one of the boys, Thomas Peters, was also coexecutor of the will. This is what annoyed Edward Barrett the most. It was this complicated will that caused problems in the Barrett family, because Edward willed some of the slaves that belonged to George to his two grandsons and this brought a family lawsuit spearheaded by Richard Barrett of Greenwood Great House against the Moulton-Barretts. Since Richard was a top barrister-at-law and was speaker of the House of Assembly, he had more clout in the courts of Jamaica than the two brothers Moulton-Barrett in London. The judgment went against Edward and Samuel Moulton-Barrett, and they had to pay back a huge sum of money to their quadroon cousin Thomas Peters, who was in fact a Barrett also, being the son of George Goodin Barrett and also a grandson of Edward Barrett of Cinnamon Hill.

The precise amount of wealth left by Edward Barrett of Cinnamon Hill to his two grandsons Edward and Samuel will never be known since no cash or cattle were mentioned, but it is said that he left forty thousand acres of sugarcane, nine sugar mills, and 3,500 slaves. No ordinary man ever owned so much, but this was only a part of his wealth. His wife Judith Goodin Barrett was left with a vast amount of cash both in Jamaica and London. His daughter Elizabeth also got a large amount of cash. These two women went to live in London after the death of Edward in 1798, never returning to Jamaica, and both died as rich women of high society London. They were still living off the proceeds of sugar and slaves from their Jamaica plantations and were settled in the exclusive neighborhood of West London known as the Portman Square enclave. They lived a life of wealth and were the envy of those partially rich Londoners who had nothing compared to the family of the Jamaican sugar barons.

Edward Barrett of Cinnamon Hill set the pattern for the Barrett family of frugal living. Even with his wealth, he wore patched clothes but saw to it that his family never did. He was not ashamed to do so, and had his descendants followed his pattern, some of the problems his grandchildren fell into would not have happened. Not all his descendants became poor. Some today are as wealthy as he was, and the name of Barrett became a household word for good or for evil. World-famous people are descended from him, such as Elizabeth Barrett Browning, who is a household name in poetry; her father Edward Barrett Moulton-Barrett, on whom books have been written and movies made; Pinkie, the most beautiful postcard star; great generals of the British Army; and a host of other famous people. The family of the Barretts was made much better off by the coming into existence of Edward Barrett of Cinnamon Hill. Even though he was one of the great slave traders and sugar barons of the eighteenth century, he did what was common to Europeans in those days. And during the present century, when slave holding is taboo, people will have to look back and say it was the peculiar institution of those times.

It is not because the author is descended from these Barretts that he may be saying these things in a slightly different manner; he knows that slavery was immoral. What we now have are historians attacking individual countries but will not attack the two major churches that dealt with the slave trade. The people who manned the barricades on the west coast of Africa during the dirty days of slavery were church leaders. They were the ones who preached Jesus Christ to them then sold them to slave dealers, and those churches retained the profits. These churches are still in existence today and teaching morality, yet they never said slavery was immoral, because this was their source of wealth. When the Quakers and the Baptists and other churches were fighting against slavery, those two churches called them heretics. Most slave beaters went to church on Sundays after beating their slaves on Saturdays, then go back on Mondays and throughout the week to start beating them again. One of those churches that owned slaves said that black people were not real human beings. Give me a break! Edward Barrett of Cinnamon Hill treated his slaves better than many churches did.

Chapter 4

Edward Barrett Moulton-Barrett

If even there were a child who was born with the proverbial gold spoon in his mouth, Edward Barrett Moulton would be one of them, or could be the only one. The place where he was born on May 28, 1785, is still obscure in the mind of Jamaican and British historians, including this writer. It took several years to find out where this Cinnamon Hill Great House was located, and if famous people like Johnny Cash had not lived there, it would have taken much longer to find.

Johnny Cash, the great singer who owned the house for over thirty years, was held up by robbers there, and the international press had a field day about robberies and murders occurring on the small island of Jamaica in the West Indies. It was this unusual incident that opened the eyes of this writer to where Cinnamon Hill was located. Few people, if ever, knew that the father of Elizabeth Barrett Browning was born in Jamaica, and less than few knew where. Before the Cash ordeal, this writer came in touch with a book purporting to be the diary of Elizabeth Barrett Browning, and he looked at a significant date in December 1831 when Sam Sharpe led a slave uprising on the north coast of Jamaica. Elizabeth Barrett Browning was writing her usual entries when she reportedly wrote the following quotation, "I am glad that my father's estates were not destroyed by the recent uprising in Jamaica. Even though he had properties in Trelawny and St. James parishes, his substantial estate was in the parish of Cambridge."

There is no parish of Cambridge in Jamaica, but when this writer racked his brain, he remembered his old teacher, Ina Patrick Wilson, told him when he was nine years old and in the third grade in elementary school that there was a governor who came to Jamaica in 1866. His name was Sir John Peter Grant, and he did two things. He extended the railroad from Spanish Town to Old Harbor, and he reduced the twenty-two parishes to fourteen. These are the same number of parishes in Jamaica today. Bearing this in mind, it was found out that one of the former twenty-two parishes was Cambridge. Further investigation found that Cambridge was connected to St. James, somewhere to the south and east.

Having said all this, Cinnamon Hill could not be found until a book written by Jeannette Marks entitled *The Family of the Barrett* stated that Rose Hall Great House was supplied with water from a spring located on Cinnamon Hill property owned by Edward Barrett, who was cousin to the Honorable John Palmer, custos of St. James, who owned and lived at Rose Hall Great House during the eighteenth century. This brought about the end of the search for the location of Cinnamon Hill. With the robbery of the great house owned by Johnny Cash, most people who were interested got to know where Cinnamon Hill was. This writer, in the year 1987, got permission from Johnny Cash to pay a visit to the great house, which he did in April of that year, and so Cinnamon Hill Great House became his location for almost ten hours.

Now this man known as Edward Barrett Moulton was the second child born to Elizabeth Barrett, daughter of Edward Barrett of Cinnamon Hill, and Capt. Charles Moulton, who had addresses in London and New York, as well as Jamaica. From the evidence explored, when he was in Jamaica, it appeared that he lived with his wife Elizabeth at Cinnamon Hill. The old great house was expanded by an extension in 1768, and it was large enough to hold more than one family. Since all of Elizabeth and Captain Moulton's children were born at Cinnamon Hill, by extrapolations, deductions, and conclusive presumptions, historians can say outright that this was the home of Elizabeth and her husband. To say that Edward Barrett Moulton was born with a gold spoon in his mouth was not very accurate until he was about ten years old. He had two other siblings at this time. His third died shortly after birth, so he had no say in the order of things.

Sarah Moulton (Pinkie) was the first, Edward was the second, and Samuel the third. Of the four children his parents had, three were alive when Edward was ten, and all three were adored by their grandparents, Edward Barrett of Cinnamon Hill and Judith Goodin Barrett, the lady of Cinnamon Hill. Some statements here sound repetitious but there are so many people with the same first names and clarity is essential, so repetition will have to be overlooked. This adoration would cause problems later in the lives of two of these three grandchildren. Sarah Moulton died shortly after arriving in England in 1795. Now, Edward Barrett of Cinnamon Hill was now free to do something different with his will that he started earlier on.

Capt. Charles Moulton, the father of the three children mentioned, was an enigma wrapped in a riddle and submerged in a puzzle. From the birth of his children between 1783 and 1788, he was seen infrequently at Cinnamon Hill. After the birth of his last child, no one knew where he was. Rumor had it that he had a mistress in New York, so on his way to London he would stop there and did some trading. He then went on to London, where it is rumored he had more than one mistress. These were all white. On his return to Jamaica, he had more than one mistress. None of these was white. They were all mulattoes and quadroons. He had about five illegitimate children with his Jamaican mistresses, and these were known to the Barrett family. Nothing could be done on the north coast that a member of the Barrett family did not know of. In fact, it was stated that his brother, Robert Moulton of Trelawny parish, had over thirty-six children by mulatto and quadroon women, so Charles with only five that were known did not even come close to Robert, his brother. This kind of behavior annoyed Edward Barrett so much that he decided to do something about the situation of his adorable grandchildren.

In 1795, he arranged for his daughter Elizabeth Moulton to take her three children to England, where they should go to school since Jamaica at that time had no worthwhile schools. These grandchildren had paid tutors at Cinnamon Hill, where they were taught as best they could. Sarah was twelve years old, Edward ten, and Samuel nine. They all had an education enough to enter some of the high schools in Britain, and the millionaire from Cinnamon Hill took control of his grandchildren away from their biological father, and he was happy to do so because no one cared about this inconsequential ship captain anymore. No one heard about him aside from news getting to Cinnamon Hill that he was siring some quadroon illegitimate children someplace along the north coast of Jamaica.

More disaster would engulf the Barretts of Cinnamon Hill, because as the children landed in Britain, the lady of Cinnamon Hill, Judith Goodin Barrett, requested a painting of Sarah Moulton (Pinkie) by Sir

Thomas Lawrence, the great portrait painter at that time. Before he completed the job, Pinkie died, after only being in Britain three months. So grieved was Judith that she gave Lawrence permission to do what he wanted with the portrait, so he put it on exhibition in London, and it was such a hit that people paid an immense sum of money to acquire it. It became world famous, and the price went to millions of dollars and was acquired by Colis P. Huntington of San Moreno, California, where it is a part of his museum. Prior to his acquisition, the Woolworth Company had it and made millions of postcards bearing the portrait of "Pinkie." So Pinkie became much more famous at death than had she lived. She was and still is a great memorial to the Barrett family.

Edward Barrett Moulton went to one of the famous schools in England at the time. Harrow was one of the best and only rich people could go there. Samuel went to another school because of his age. Even though their mother was in Britain, she had not much control over them. They were under the care and protection of two prominent men who lived at Newcastle-upon-Tyne. They were James Scarlett, who later became Lord Abinger, and John Graham-Clarke, who got the job to change the boys' names by deed poll from Moulton to Barrett, and to carry the coat of arms of the Barretts. It was not legal under British law at that time for anyone to inherit property from a grandfather, unless that person had the last name of the grandfather and was permitted to carry the coat of arms.

This took about three years to do, and John Graham-Clarke hurried it along as much as he could so that their grandfather could amend his will to make them heirs and successors to Edward Barrett of Cinnamon Hill. Edward was also very happy that he had removed his favorite grandchildren from a conflict that was brewing between white slave owners and the Maroons who were freed by the British in 1739, and they were constantly threatening to attack. It is no wonder why so many of the Barretts entered into the military. They had to defend several square miles of property because the land owned by the Barretts was easier to be measured in square miles than by acres and hectares. So the Barrett family was on edge whenever the Maroons threatened. At this juncture, it gives this writer great pleasure to inject that he is a direct descendant of the Maroons as well as a direct descendant of the Barretts. Here are two groups of people, one white and the other black, confronting each other in hostile array, and even engaged in warfare, and here is a descendant of both groups, some 313 years later, writing about his ancient ancestors. This is incredible and unusual, and more so unusual is the fact that this writer knows about it.

As the story of Edward Barrett Moulton continues, he was not a very brilliant scholar, which could be attributed to the fact that as a boy he had too much money and too many famous people rallying around him. He was not as brilliant as his uncle George Goodin Barrett, who was matriculated at Oxford University at the age of fourteen, graduated at eighteen with his bachelor's degree, then went on to the Inns of Court, where at age twenty he became a barrister-at-law and was one of the youngest to do so throughout the British Empire. What Edward had to do was supervise his inheritance, which was for his younger brother and himself. His younger brother had to continue in school while he and the caretakers talked business. It was not until January 2, 1798, that John Graham-Clarke got through with the change of names by deed poll for his brother and himself, and it took three months to get to Cinnamon Hill, where Edward Barrett, with pen in hand, was waiting to change his will.

Upon getting the good news that his two grandsons Edward and Samuel by his favorite daughter Elizabeth now had the surname Barrett, Edward amended his will to give them forty thousand acres of sugarcane, nine sugar mills, and 3,500 slaves. This was an enormous amount of wealth to give two grandsons, but he did it anyhow. Many more relatives got fortunes from Edward Barrett, and the amount of cash he appropriated to relatives were in the hundreds of thousands of pounds, and cattle and other real estate holdings were also in superabundance. After altering the will, he saw the travail of his soul and was satisfied. He did not survive the remainder of 1798, but he made a great mistake with the slaves, because some of them belonged to his son George Goodin Barrett, who made a will as to the slaves' disposal. This was to later haunt and oppress the two grandsons some twenty years later, when the son of George Goodin Barrett challenged the will, aided and abetted by Richard Barrett, the speaker of the House of Assembly.

Now that the change of names was successfully carried out, the two boys had all their documents changed and from henceforth and forever, the their names and that of their descendants would be Barrett, and they would bear the Barrett coat of arms. Edward from now on would have the name Edward Barrett Moulton-Barrett.

As was mentioned before, it was John Graham-Clarke who did the proceedings to get the names changed. He also had his eyes on Edward. He was an overseer of the boys while they were growing up, and he was privy to the changes made in the will of Edward Barrett of Cinnamon Hill. And as soon as Edward Barrett Moulton-Barrett was twenty years old, Graham-Clarke gave him his first daughter, Mary Graham-Clarke, to wed. The marriage was done in a rush, and no one knew whether something was going on between the two young people or not. However, she was four years his senior, so her father wanted her married fast, because in those days a twenty-four-year-old woman was considered past her peak for producing her first child. Not only was young Edward eligible, he was also rich, and John Graham-Clarke was an astute businessman, so he would not let go of as good a catch as Edward. No previous historians, as far as is known, ever commented on this alleged kidnapping.

Edward Moulton-Barrett, as he will now be called, was one of those old-fashioned Englishmen trained in etiquette that even had he wanted to say no to John Graham-Clarke's request or command to marry his first daughter he would not have said so. As it turned out, Elizabeth, Edward's first child, defied his order not to marry during his lifetime. This act of Elizabeth caused two more of his children to defy Edward, who was so adamant that none of his children should marry while he was alive that he disinherited all three who did so.

We now look at the condition under which Edward had to say yes to John Graham-Clarke. It was John who changed his name so that he could inherit from his grandfather, Edward Barrett of Cinnamon Hill. It was John who was his caretaker and guardian while he went to school, and it was John who made the necessary recommendations for his wellbeing while he was in England. John played the role of father to him since his biological father was roaming the world and having affairs with women in whom the tar brush was evident. Taking all these into consideration, an obedient lad would obey those he thought had his interest at heart, whether or not those people would handsomely benefit. So the die was cast, and Edward decided to marry his playmate even though she was four years his senior. In contrast, his daughter Elizabeth married Robert Browning, who was six years younger than herself, so she followed in the footsteps of her mother by choosing a much younger man. As the saying goes, when the ground is level, a fruit never falls far from the tree.

It was on that memorable day, May 14, 1805, that young Edward Moulton-Barrett married his mature sweetheart Mary Graham-Clarke at Gosforth Church in Northumberland, and the following year they started one of the largest Barrett families superseded only by old Samuel Barrett and Elizabeth Wisdom at Cinnamon Hill some eighty years earlier. Samuel and Elizabeth were the great-grandparents of Edward Moulton Barrett.

Since there is so much to be said about Edward, the children will be listed in order of birth, and one or more of them will be the subject of another or more chapters. Their first child was Elizabeth, born at Coxhoe Hall, Durham, March 6, 1806; Edward at Coxhoe Hall, June 26, 1807; Henrietta, March 4, 1809, at Hope End, Herefordshire; Mary, September 26, 1810, Hope End; Samuel, January 13, 1812, Cheltenham; Arabella, July 4, 1813, Hope End; Charles John, December 28, 1814, Hope End; Geoge Goodin, July 15, 1817, Hope End; Henry, August 19, 1819, Hope End; Alfred Price, May 20, 1820, Hope End; Septimus James, February 22, 1822, Hope End; Octavius Butler, April 12, 1824, Hope End.

Hope End was a large property bought by Edward Moulton-Barrett in the parish of Ledbury in the county of Hereford. It had a large house surrounded by hundreds of acres of land. All the boys were surnamed Moulton-Barrett and also carried the middle name Barrett. For example, Charles John's full name was Charles John Barrett Moulton-Barrett. The girls did not carry the name of Moulton. All eight boys had their last name hyphenated, but the girls only had Barrett as their last name. Elizabeth hated the name Moulton in such a way that she said it with disdain. She added another Barrett to her name and called herself Elizabeth Barrett Barrett. She signed her initials EBB. Enough on the name Barrett.

When Edward Barrett Moulton-Barrett had sired twelve children, eight boys and four girls, by his wife Mary, he thought she had had enough. She must have been the one to cry out loud. Even though they inherited much wealth, the health of Mary took a downtown, and four years after giving birth to her last child, she died on October 1, 1828, and left behind twelve children. Elizabeth, being twenty-two years old, became the caretaker of her siblings, a job she did until the time of her great illness, which lasted many years. Her father did not remarry, so the older ones had to take care of the younger children.

When George Goodin Barrett died in 1795, he left a funny will freeing his slave mistress Eliza (Elissa) Peters and had all his slave children taken care of in his will. The will was most reasonable and excellent, but in the eyes of Edward Barrett, his father, the will was funny. In those days, illegitimate children could not inherit anything, more so slaves and their mulatto and quadroon offspring. The whole story is this: George Goodin Barrett was a barrister-at-law and was one of the most brilliant brains a Barrett could produce. He decided to buck the old system and take care of his colored offspring, but his father did not agree, so he did many things to circumvent the wishes of his son and ended up willing some of his son's slaves and property to his favorite grandsons, Edward Moulton-Barrett and Samuel Moulton-Barrett. These two grandsons were now going to pay dearly for their grandfather's mistakes.

Now, at this time, George Goodin Barrett's children with slave mothers were in England being educated under the guidance of John Graham-Clarke, the father-in-law of Edward Moulton-Barrett. What a conflict! John Graham-Clarke was the protector of Thomas Peters, who was the son of Eliza Peters and George Goodin Barrett, who died in 1795. From 1802 onward, multiple lawsuits were filed by many members of the Barrett family against each other, and these lawsuits, both in England and Jamaica, continued until around 1826, when the two grandsons of Edward Barrett of Cinnamon Hill were confronted in court by his other grandsons. The first was Thomas Peters, whose surname was really Barrett but because he was the son of the slave Eliza Peters he had to take her last name. The other grandson was the notorious Richard Barrett of Greenwood Estate, a top barrister-at-law and three times speaker of the House of Assembly. He was also custos of St. James parish and had great influence among the bigwigs of those days. When he joined the lawsuits against the Moulton-Barretts, the result was a forgone conclusion. He was so powerful in Jamaica that few could challenge him in court. He was one of the brilliant legal geniuses of the Barrett family, so all the important judges knew him well. When the cases against the Moulton-Barretts finally came to a close, they had to pay back thousands of pounds in cash to the other Barretts, foremost Richard himself and Thomas Peters (Barrett). Had it been only Peters' case, the Moulton-Barretts would have gotten off much easier, but the great Richard was their first cousin and inveterate enemy. The Moulton-Barrett family hated him for the rest of his life.

Were it for Thomas Peters (Barrett) alone, his protector, John Graham-Clarke, would have brought about some form of compromise since his daughter was the wife of Edward Moulton-Barrett. This was not to be, because Richard (the Lionhearted) Barrett was on the case. He lived in Jamaica, and the case was settled in Jamaica by judges who lived in Jamaica. This was the earlier part of the nineteenth century, and even now in the twenty-first century, if one lives overseas and some other family member captures one's property and a court case arises, the judges in Jamaica always rule in favor of the one who still lives in Jamaica. They consider the one overseas as a foreigner who is always picking up money off the streets or taking it from trees, so the property in Jamaica belongs to the one who lives there. What a travesty of justice! Edward and his brother Samuel lived in England, so the suit brought against them was loaded in favor of the Jamaicans.

With this shock in the lives of the Moulton-Barretts, Edward had to sell a part of his beloved Hope End property in Herefordshire to pay up the money the court had imposed on him. It is difficult to find the total amount, but it was upward of eleven thousand pounds for use of 131 slaves over many years, in addition to the use of other properties. This is according to Jeannette Marks in her book *The Family of the Barretts*.

Samuel Moulton-Barrett had no such difficulty. He had plenty of cash because he was unmarried and had no children, but Edward, even though he was rich, had twelve children and had spent most of his cash to buy the Hope End property, which consisted of many hundred acres and a large house.

The move from Hope End was a devastating blow to Edward Moulton-Barrett and his children. They had plenty of lakes and springs with water flowing throughout the property and plenty of land in which to room and a large flat area to play cricket and football (soccer). On these flat areas, Edward and his children played and rode horses over many acres. They all loved Hope End, and this was where Elizabeth Barrett Browning started on her poetic career.

The first move was to Sidmouth near the sea, then to the west end of London at Gloucester Avenue in the Portman Square area where the Barrett and the Lawrence families owned extensive real estate holdings. These two families, earlier on, had intermarried. Edward's grandaunt, who was married to Ezekiel Lawrence, lived there, so it was a kind of homecoming for the family. He then left Gloucester Avenue and bought

50 Wimpole Street, where he lived until his death in 1857. It was at this place that the love letters of Elizabeth and Robert Browning were written and received while Edward was away at work in his office at another section of London.

During this period of relocations, the surrogates working for the absentee landlords Edward and Samuel Moulton-Barrett were robbing them because of their absence. The production of sugar and rum had decreased to such a point that the two brothers were barely breaking even. Edward then came upon a scheme whereby one of the brothers had to go to Jamaica to take over the administration of the properties.

Samuel was now completing his second term in the House of Commons, representing a Yorkshire constituency. As a sugar baron, Samuel was probably elected under the rotten borough system. This was a fraud in English parliamentary system. It went like this: a sugar baron who lived on a large farm with a big manor house had five hundred employees, and these were all voters. The powers that be made this big manor house and property a constituency to elect a member of parliament. All the owner of the property had to do was tell his workers and those of their families who lived in outlying districts to vote for him. Since he was the chief employer in the districts surrounding his property, if he lost the election, those workers would be fired. If the manor house was large enough to employ more than 500 voters, the manor house and property would make a constituency. These were called rotten boroughs. The other boroughs that were outside these manor houses consisted of more than five thousand voters. So the constituencies that send members to the House of Commons varied between five hundred and ten thousand voters. The members of parliament who were calling for the abolition of slavery were from these more populous constituencies, and those who opposed were from the rotten boroughs. Most, if not all, of the manor house constituencies were absentee landlords who owned slaves and sugar plantations in the West Indies.

When the House of Commons finally passed the Reform Act of 1832, something great happened. What the Reform Act did was equalize as close as possible the number of votes in each constituency so that no manor house workers could alone be the electors of a member to the House of Commons. This caused a drastic change in the make-up of the members. The next election saw quite a number of abolitionists enter the House of Commons, so that by 1834 the Abolition Act was passed, granting slaves their freedom. Were it not for the Reform Act, that act for freeing the slaves could not have been passed, and this could have been the reason why Samuel Moulton-Barrett was so willing to quit his seat in the House of Commons and return to the place of his birth, Cinnamon Hill in the parish of St. James.

When he returned to Jamaica and took over the properties, a great turn-around in the fortunes of the Moulton-Barretts took place. He made a greater reform on his properties than the one in England. He sent for a Scottish missionary by the name of Hope Waddell to teach religion to his slaves, and built schools for the slave children as well. This was the fist time that this ever happened, and over a period of time the first black schoolteacher was appointed. She was the daughter of a black slave *busha* (overseer) on one of his properties, one he had named Edward Barrett after his grandfather, Edward Barrett of Cinnamon Hill. This black Barrett became the ancestor of many Barretts who are in fact not related to the Barrett family. This is an irony. There were many quadroon and mulatto Barretts who were sired by the English white Barretts and these children were not and could not go by the name of Barrett, but many slaves were given the name by their owners who were Barretts. So the first black busha and the first black schoolteacher originated on Barrett properties. All these reforms were agreed upon by Edward Moulton-Barrett back in England, and he was the one who recommended it to his brother. He also became one of the leaders in the British Tract and Bible Society that sent religious tracts all over the world, and he was one of the chief financiers.

As Samuel made these reforms, the fortunes of the Moulton-Barretts recovered. The old overseers were all replaced, so the stealing stopped and profits multiplied. As things began to turn around, the Moulton-Barretts were experiencing uncertainty with their slave ownerships. They had thousands between the two brothers Samuel and Edward. Samuel was the great property administrator, and Edward the sugar merchant in London, where he sold rum and sugar for his brother and himself. He was also the self-proclaimed Christian in the family, and he supported missionary endeavors with his cash. He supported his twelve motherless children and would never marry again. He stood out in his home as a military commander as well as an ancient moralist. If you disobeyed his orders as commander, you would be severely punished. And if you obeyed, you would be rewarded handsomely. He also set the moral tone of when any of his children should get married, but not during his lifetime. He told all his children never to get married as long as he was alive. Three of them did and he immediately disinherited them.

One day, it was said that his second daughter, Henrietta, took her younger sister Arabella to her father, who was having supper in the dining room, and asked him if she could get married since she was thirty years of age and should do so. It is stated that when he answered them they both fainted and smelling salts had to be brought in and applied, and the two sisters recovered and ran back to their room. Whether this story is true or not, the next morning he addressed Henrietta alone and told her that the man she was planning to marry was too poor to marry Mr. Barrett's daughter. She did run away from home and married the man who was too poor for her. He was Capt. Surtees Cook, a bodyguard for Queen Victoria and a cousin of the Barretts. When Edward Moulton-Barrett heard of this, he changed his will immediately and disinherited her. She was not the first to get this treatment, because Elizabeth, his firstborn, was also disinherited previously but will be mentioned in a following chapter.

While Samuel Moulton-Barrett was doing excellent work in Jamaica, he got married and needed some help to run the properties, and Edward Moulton Barrett sent one of his sons, Samuel Moulton-Barrett to his uncle in Jamaica. Now there were two persons with identical names living at the same place, and in order to avoid confusion, the younger Samuel took the title of *the younger,* so one was the "Older" and the other was the "Younger." This cleared up the confusion on the properties. The Emancipation Bill was passed in the House of Commons before the Younger left for Jamaica. He now had to join his uncle in preparation for full freedom in 1838. The slaves were going through their apprenticeship period and the two Moulton-Barretts had to prepare more than two thousand slaves for their freedom. It was not as difficult as the rest of slave owners were experiencing. The Moulton-Barrett Estates had a resident missionary, Hope Waddell, and a school with a black schoolteacher and several black overseers (*bushas*) running things in order, so the transition situation on Moulton-Barrett properties was superior to any other slave owner.

It was a very great disappointment for Edward Moulton-Barrett when in 1837, one year before emancipation, his brother Samuel Barrett Moulton-Barrett died at the young age of fifty. This was a tragedy of extreme proportion for the Moulton-Barrett family. I used the name Moulton-Barrett here for the purpose of showing some form of resentment among the other Barrett family on the north coast who considered themselves as plain Barretts, or the Goodin Barretts who were the direct descendants of Edward Barrett of Cinnamon Hill and his wife Judith Goodin, who was from Westmoreland parish before she married Edward. The rivalry was that Edward Barrett of Cinnamon Hill left too much of his wealth for the two grandsons, the children of his favorite daughter Elizabeth, who married Capt. Charles Moulton of dubious pedigree who then abandoned his wife for mulatto and quadroon mistresses. The rivalry between the two Barretts was that the Goodin Barretts successfully pursued the case against the Moulton-Barretts for land and slaves on behalf of the mulatto and quadroon children of George Goodin Barrett. These quadroon and mulatto children were also the grandchildren of Edward Barrett of Cinnamon Hill, but based upon the British laws, they could not inherit any property from their father because they were illegitimate, and more so, because the tar brush was all over them. George Goodin Barrett, their father, was one of the top barristers-at-law in the country, so he framed his will making John Graham-Clarke their protector, and he was instructed by the will that if the children did not get the inheritance, it would still be under his control. How much the children got we do not know, but the case in court was settled in their favor. We suppose that while they were living in England they were no longer Negroes, because in England at that time people who were the inheritors of some sugar money were no longer considered as black.

The death of Samuel Moulton-Barrett the Older placed a strain upon Samuel Moulton-Barrett the Younger. He now had to take on the whole business of running the properties, and the Older left behind a wife who was in his will with a share of the Moulton-Barretts' estate. Young Samuel had to deal with this and the abolition of slavery. When slavery was abolished in 1838, the planters of Jamaica began paying the freed slaves sixpence per day. Some planters drove the slaves from their properties and took away their cultivations so that they had to work for the sixpence or suffer starvation. Even though young Sam agreed and started paying his former slaves the sixpence per day, he still allowed them to keep their provision grounds, so his former slaves worked almost as hard as when they were in servitude. Now sixpence in those days was one-eighth of a dollar. Forty-eight pence was equal to one United Stated dollar.

When Edward Moulton-Barrett of London heard about the day's pay, he invoked his Christian principles, chided his son, and told him to double the day's pay to one shilling. One shilling was twelve pence. This caused a great furor with the rest of the planters, who said that the Barretts were spoiling the Negroes. There was no turning back for the Barretts, who said that they got more work out of the Negroes when you pay them one shilling per day. This proved to be economically sensible because production on the Barretts' estate increased proportionally to the higher wages. Even some of the hill land was sold to those who had sufficient money to buy. So the Moulton-Barrett estates prospered during emancipation as it did during slavery. The Moulton-Barretts also had a lot of cash in hand because Queen Victoria signed the bill that gave slave owners over £22,000,000 for the slaves' freedom. This was distributed according to the number of slaves one possessed, and the Barretts had many slaves.

As soon as things settled down for Edward Moulton-Barrett, who still sold rum and sugar on the world market from his office in London, tragedy upon tragedy struck again in the year 1840. This was the worst year in the life of Edward Moulton-Barrett. He was planning to send his first son, Edward Moulton-Barrett Jr., to join Samuel in Jamaica, but by the time this was materialized he got the news from Jamaica that Samuel Moulton-Barrett the Younger had suddenly died. It took sailing ships sometimes over two months to travel from Jamaica to London, so when the news got there, Samuel had been dead over two months. Young Samuel died on February 17, 1840, from the terrible plague of yellow fever brought on by the sting of the *Stegomyia fasciata* mosquitoes. When this mosquito stings, it was like the Black Death brought about by rats in an earlier period. Upon hearing about this death, Edward Moulton-Barrett Sr. almost lost his mind. He had a sick daughter, Elizabeth, living in Torquay, some distance away from London, and his first son, Edward Junior, was staying with her. His home at Wimpole Street was now in the hands of other children for whom there was not much fondness except for one son who was barrister-at-law and was not always home as he was out trying cases all over the country.

How Edward's estates fared in Jamaica was in the hands of his attorney, the famous Matthew Farquharson of the parish of St. Elizabeth, who resided at Font Hill Estate, a few miles west of Black River, the capital of St. Elizabeth. It was this man who saw to it that the Moulton-Barretts' estate did not go into decline. For all intents and purposes, this lawyer, unusually, was an honest Scotsman whose integrity stood out untarnished. He was one of the Scots who landed in Jamaica after his ancestors laid the foundation in the parish of St. Elizabeth. Col. John Campbell of Scotland went to establish a Scottish enclave in Panama at a place called Darien in 1699. The settlement failed, so he came to Jamaica in 1700 and married a rich woman who owned plenty of land, finally settling at a place near Black River called Hodges Pens. He died and his tomb is still on the property. He later became a member of the House of Assembly representing the parish of St. Elizabeth and later became custos of that parish. He was one of the Scottish pioneers to the island of Jamaica, and many others followed, including the ancestors of Matthew Farquharson. That is why so many villages in Westmoreland and St. Elizabeth have Scottish names, such as Culloden, Aberdeen, Kilmarnock, Auchindown and Ben Lomond, and many others. These people and their descendants played a very important part in the intellectual development of Jamaica, and Matthew Farquharson was one of them. He saw to it that the Barrett estates were run properly, and Edward Moulton-Barrett Sr. trusted him very much.

Edward Moulton-Barrett Jr. was now considered the best one to send to Jamaica, but Senior had great consideration for his sick daughter Elizabeth who thought she would die if Edward Junior was sent to Jamaica. Before any decision could be made, tragedy struck again. On the eleventh of July 1840, Edward Junior went on a boating trip with some friends. The boat overturned and they all drowned. The bodies of the friends were found but Edward's body was not found. The anguish this caused among the Moulton-Barrett family could not be told in any one chapter of a book, so this will be left to the imagination.

All the hopes of Edward Senior were now dashed and he teetered on the brink of insanity. Few human beings could have withstood such tragedies and still keep somewhat of a sound mind. His actions, which were to be described later as tyranny, should be looked at in a different light, when all the circumstances are placed in proper order. It is not to be understood here that this author is defending him, but based on the many circumstances, he should have been treated a little less harshly.

The death of Edward Junior caused the Senior to change his plans. He had to recall Elizabeth back to 50 Wimpole Street and he had to send another son, Charles John Moulton-Barrett, to Jamaica to take over the administration of his properties. These were hard nuts to crack. Elizabeth placed the blame upon herself for the death of her brother, and became so disoriented that she never talked or wrote about the incident in all her writings. Edward Senior did not publicly blame anyone for his misfortune, but he later showed by his behavior that Elizabeth had something to do with the drowning of her brother. We now come to the point where Robert Browning entered the picture.

As soon as Robert entered the picture, things began to change in the life of the Moulton-Barrett family at 50 Wimpole Street. A regular correspondence between Robert and Elizabeth started. This invalid woman was immolating herself over the death of her favorite brother Edward and had turned herself into a virtual recluse and bemoaned her bad luck within the walls of her room, and did not want to see any stranger for many years. As Robert read the poems she had written, he began to commend them to her and also recommended some minor changes. The changes were not significant, because linguistically she was more educated than he was because her father had plenty of money and the will to employ private tutors for her.

After many months of writing letters, he invited himself to 50 Wimpole Street, which took many more months to materialize. He lived in Camberwell and she lived at Portman Square, a good distance away, which would take a very long time for him. Historians did not say what kind of transportation he used but this author visited both places and Camberwell is in southeast London and Portman Square is in the west end, so the presumption is that he took the trains or carriages and most likely he walked the many miles, which by ordinary standards of walking would take him about four hours to do. It is not the walking that was amusing but the frequency of his visits on a weekly basis. Sometimes he was there more than once a week.

As his visits became more frequent, it came to the knowledge of Edward Moulton-Barrett, who was at his office six days each week in downtown London by the wharf side, selling sugar and rum at wholesale, and waiting for the arrival of his ships from Jamaica and sometimes from Egypt because he did some trading too in the middle East. Now that Edward found out that this daughter was being visited by another poet, he became interested in this person. He wanted to know what a man would be doing in his crippled daughter's room. One thing he did not know was that Robert Browning was some kind of psychoanalyst. He got Elizabeth to walk on his first visit to her, but she kept it from her siblings, and more so, from her father Edward. She hid her recovery for many months, and when her father came home at nights and visited her room, she pretended she was as sick as he had left her that morning.

When Edward found out that Robert was visiting too often, he paid two of the boys to report to him on a daily basis when Robert visited. On finding out that Robert was at his house every week almost, he surmised that he was not only there for poetry discussion, maybe he was there to steal intellectual property as well. He also thought of many things, such as should there be a miraculous recovery for Elizabeth maybe Robert would have the audacity of proposing to her, and as he always said, "These men are too poor to marry Mr. Barrett's daughters."

It was now time for him to act. He first contacted a genealogist, Dr. Frederick Furnivall of London, to do a genetic check on Robert Browning and his ancestors and report to him in writing on his findings, and he would be paid handsomely for this job. Furnivall went to work and made contact with people from St. Kitts and Jamaica in the West Indies, and also Germany, where his mother's ancestors were located, and he found just what he wanted. When he made the report to Edward Moulton-Barrett at his London office, Edward was very satisfied because from what he heard it would not be correct for any of his daughters to get involved with him.

Dr. Furnivall's report was very comprehensive. It stated all the relevant good things that anyone would like to hear about a person in whom one is interested, and when all was said in a written report, the great conjunction appeared. The report made it clear that Robert Browning was qualified in all respects but the tar brush passed nearby. This is the report that sealed adversely the relationship between Robert Browning and Elizabeth Barrett in the eyes of her father and family. To make matters worse, both Elizabeth and her father were suspicious of their own ancestry in the person of Charles Moulton, Edward's father. Elizabeth in her speaking and maybe her writing gave the impression to many that the tar brush also passed nearby. There were, and still are, many contradictions in this saying but no one knows for sure who did or did not have a touch of the tar brush. This term is used very frequently in this chapter because it is the reason why we have the rooms without doors at Cinnamon Hill Great House, and this terminology will be used many more times as the chapters develop.

Now that Edward had his document, he only became cockier in his attitude toward his children because he thought he was protecting them from the evils of the world. He also laid down his rules against marrying. He said that none of his children should get married during his lifetime or else they would be disinherited. He repeated this statement like a Bible verse each week, and even if some of them were deaf, they all would have heard. Three of them did get married, and they were all disinherited.

Even though he had the Furnivall report, he did not show it to his children. This was only found in his archives after he died. He only put a greater watch on Robert Browning's visit, and each day when he returned from the office he inquired of his spies whether Robert came to Wimpole Street. He knew that Elizabeth was very sick, so for months he tolerated Robert's visits, and even though he was angry, he behaved like an English gentleman and kept every dislike within his heart because he did not want to upset Elizabeth. He adored her intelligence, and she was putting the Barrett name all over the world by her poetry.

People did not know anything about the Moulton part of the family because Elizabeth hated it and signed her name as Elizabeth Barrett Barrett, and used the acronym EBB. From further investigation, it was learned that she knew the tar brush passed nearby her grandfather Charles Moulton. The question now arose whether she knew that Robert Browning had this same connection. Or was she somehow not going to have any children of her own? All this thought might not have come to her mind because she did not know that Robert was thinking of eloping with her. No one thought that a sick woman like Elizabeth would consider getting married. Her father did not even have the faintest idea about such a thing or else he would have acted. When Robert's visits became unbearable to Edward Moulton-Barrett, he decided to move the family to a far distant place so that the poor man Robert could not visit so often, and this decision to move made Elizabeth and Robert's elopement more feasible. It took on more urgency than ever before.

It was a great risk that they were taking when they decided to get married and elope. She was still recovering from a bout of tuberculosis and was very weak. She was also prescribed large doses of laudanum and morphine by her doctors and the question arose whether she would be able to get these drugs in Italy where they planned to reside. The day was fast approaching when Edward Moulton-Barrett was going to move the family from Wimpole Street to a place called Little Bookham in another county many miles away. This, in the mind of Edward, would stop the frequent visits by Robert Browning to his daughter Elizabeth.

On Monday, the twenty-second of September 1846, the Barretts were to leave for Little Bookham, so Elizabeth had to go with the family or flee with Robert to Italy. So on September 19, 1846, Elizabeth and Robert were secretly at Marylebone Church, the same place where her grandmother Elizabeth Barrett Moulton was buried. That day was Friday, and by midnight Saturday the Barrett household at 50 Wimpole Street knew that Robert and Elizabeth had eloped with her dog Flush and her special maid named Wilson.

When Edward Moulton-Barrett knew what had taken place, the Calvinist despot got into a rage and called his children together and inquired who knew what went on before the flight. They did not know what and how to tell him. Some of them fainted and some came up with all kinds of excuses. Elizabeth's two sisters knew what went on but would not talk the truth. Two of her brothers who were actual spies did not know anything. He then called his son, the lawyer George Goodin Moulton-Barrett, and amended his will to exclude the name of Elizabeth from every part of it. He did the same on two other occasions, one in the case of his daughter Henrietta and the other in the case of his son Alfred Price Moulton-Barrett. These two were also guilty of marrying during the lifetime of their father. Now, Edward hated close family getting tied in a marriage, and Henrietta married Capt. Surtees Cook, a cousin of the Barretts, and Alfred married his granduncle's daughter, Georgina Barrett.

Edward Moulton-Barrett has been called many names such as *tyrant*, *despot*, and a host of other derogatory names, but one must look at the conditions surrounding why he behaved that way. It is easy to say bad things about people, but the good things they do are always put on the back burner, and when they do come to focus, it is with envy and strife. Certainly, this author is not defending him. What is now in the mind of the writer is the great number of Barrett descendants he is looking at who have the same tendencies as Edward, and these tendencies seemed to have transcended many generations. Elizabeth was his idol and he did not even know that she had recovered sufficiently to walk, much more to arrange a secret marriage and flee the country. He was so annoyed at her and also the rest of her siblings that he felt betrayed by his children. Even those that he paid to observe the situation on his behalf did not know what was going on, and he thought it a great conspiracy against him. These conspiracies were not unusual in the Barrett family. They fought among themselves sometimes, and so vicious were some of the fights that outsiders were drawn into some of them. The problem with Edward and his children was his pronounced attitude of control, which he displayed over them and treated them as decent slaves all during their adolescence. This brought about the attitude of his children toward him, and when sexual desires overcame some of them, all they had to do was run away, just as a real slave would.

It is now very important to look at some of the reasons why this so-called tyrant should behave the way he did. Sometime around 1826, he lost a family lawsuit that set him back greatly at a cost of about £25,000. He had to sell part of his beloved Hope End property to pay the bill. In 1828, his adorable wife Mary died and left him with twelve children to take care of, the oldest being Elizabeth, the poetess, at the age of twenty, and the youngest at age four. Then again in 1831 there was a slave insurrection on the island of Jamaica where his brother Samuel was in charge of the estates. Even though none of his properties was destroyed, the fear of destruction and the safety of his brother were foremost on his mind. In 1834, the Emancipation Bill passed the House of Commons to free all slaves in the British Empire within six years, and he had many slaves. The apprenticeship period before full emancipation was cut from six to four years, and by 1838 all slaves were to be freed. In 1837, his favorite brother in charge of the estates in Jamaica died, one year before full freedom, and Edward was at a point of insanity. His young son, also named after his brother Samuel who died, was not fully equipped to handle all those properties. The move from Hope End to London in 1832 was also heavy upon his mind. But this was not all. When all his slaves were fully freed in 1838, new problems developed in the operation of the estates, but he circumvented those problems by paying the former slaves twice the pay as other property owners, so the problems were solved with respect to labor. Because of Elizabeth's illness, he requested her eldest brother Edward to be with her at Sidmouth, which the father reluctantly agreed to, and shortly after young Edward got there, he was in a boating accident and drowned. This was the heir and successor to his father, and the grief was so great that it almost paralyzed the Moulton-Barrett family. The father, in his mind, blamed Elizabeth for this. Elizabeth, in her mind, blamed herself. No member of the family wanted to talk about it. This was July 1840. They were still mourning the death of another brother, Samuel, who died from yellow fever in Jamaica in February of the same year but the news did not get to them until three months later. At the same time that Edward Senior wanted to send Edward Junior to Jamaica to replace Samuel who died, Elizabeth imposed on her father to send him to her instead of Jamaica. Elizabeth won the argument with her father, so the properties in Jamaica were left to attorneys until the decision was made to send Charles John Moulton-Barrett, another son, instead.

All these tragedies came upon Edward Moulton Barrett and people are still wondering why he behaved the way when Elizabeth decided to elope with Robert Browning, whom Edward knew was a poor man, and worst of all, that the tar brush passed nearby. The tragedy of Elizabeth's elopement in 1846 was one of the greatest shocks in the life of Edward Moulton-Barrett. She got more care and money from her father than anyone else, and even though she inherited much money from her grandmother Elizabeth Barrett Moulton and her uncle Samuel Barrett Moulton-Barrett, most of the money spent on her illness came from her father. And the fact that she did not tell him she was recovering made him feel a bit let down. Her brothers did not side with her in the elopement, and very few corresponded with her during her stay in Italy until her death. Even though her father did not open any of the nine letters she wrote him from Florence in Italy, presumably asking forgiveness, the males in the family agreed with him for the behavior he displayed. It is the belief of many that had he been properly examined by a psychiatrist the findings would have been that he was having something like a mental breakdown. Enough had happened to him for this diagnosis to have been handed down, but many of the family, two hundred years afterward, are seeing the same behavior in relatives who are considered quite sober. Many believed it to be the innate disposition of the Barrett family.

During the time that Charles John Moulton-Barrett was in Jamaica, the work became too difficult for him, so his father sent help in the person of another son, Septimus, to help in the operation of the properties, but this was a grave mistake. This move heralded the decline and fall of the Moulton-Barrett empire. Septimus did everything that was evil and disastrous in the Moulton-Barrett family, and Charles John had to bail him out of debtor's jail. He went all over the parishes of St. James, Trelawny, and St. Ann creating debts upon debts, until he was bound for the debtor's jail in Spanish Town. Charles John sold properties to save his brother.

It was a good thing that old Edward back in England had entrusted his wealth in the hands of his lawyer son, George Goodin Moulton-Barrett. The London side of the wealth was preserved in good hands. George, who became a circuit court judge, resigned his position to take care of his father's wealth and to amend his will three times. First, to disinherit Elizabeth in 1846, who eloped with Robert Browning, then next to disinherit another daughter, Henrietta, who married a cousin, Capt. Surtees Cook, in April 1850, and then to disinherit his son Alfred, who married another cousin, Elizabeth Georgina Barrett, in August 1855. All three were disinherited because their father said no one should marry during his lifetime, and he made sure he carried out his threat. After his death, three sons got married, Henry, Charles John, and Octavius, who married twice. So we have three married before and were disinherited and three after who inherited. This is a very strange story and should be analyzed by historians all over the world. This story of the first Edward Barrett Moulton-Barrett is an enigma placed into a puzzle that became an interesting riddle. Sir Winston Churchill is to be credited with saying something almost similar when he was confronted by the Germans in the Second World War.

It came to the point when old Edward could do nothing more than hand over his wealth and operations to his barrister son George Goodin Moulton-Barrett, and so on the seventeenth day of April 1857 he died a disappointed man from the fact that some of his children disobeyed him. Those who did not and survived after his demise inherited his wealth, while Charles John had to sell most of the wealth in Jamaica to keep Septimus out of jail. He drank out the Jamaican wealth of the Moulton-Barrett family and died a pauper. Charles was left with only two small properties and had to sell the great house at Cinnamon Hill, thus passing the possession of the Barretts' ancestral home into the hands of strangers. It was a sorry ending to the Jamaican side of a great family. Scores of books have been written about this family and a novel entitled *The Barretts of Wimpole Street* was written around 1831 by novelist Rudolph Besier, which was made into a movie with the same title. The movie now goes by the title *The Forbidden Alliance.* It is true to a point but incorrect historically. So ended the life and times of Edward Barrett Moulton-Barrett.

CHAPTER 5

Elizabeth Barrett Browning

The story of Elizabeth Barrett Browning is the most difficult to understand. It is like a puzzle based on an enigma, riddled with controversies. This is a phrase once used by Winston Churchill when he was describing some aspect of the Second World War, during which he was prime minister. The phrase, as the author remembers it, was not exactly as mentioned above but it went somewhat like it, so he must give credit to this eloquent prime minister who used phrases and speeches to sag up the declining morale of the British people during the Great War.

Let us look at her life in a different way. Her life story was like an atom with a nucleus around which revolved neutrons, protons, and electrons, with some of these revolving in a contrary way. So difficult is her life to explain that not even her relatives and friends could explain it. When they tried to explain it one way, she would come up with something else to make that explanation obsolete. She herself could not explain herself satisfactorily. So as an attempt is being made here to explain some of her behaviors, the writer can only leave it to the readers to guess who she was. Books cannot contain her life story, much less a little chapter in a little book, but some key historic points will be made to show what a character she was.

She was the first child born to Edward Barrett Moulton-Barrett (sometimes called the tyrant of Wimpole Street) and Mary Graham-Clarke, after their marriage, or may we say *business marriage* because she was four years his senior and her father, John Graham-Clarke, was the protector of young Edward and his brother Samuel, who had inherited vast wealth from their grandfather Edward Barrett of Cinnamon Hill, Jamaica. At that time, the couple was living at Coxhoe Hall in the village of Durham in the county of Kent, and on March 6, 1806, a girl was born whom they named Elizabeth after her paternal grandmother, Elizabeth Barrett Moulton of Cinnamon Hill above, and also for her great-great-grandmother Elizabeth Wisdom of St. James parish, Jamaica, who married Sam Barrett, who started the north coast dynasty of Barretts in the island of Jamaica.

From this dynastic empire, Elizabeth was born into wealth. And as the first child, she inherited great wealth from her grandmother Elizabeth, who willed a large sum to the firstborn child of her firstborn son Edward. There is dispute as to how much wealth, which was not stated, but from her spending habits, it appears to have been substantial. She also inherited wealth from her uncle Samuel Barrett Moulton-Barrett, and also from her writer cousin, John Kenyon, also from the island of Jamaica. These benefactors were all sugar barons in the days when sugar was king.

There were many descriptions given about this little girl, and some sound preposterous, while others seemed from the sublime to the ridiculous, but on a whole, her description was as confusing as her life story. According to Jeannette Marks in her book *The Family of the Barrett*, she said that Elizabeth was called the little Portuguese—tiny, fragile, dark complexioned, dark haired, the vivid Creole flower of many generations of Barrett background. To this writer, the word *Portuguese* is suggestive. Portuguese was the derogatory decent name for Europeans of black ancestry. This goes back to the days of the Arab conquest of Spain and Portugal, which were under the rule of the Moors.

Sometime during the eleventh century AD, the Arabs captured the whole of North Africa, miscegenated with the population, and their descendants were called Moors, and these moved over into Spain and Portugal and ruled for over four hundred years. The miscegenation was so severe in Portugal that European blood almost disappeared and results can be clearly seen today. In Spain, sometime around 1475, after the marriage between Ferdinand of Aragon and Isabella of Castile, these two provinces were united and they turned their combined forces against the last Moorish kingdom of Granada, defeated it, drove the Moors out, and made Granada a province of greater Spain. These persons were the benefactors of Christopher Columbus.

The country of Portugal was not so. It produced a lineage of kings who were predominantly Moorish. Of particular note is King John, the father of Prince Henry the Navigator. King John, according to J. A. Rogers in his book on world history, had a daughter who married in the royal household of Saxe-Coberg-Gotha, and she produced a lineage of monarchs such as Queen Charlotte, the wife of George III and also grandmother of Queen Victoria, hence the darkening of the British royal family and all of present-day Europe's royal families. It is said that the American colonists knew that their Queen Charlotte was Moorish, hence of black ancestry, and that they revolted with greater urgency than for the mere fact of taxation without representation. No one ever publicly said this, so the racial connotation is left to be analyzed by the readers. It is also said that European royal families sometimes went to Africa to get dark complexioned mates for their children so as to give their dynasties a better complexion. That was the days before African slavery when black people were considered as equal.

This complexion of Elizabeth is so complicated that there are several versions. In her book *Dared and Done*, author Jean Marcus of Hofstra University said she believed that Elizabeth had a touch of black in her. She said that Elizabeth, in her collection of poems *Sonnets from the Portuguese*, created a character that could have been herself. The character wished she was from a purer race. This then suggested that she was not of pure race. This can be construed to mean that somewhere in her family lineage the tar brush passed nearby. We cannot be sure of this because no one has said exactly that it was so. We are now back to Jeanette Marks again. On page 291 of her book already mentioned, when Elizabeth was fourteen years old and after she published her first book of poetry entitled *The Battle of Marathon*, she personally described herself to a friend as, "My hair is very dark indeed, and always was, as long as I remember, and also I have a friend who makes serious affidavit that I have never changed (except by being rather taller) since I was a year old." It could not be said here that because her hair was black she was also black, but she has made other references where she indicated her dark complexion. According to this same book, on page 304, Elizabeth looked like her father Edward, who had a massive head with the look of power, dark hair, dark skin, odd mouth, and receding chin. Also she had about her to an unusual degree the luster of the Barretts on her dark cheeks the color of the wild rose, and flashing from the irregular mouth when she smiled, white teeth resembling that of the Creole and not of an English girl. This description is rather funny. Elizabeth again placed historians into confusion over her complexion. Jeanette Marks really covered her extensively. In her book, on page 312, is a significant statement by Elizabeth. She said she would rather give ten towns in Norfolk (if she owned them) to own some purer lineage than that of the blood of a slave. This is a very damaging statement to the defenders of her complexion as being purely Anglo-Saxon. What she really meant, one cannot be sure. She also added a curse to her family after the statement. The question is still out. Was she mixed?

This writer has checked out her family lineage from the side of the Barretts and as far back as the Norman Conquest in 1066 when the first Barrett came to England from Normandy. There is no trace of African blood in them, but no one can be sure. The Moors did not enter Europe as yet, but since all races of mankind are related and since they all were traveling around the countries where they could walk, we must remember that Africa was connected to Asia and Europe by land. It is only with the cutting of the Suez Canal in 1869 that Africa was separated, and that's just the other day.

We also learned from unofficial sources that in 1596 Queen Elizabeth I signed a law preventing more black people from coming to England because there were enough of them in England. It is said that she also had black women working in her household. These could have been some of the Moors fleeing Spain after 1575 when Ferdinand and Isabella destroyed their stronghold of Granada. Also, the *asiento* was in full force and African slaves were being transported not only to the West Indies but also to Europe itself. Liverpool in England was at one time a slave market.

All these movements of the two races could have brought about miscegenation. From the Barrett side it seemed difficult to have picked up this dark complexion even back to their fourth generation. When Edward Barrett of Cinnamon Hill married Judith Goodin from Westmoreland parish, we have very little to go by, and she was Elizabeth's great-grandmother. All the areas to the Barrett family and Elizabeth's complexion seemed to be out of place. We will now look a little closer at her grandfather, Charles Moulton.

In trying to find Negroid connection in Elizabeth, the examination now turns to the family of her father's father. All the evidence is now pointing toward Charles Moulton, her paternal grandfather. Historians have checked back to 1535 and cannot find an ancestor with African blood. Nobody can be sure about this. They only do not know. If a black person produced a mulatto with a white person and that mulatto married a white person, and each offspring continues to marry white for four generations, it is only a genetic accident that can produce someone black. It can happen. It is not impossible.

Now that we can trace genes backward, I am not sure there is a pure race anywhere anymore. We are all mixed, having descended from only one source. All the evidence that is available has not pointed out any black genes coming from the Moulton family that produced Elizabeth. So if the Barrett family had no Negroid connection and the Moulton family had none, then where did Elizabeth get her dark complexion? She said so many times in describing herself. We will now turn to some deductions from the extrapolations and conclusive presumptions.

Elizabeth's mother was Mary Graham-Clarke. She was the daughter of John Graham-Clarke. Now John Graham-Clarke had under his care and protection four quadroon sons of George Goodin Barrett of Cinnamon Hill, who died in 1795. According to Jeanette Marks in her book *The Family of the Barrett*, they were named Thomas, William, Samuel, and Richard. These were the sons of Elissa Peters (the mulatto slave) and sired by George Goodin Barrett. They all were in his will and instructions were given that they should not return to Jamaica after schooling. They should remain in England and John Graham-Clarke should bring them up until adulthood. There were girls too but this author is only interested in the boys at this time. These quadroon boys were all Barretts even though they had the last name Peters. They were born out of wedlock, so they had to use their mother's surname. Both children of John Graham-Clarke and these quadroon boys grew up together in the same large house in the place called Newcastle Upon-Tyne. It must also be noted that Thomas Peters had the title "esquire" behind his name. He must have been a lawyer or some educated person to have that title behind his name.

Thomas Peters and his siblings were about the same age or older than Edward Moulton-Barrett, who was a little over nineteen years when he married Mary Graham-Clarke. We do not know whether any of at least five Peters' children were invited to the wedding since they were quadroons. One thing we have to remember is that when sugar was king, quadroon children of sugar planters in the West Indies were considered the equal of whites when they went to England for schooling, and the boys were more in demand by the white girls than their English counterparts, who were considered poor in relation to the West Indians.

There was a story that was always told to West Indians when they went to school in England. Two blond-looking men were traveling on a train near London when one looked upon a hillside and called the other's attention to this house and said, "Imagine this large house I understand is owned by a nigger from Jamaica. He must be one of those sugar barons' sons I suppose." The man replied, "I suppose so. However, I am having a great party at my house tonight. Do you mind coming?" The other blond told him yes and they both exchanged address cards, and when they parted company at the railway station, each promised to see the other later. At about ten o'clock that night, the visitor showed up with his wife, and when the music started and Jamaican rum punch began to take hold of the senses, the host took his racist friend to the back of the house that overlooked the railroad they were on earlier and showed him around in the moonlight and said, "You remember showing me this house while we were traveling together earlier on? Well, I am that nigger from Jamaica." The visitor disappeared shortly without saying a word. This story goes to show that there are black people who looked like that gentleman from Jamaica.

Even though the marriage of Mary and Edward took place on May 14, 1805, and Elizabeth was born on March 6, 1806, everything according to date seemed to have been right, but since the description of her being dark, anyone can conjecture that something funny could have happened. Thomas Peters was older than Edward and presumably was handsomer and was more educated based on his title. And we know that Edward dropped out of Cambridge, not because of money, because he had plenty and John Graham-Clarke was not afraid to use it since Edward was under twenty-one, so many conclusions could be drawn here. John just selected the richer one who was considered white. However, four years older than the man, some cultures would consider that as cradle snatching, but in times when women appeared to be more numerous than men, a few years older would not change anything.

So John Graham-Clarke, knowing the wealth that Edward was to acquire at age twenty-one, could not wait to arrange that marriage. It must also be remembered that they were growing up together at the same place, even though for a few years Edward was away at Cambridge University and Mary was at Newcastle-Upon-Tyne. John's influence was very great both in Jamaica and in England. He was so well known that many Jamaican sugar planters who were absent from their families in England employed him to look after their families during their absence. Since he had so many children under his care, he knew the best one to select for his daughter Mary, so it was not strange that he got hold of Edward very early.

After the marriage took place, the couple lived in close proximity to the children of Elissa Peters. It is presumed that they came in contact with each other even though historians will not write it. We know that Mary was married twenty days over nine months before Elizabeth was born, so if there were any shenanigans going on they would have to have been after the marriage. That is not impossible either, even though it may seem to be highly improbable. The only focus now is that as Elizabeth grew up she bemoaned her complexion and suggested she had some blood of slaves. The only blood of slaves she could have had was if her ancestors were mixed with slaves, which historians have no proof of. But if you were the only one born dark out of twelve, then the only conclusion is that some quadroon passed nearby one of your parents. If say it was one of the Peters boys, then all four were Barretts with the familiar Barrett features that Elizabeth also had. They were first cousins to Edward, so Elizabeth could have gotten the Barrett features from any one of the cousins. Enough presumptions have already been made, so the readers will have to think for themselves, but the writer still wants to know why only Elizabeth was dark complexioned and there were eleven others who were not. We just have to move on from here.

Elizabeth was only about four years old when she was relocated from Coxhoe Hall to Hope End. This house was very large and was situated in 477 acres of land. There were lakes and streams running all through the property, and as the family grew and expanded, there was enough place to play and roam. Nine of Elizabeth's siblings were born at Hope End and she had a wonderful time there until disaster struck the family and they had to sell part of the property with the house and move to areas nearer to London, where her father had an office to sell his rum and sugar from Jamaica.

The disaster was a lawsuit that had been running for many years. Thomas Peters, her quadroon first cousin once removed, was now at age twenty-one a mature person by law, so he became coexecutor with her grandfather John Graham-Clarke. Her father and Samuel

Moulton-Barrett his brother had illegally inherited slaves from their grandfather, Edward Barrett of Cinnamon Hill, and these slaves really belonged to Thomas Peters and other members of the family. Because of racism, Edward Barrett did some illegal undertaking and passed them to his grandsons so that the people with tar brush passing nearby would not inherit their father's property. The lawsuit, which lasted over twenty-one years, finally ended, and Elizabeth's father and uncle had to pay a huge ransom. This caused a real economic setback to Edward Barrett Moulton-Barrett and he had to sell assets to pay up. It was of significant note to see her grandfather John Graham-Clarke, her mother's father, joining with her cousin to fight against her own father, his son-in-law, to the detriment of Edward Barrett Moulton-Barrett. Her grandfather had to do it because he was executor of many Barrett wills. He had his hands in too many pies and he was up against the top barrister in Jamaica who was a friend of most of the judges, especially the one who was trying the case. This barrister was none other than Richard Barrett, speaker of the House of Assembly, the one who owned Greenwood Estate, a grandson of Edward Barrett of Cinnamon Hill and first cousin to Elizabeth's father. The whole family was in turmoil over this case, and some portion of the family never spoke to each other again until several generations had passed.

This was somehow a great setback for her family, but she, as the first child, inherited much from her grandmother, Elizabeth Moulton. She had enough money to pay for her private tutoring, and when the family had to move, she missed her country upbringing and her family and close friends who were living at Newcastle-Upon-Tyne. There was no place around that the Barretts did not have family, so when they moved from one place to the other, some section of the family was always there to welcome them.

It was at Hope End, however, that Elizabeth made one of her decisions that would affect her till the end of her life. She seemed to have found out that her lineage had the blood of slaves and wished she was from a purer lineage. She, at that time, did not say where this Negroid connection came from, but by all intents and purposes she was pointing to the Moultons and not the Barretts. Many historians defended the idea that she had no blood of slaves, but she constantly pointed to her impure race. There is also no recorded connection anywhere, but it is known that white historians will always hide the true racial connection of famous people. Sir Winston Churchill and most of Europe's royal families are all connected to different races, and may it be said, all of Europe's royal family who came out of King Christian IX of Denmark and Queen Victoria of England were all connected to Africa, the Middle East, and American Indians.

One reason why it seemed that Elizabeth was pointing fingers at the Moulton family for her impurity, as she called it, was because she dropped everything in her name that pertained to Moulton. Were it not for a deed poll, her father would have been still Moulton, but her grandfather John Graham-Clarke got the name changed so that he could carry the coat of arms of the Barretts. She would have been Elizabeth Barrett Moulton.

She disdained the name Moulton, especially when she was made aware that she had black aunts and uncles back in the island of Jamaica. Her grandfather Charles Moulton, even though not divorced, had several mulatto and quadroon children by black and colored mistresses all over Jamaica, especially in the parish of St. Ann where he rose to prominence and even became the custos of that parish, making him the chief law officer and gentleman.

In modern days people curse officials for having adulterous affairs, but in those days they only made them more popular. Elizabeth was only made angrier about her grandfather's escapades and from then on her initials became only EBB until the time of her death. She doubled the name of Barrett in her initials. Elizabeth did not consider why she was the only dark one in all of twelve siblings when her father was first cousin to at least five quadroon boys, some as old as he was, and all were living at the same place under the guidance of her grandfather John Graham-Clarke. These quadroon young men were all Barretts, even though they went by different names. So if one of these was her biological father, she would still carry the Barrett genes and could still resemble her father.

No one here is suggesting anything, but she complains too much about her complexion, and there were many quadroons around living at the same place. The great question is, could she have been fathered by one of her father's quadroon cousins? The readers will have to decide this.

Elizabeth was a special girl, so she was tutored at home by teachers who came there. She was taken to the home of others as well. She was so brilliant that at the age of fourteen she published her first set of

poems known as *The Battle of Marathon.* Her father was fully behind her
and boasted that she was a prodigy. She was not the first in the family
because her granduncle George Goodin Barrett of Cinnamon Hill,
Jamaica, attended Oxford University at age fourteen and graduated at
age eighteen. It is not known whose money paid for her education and
publication, but we all knew she inherited plenty of money from her
grandmother Elizabeth Moulton.

Even at that tender age she was secretly against slavery, and out of
slavery came her wealth. There are many contradictions in her life, as
well as that of her father. Her father's household all became Methodists,
a denomination that was based on Calvinistic theology, which included
predestination and made prominent in England by John and Charles
Wesley. This organization was vehemently against slavery and all that it
forebodes, and how one of the largest slave owners in Jamaica at that
time could have been supportive of such a religion is a puzzle within an
enigma, as Winston Churchill would have said.

There was great sympathy shown by the Moulton-Barretts toward the
treatment of slaves. The first black overseer on any property in Jamaica
during the time of slavery was that owned by the Moulton-Barretts. The
first black schoolteacher on any slave property to teach slaves and black
freedmen to read was on the same properties. The first missionary sent
by slave owners from England to Jamaica was sent by Elizabeth's father
and uncle Samuel Moulton-Barrett. Did young Elizabeth have anything
to do with this? Yes, she may have had. Both father and uncle adored
her, and when their mother Elizabeth Moulton died, they looked to
Elizabeth Barrett as a role model. The Wesleyan Methodist Church
could also have been a part, or perhaps the better part, of the influence
that made the slave owners tick. No one knows for sure, but there was
some undue influence around.

At age twenty, young Elizabeth found herself at the head of a home
with twelve siblings. Her dearly beloved mother died and she was left as
the eldest child in the home to see things right since her father was most
of the time away on business. She seemed to have handled it very well
until disaster struck. Her father would not remarry, and the running of
the home was left in her care, as well as looking after so many teenagers,
and teenagers in 1828 were still teenagers. All was not left to Elizabeth
alone because other cousins were there who were older than she was,
and as the Barrett families are always closely knit even when fighting
each other, the smooth running of the household continued.

It was not very long after her mother died that another tragedy struck the Moulton-Barrett family. In 1831, the matriarch of the family, Elizabeth Barrett Moulton, died. And even though this left Elizabeth with some kind of grief, it also left her with some form of wealth. It was upon the death of her grandmother that she inherited most of her wealth in addition to what she got as the firstborn grandchild. She was not too fond of her grandmother but she kept it concealed. Her death affected Elizabeth as it would have any other person she knew, but she became thankful for the inheritance, which saved her from undue embarrassment in her flight from 50 Wimpole Street some fifteen years later.

After the disastrous lawsuit against her father in which he had to sell part of Hope End property, she had to move from her comfortable home to places unknown to her. Her next home was at a seashore town called Sidmouth, where Elizabeth was very happy during their short stay because of the seashore. She loved being near the sea, as her many letters to her friends would indicate. She was part of a moving family from 1832 when she left Hope End to Sidmouth. By 1835, her father moved again, coming closer and closer to London where his business was, and settled at several places in Portman Square area of London's West End. Now most of Portman Square was owned by the Barrett family, so he was right at home where his aunt Margery Lawrence lived. She was the sister of Edward Barrett of Cinnamon Hill, and daughter of the pioneer Sam Barrett and his wife Elizabeth Wisdom. There were many other Barretts there too, and the host of the north coast Barretts of Jamaica settled in close proximity to Portman Square.

As Elizabeth reached the prime of her life around age thirty-nine, she was struck with a kind of tuberculosis that did not seem to be contagious. This is a strange thing to say, but since she was among so many people and associated with more outside of her family but there is no report of any other person having caught the disease, then it could not have been of the contagious type. It would have been impossible under those ancient conditions for others not to have contracted the disease. There have been so much stories about her illness that it seemed ridiculous. There was no antibiotic to treat this disease and some of the ridiculous treatments given her made it impossible for reasonable people to believe all of this crap. However, some of the treatments were donkey's milk, a tankard of porter daily, opium, laudanum, morphine, and worst of all, leeches sucking her blood. These were given to her by her so-called reputable doctors, foremost among them was Dr. William Frederick Chambers, BA, MA, MD, all from Cambridge University. He was also chief medical officer to King William IV and Queen Victoria.

We have had all kinds of legends about Elizabeth's illness, foremost among these was that a saddle fell on her when she was about fifteen years old and damaged her back, but all through her adolescent life no one ever heard of this. Could this tuberculosis scare be also a legend? We have also reports of broken blood vessels that Elizabeth had in 1838 when her favorite uncle Samuel Moulton-Barrett died in Jamaica on the twenty-third of December 1837. This death news did not reach her until February of the following year. Based on previous information, she loved her uncle more than her father, so that death was a great shock to her, and she, in her supposed frailty, could have broken anything, so this mishap would not be very surprising.

The peculiar institution of slavery was always abhorrent to Elizabeth and she openly said so to the annoyance of her family who had many slaves. That she really hated slavery from whence she got all her wealth can be seen in a letter she wrote one Mrs. Martin. Jeanette Marks, in her book *The Family of the Barrett*, said that Elizabeth wrote the following, "Of course you know that the late bill (the Abolition Act of 1834) has ruined the West Indies. That is settled. The consternation here is very great. Nevertheless, I am glad and always shall be that the Negroes are—virtually—free!" A statement like this coming from a slave owner is very significant. At the back of her head, as well as that of her family, was the idea that cheap labor was more appreciated than forced labor. Economically speaking, it was also more profitable. The major difference was that cheap laborers could not be sold for cash and the former owners lost their property rights. They were no longer goods and chattel.

That seemed to be something reasonable, so the British government embarked upon it. They paid former owners £22,000,000 pounds, which in those days made poor slave owners rich. The Barretts had so many slaves that the portion of money granted to them for each slave made every member of the Barrett family wealthy. That is why so many of them returned from Jamaica to the mother country basking in the sunshine of their newfound wealth.

Let no one mistakenly think that this was not a blessing in disguise. Most of them went back to England and became great businessmen and gave up sugar production. Those who remained bought up or leased the properties of returning Englishmen, paid the ex-slaves one shilling per day and produced sugar at a profitable cost. They then became rich, and some of the landlords' descendants returned to the island much more educated than their ancestors and did much better than they at agriculture and prospered.

With all of this happening around her, Elizabeth seemed to have basked in the sunshine of happiness, knowing that the inherited money she was spending was not coming through the sweat and blood of slaves. When the slaves were finally freed in 1838, her father had a great haul since his brother Samuel died and most of these slaves were eventually turned over to him. Even though she got a good sum from her uncle's will, just two years hence and two tragedies struck her again. One brother who was in Jamaica died from yellow fever on February 17, 1840. He was Samuel Barrett Moulton-Barrett, the fifth child of her father. Then on July 11, 1840, the first son of her parents, Edward Barrett Moulton-Barrett, drowned while he was with her at Torquay. With these two tragedies happening in less than six months, Elizabeth began cursing her family's lineage again and said that God was angry with them for having the blood of slaves. Her anger was so great that this was why her illness was prolonged. Her mind was not at peace and the body would have to react adversely.

The author does not know anything about dealing with sick people, but this is just a common-sense idea he learned long ago. A sound mind exists within a sound body and vice versa. But where did Elizabeth get all this vitriolic criticism about her family? Many people are interested to know. Was she looking at her quadroon cousins and their close association with her mother? Or was she looking at her father and his father also? Now that we have DNA testing, maybe someone could do a test, but the family is now so mixed that all tests may come back with the blood of slaves. The emphasis is being compounded here because of the title of this book and the reason why there are rooms without doors, and the blood of slaves had a lot to do with it. However, economics has more to do with racism than the color of the skin of another. When you control the wealth, you control most of the prejudices.

The month of September was very significant in the life of Elizabeth Barrett Browning. She is one of the unique Barretts, and why September came up so often in her life would take some great psychic to decipher. In September 1832, she left her favorite abode, Hope End, for Sidmouth.

In September 1838, after slavery was abolished, she left Sidmouth for
Torquay from whence her brother Edward went to sea and drowned. In
September 1841, she finally settled at 50 Wimpole Street. In September
1846, she married Robert Browning secretly and fled that same month
to Italy. Could all these September movements be coincidental? No one
seems to have an answer, and if one does, where was it written?

There were many writers contemporary to Elizabeth who thought
that her family was of a class all their own. There is one quotation
recorded by Jeanette Marks in her book *The Family of the Barrett* in which a
writer by the name of M. R. Mitford described the Barretts as belonging
to that best class in the whole country, the affluent and cultivated gentry
of England. Marks also said that it seemed that the majority of the
Barrett children were intellectually superior. Two of Elizabeth's brothers
went to Glasgow University and graduated in three years instead of
four for their bachelor's degrees. When they were accepted, one was
fourteen and the other seventeen. There were also other Barretts who
matriculated at Oxford University at age fourteen, and there were scores
of them who had university degrees before the age of twenty. Many were
barristers-at-law before they were twenty. Since the author is a direct
descendant of this family, he is only doing a little bragging here. It
cannot be considered as arrogance since the story is 100 percent true
and arrogance has to do with some form of dishonesty about oneself.

As she wrote her poetry, she became most admired by friends of the
same calling, but she seemed to thrive on sympathy from these persons,
as well as from her father. Sometimes her illness caused her to spit blood,
a sure sign of tuberculosis, and the treatment given by her doctors Scully
and Chambers was the old-time prescription for that disease. She was
given laudanum, the alcoholic tincture of opium, and this was also
addictive medicine that adversely acted upon her brain cells. It reached
the point where she behaved in such a manner that it could be said she
was pretending to be much worse than she really was. If she was up
and around sometimes, as soon as her father came home she was sick
unto death. He adored her for her intellect because she was bringing
fame, although very little fortune, to the family of the Barretts. Up to
the present moment, her fame is greater than any other known Barrett.
She has placed the family's name all over the world where literature is
concerned, and despite all her behaviors and attitudes, she will remain
a famous personality.

The coming of Robert Browning into her life in 1845 made great improvement to her health. One of the things she needed most was physical exercise, and he gave it to her. When he met her in the condition she was, he played a psychic trick on her and demanded that she leave her bed and walk to him. In supposed ecstasy, she did. From that moment on, within twelve months she was ready for an amorous relationship with Robert. Her father still thought he had a cripple on his hands, but Elizabeth was crying out for sexual love. Many questions are being asked whether Robert was a psychic. He made this sick woman walk from the first visit and threw her mind into romantic convulsion. This had to be from a man with some kind of supernatural power. Be that as it may, we have something unusual here, and Elizabeth was responding to suggestions she had pent up for thirty-seven years.

Were she a healthy woman, she would still be in a worse predicament where lovemaking was concerned. Her healthy sister over thirty-eight years old went to her father and asked permission to get married. She took her younger sister with her. When he gave her the answer, both sisters fainted. No one has ever come up with the answer he gave them; however, it was his oft-repeated rule that no one of his children should get married during his lifetime or else they would be disinherited. Some did and paid the consequences.

Now, Elizabeth knew her father very well, so a plot would have to be made up by Robert and Elizabeth to circumvent the rule of her father. She had several strikes against her should she desire to marry Robert. One, he was too poor to marry Mr. Barrett's daughter; two, Robert had the tar brush passed nearby based on the information her father had. Marrying in his lifetime would be the third strike, and she did so and struck out. Could she manage a situation like this and survive? Yes, she could, and she did. One fact to the whole affair was that Elizabeth had income left by her grandmother of the same name. Her uncle Samuel left her money in his will, and her cousin John Kenyon also assisted her financially. He was also a poet and friend of Robert Browning.

There was a plot of sorts brewing in the minds of Elizabeth and Robert, but came first in the mind of her doctor, who was not considering any plot at all. He was only recommending, based on his experience, that should Elizabeth go to a warmer climate she would recover from her disease. This doctor is none other than Dr. Chambers, the said doctor who attended Queen Victoria. The city of Pisa in Italy was the place at issue. When the suggestion got to her father, he refused to let it happen. He had control of Elizabeth's money given to her by his mother, and this money was a part of a larger amount he had under his control. There was enough money to pay for a one-year stay in Pisa, which Elizabeth had of her own but he did not want to see any of his daughters escape from his control. Because of his refusal to send her, Robert and Elizabeth began to craft their own way of escape.

There were many friends of Robert and Elizabeth already in Italy. Some were at Pisa and some were at Florence. They all encouraged Elizabeth to make the trip, and some suspected that Robert would be there too. Her cousin John Kenyon, a friend of Robert, encouraged her to go. He knew that his cousin Edward would not easily accept this suggestion, but John was also afraid to talk to him since he knew the character of his tyrant cousin. They were both Jamaican planters and grew up together as boys on the north coast of Jamaica. He was a friend of Robert Browning and did not mind having him as a cousin-in-law. He also would help to finance the journey to Italy if Elizabeth could not find the cash. It was his delight to see them go.

One evening, Edward Moulton-Barrett came home, and after interrogating his youngest daughter Arabel, he went upstairs to Elizabeth, who had on a white dress, and asked her whether Robert had spent the entire day at Wimpole Street. She told him that the weather had been bad and it held him there much longer than normal. He began to suggest all kinds of mean motives, but Elizabeth kept her cool. As the plot between Elizabeth and Robert thickened, the tyrant decided to have 50 Wimpole Street emptied for major repairs. He then sent his barrister son, George, to take a house at Dover, some twenty miles or more away, so that the family could move immediately. This would thwart the plan and lessen the visits of Robert Browning. The swiftness of this move had the entire Wimpole Street in disarray. Now that the house was rented, Robert and Elizabeth had to up the ante. Instead of Dover, George took a house at a place called Little Bookham, and on the twenty-second day of September, all the Barretts were to leave 50 Wimpole Street.

When the news got to Robert that the Barretts were moving on the twenty-second of September, he arranged for Elizabeth to start packing secretly. She either had to leave with the family to Little Bookham on September 22 or leave with Robert some day before. The packing was not done in secret because all the Barretts were packing. Robert made the plan for flight as well as the marriage, and when Edward Moulton-Barrett thought everything was going his way, Robert was preparing to give him one of the greatest shocks of his life. On September 12, 1846, Robert had everything arranged for his wedding at Marylebone Church, some short distance away from 50 Wimpole Street, to Elizabeth Barrett. This was the same church her Jamaican grandmother Elizabeth Barrett Moulton was held in state at and was buried in the church's graveyard. The day of the marriage was a Friday, and Elizabeth came back to Wimpole Street for eight more nights. She slept in her room on those eventful eight nights without her father knowing she had become Mrs. Robert Browning. Some of her siblings knew but some unknown forces must have kept this secret from him. On Monday the following week, at about three thirty in the afternoon, Elizabeth fled Wimpole Street to the Vauxhall Station, where Robert joined her. They arrived at the Royal Pier, Southampton, and left by ship at nine o'clock to Havre, France. She had her dog Flush and her servant Wilson with her.

Even though Elizabeth was not as well as any woman her age could be, she was overcome by a love for Robert Browning that cast aside all forms of illness for the passion of love she could not enjoy while at Wimpole Street under the straitjacket of her father, who treated her as either a slave or a juvenile delinquent. All her other siblings were under the same rule, so she was not alone. She called upon her ancestral genes and did exactly as her forbears did when under pressure. As a descendant of Vikings, she goaded up enough courage to do as her ancestors did. They moved from country to country and from situation to situation, not knowing where they would end up. First her Viking ancestors came down from Norway to France in order to find warmer climates in southern Europe, and to capture and conquer as they went along. Their hordes settled at a place called the land of the Northmen, which became Normandy. This land was given to them by a King Francis of France by a treaty in the year 911 AD. This was to prevent them from attacking Paris, the capital. They settled there until 1066 AD, when an ambitious ruler by the name of William the Conqueror decided to claim the throne of England, saying that he was the grandnephew of Queen Emma and had a better claim than King Harold. So at the Battle of Hastings in that year, he defeated Harold and took over the throne of England and established the Norman dynasty whose blood is still in the veins of British royalty.

It is not so much history that the author would like to convey as the resilience in the Barrett genes, which are predominant with adventure and exploration, and a passion to endure hardships in order to succeed. According to Jeanette Marks in her book *The Family of the Barrett*, "In this great hour of her life, Elizabeth Barrett left the known for the unknown as did Ensign Barrett when in 1066, under the command of Colonel Henry de Ferrers, he had left Normandy for Great Britain; and as Hersey Barrett, the Pioneer, had done when in 1655, he had sailed from Cornwall to the West Indies, and Sam Barrett in the eighteenth century, when he departed from the prosperous Southside of Jamaica for the unknown of the Northside." This statement will say much about the character of Elizabeth when she landed in Italy with Robert her husband, Wilson her servant, and Flush her dog. She decided on a new life free from all the rules of the Barrett household, and to embark on a life of her own. It turned out that she wrote more poetry in Italy than she did in England. At thirty-eight, it was time for her to enjoy some kind of romantic encounter that every human being should experience, and this would free up her mental capacity to think as a reasonable human being. This is why she wrote so effectively in Italy.

The behavior of Edward Moulton-Barrett when he found out that Elizabeth had fled became more hostile. One could suppose that he became partially insane since tyranny borders insanity. Psychiatrists will differ on this statement, but most ordinary people believe this to be true. There is no evidence that the family moved to the new abode in order to have 50 Wimpole Street renovated, but one thing is sure, Edward changed his will to disinherit Elizabeth, and he had his barrister son George on hand to do the drafting of his new will. He also had to alter it two more times, since his daughter Henrietta married her cousin Capt. Surtees Cook, and his son Alfred married his cousin Elizabeth Georgina Barrett 1855.

Since he told his children not to marry in his lifetime, Edward Moulton-Barrett was confronted with two major mental adversities. He did not like family intermarriages, and this was frequent in the Barrett family, and he did not like Negroid blood within his family. First, he had to contend with Elizabeth marrying Robert Browning, for whom it was documented that the tar brush passed nearby. This was in the year 1846. Then he had Henrietta marrying her cousin in 1850, then Alfred marrying another cousin in 1855. A cyclonic explosion must have taken place in Edward's mind and the results were far reaching. He still controlled plenty of money, and it seemed that his son George got most of it. George gave up the practice of law and lived entirely on the wealth that his father left him. He died at seventy-eight in 1895.

What Edward Moulton-Barrett did to Elizabeth after she married Robert Browning is still being practiced by modern-day Barretts. They can keep malice forever. It is being practiced in the writer's family, who is descended from them, and many of the ancient habits of the family are still being carried out by members, even though they are ten generations down the line.

Elizabeth wrote to her father many times but did not receive a reply. She wrote her brothers and some did not reply, but her brother George did, even though he sided with his father against her. He had business with her since his father handed over to him the shares she had in a company owned by her father and herself, which she inherited from her grandmother Elizabeth. She got her annual dividend from George.

Robert Browning paid a visit to London some six years after the flight, and he visited Wimpole Street, where he found Edward Moulton-Barrett. He spoke to him about Elizabeth and how she had written him many letters asking for forgiveness and he did not reply. Robert was bold enough to tell him that it's time to put away his stupidity and reply to his daughter's longing. Edward went into his room and came back with nine unopened letters from Elizabeth and gave them to Robert with the request that he should give them back to Elizabeth. It is not known what Robert did with them, but it did not seem that Elizabeth saw them on Robert's return to Italy. Edward never read any of those letters. One can see the hatred and the malice from this action.

Elizabeth, after several miscarriages, had a son whom she named Robert Weideman Barrett Browning, and he grew up to be a businessman in Asolo in 1912. He was married but had no one to bear his name. It was rumored that he had two daughters in France, but no one seemed to know what had become of them. So the name of Browning coming through this lineage died.

It is not the purpose of this book to give anything near a complete history of the Barretts. Its purposes are to define certain idiosyncrasies of the family in relation to racism that will make the reason for the title *Rooms without Doors* relevant.

When Elizabeth died in 1861, it seemed she had acquired a goodly sum of money, which she left to her only son because he bought a large castle in Italy where he lived and died. He also earned money from the sale of the love letters of Robert and Elizabeth, which have been published in two volumes. The reason why it is believed that Robert did not give Elizabeth the nine letters returned by her father was that her son would have published them as he did the love letters. Historians, however, learned that these letters came into the possession of one of her nephews, Col. H. P. Moulton-Barrett, who was very angry at her son Robert for publishing the love letters, so he destroyed Elizabeth's letters to her father. This writer expects some forgery of these letters someday if in fact they were destroyed. Based upon Barretts' pride, it is truly believed they were in fact destroyed.

Elizabeth, if she did not love Italy so much, could have been buried in Westminster Abbey like her husband Robert Browning, but she chose to be buried in Florence, Italy. The escapades of Elizabeth and Robert Browning have been written in many books, but most people did not know of their common Jamaican ancestry. Robert is descended from the Tittle family at Half Way Tree in St. Andrew parish, and Elizabeth from the north coast Barretts of Jamaica. It seemed both of them had the tar brush passing nearby. Robert's own has been certified, but Elizabeth's is suspect. She herself said many times that she was of dark complexion. She had many quadroon cousins of her father who were really Barretts under the protection of her grandfather John Graham-Clarke, and growing up with her mother and other family members, so Elizabeth, as the only dark child out of twelve, seemed to be, according to Sir Winston Churchill, a puzzle in a riddle encased in an enigma. So historians will have to judge this contradictory situation.

CHAPTER 6

Robert Browning (Poet)

Had the great earthquake of 1692 that struck Jamaica and destroyed the wicked city of Port Royal, the buccaneers' headquarters in the West Indies, not spared the lives of Edward Tittle and his son Edward, the name of Robert Browning, the poet, would not have been known. To many people of letters, few knew that this great man had his roots in the island of Jamaica. There were many Robert Brownings but this one will be called "The Poet" because he was the only one who was. Three Robert Brownings will be mentioned in this chapter.

Port Royal was considered the wickedest city in the world sometime after 1670, and it became the capital of the most vicious pirates of the then British Empire. Now, the British took Jamaica from the Spaniards in 1655, and it is presumed that pirates were encouraged to go there by the government of Britain in order to help defend the new colony. Foremost among these was Henry Morgan, who was of Welsh descent, and became the most notorious of all the buccaneers. When the British government wanted to control them it had to make Henry Morgan governor of the island. It made him a knight, and he became Sir Henry Morgan. It is of significant note that New York's great moneyman J. P. Morgan has in his family tree this great buccaneer.

As Port Royal became the utmost in wickedness, Christian historians suggested that it was by the judgment of God that it was destroyed. It is said that those inhabitants of Port Royal did every evil that could be devised by man. Many Barretts lived there during that time, and when the earthquake struck, none survived but a Jewish family by the name of Tittle. There were many families of Jews living all over the western hemisphere because this was the time of the Inquisition in Europe,

and many had to join the early explorers. In fact, some of the explorers
were Jews who pretended to be Christians. Based on the letters of Diego
Columbus, his father Christopher Columbus was a Jew from Italy. These
letters may be found in the archives of Madrid, Spain.

The Tittle family that survived had a father and son by the name of
Edward. Both Senior and Junior lived with their family on Jew Street in
Port Royal, four streets or more from the western seashore. There were
three seashores since the city was located on the Palisadoes peninsula.
There were north, south, and west. Edward Senior was an assistant to John
Waight, the cordwainer of Port Royal. The name *cordwainer* is ancient
but it sounds romantic. It means a person who deals with leather goods,
such as bags, shoes, boots, reins for horses and carriages. It is much
more than being a shoemaker. When John Waight, the Englishman who
came with the British forces in 1655, died, Edward Tittle Sr. took over as
cordwainer. This Edward also had property in Liguanea at a place called
Half Way Tree, now in the parish of St. Andrew and is its capital. It is of
significant note that at this point in time and place the Barretts and the
Tittles were on opposite sides of Eastwood Park Road doing business.
The Barretts had a general store, and the Tittles a leather goods shop.
Both families purchased goods from each other, but none were prophets
who could predict the future. These two families were the ancestors of
Robert and Elizabeth Barrett Browning, who gave the world the greatest
elopement story of modern times.

Even though there were two Edward Tittles, father and son, there
was a son whose name was John, oldest of the children, whom the
father would like to go away. He was the son of an African slave woman
who was born before any of Edward Senior's legitimate children. He
was an enigma in his father's household, but he had all the physical
characteristics of his father. And being a fair-complexioned mulatto,
he was sometimes indistinguishable from the rest of the family. Edward
Senior saw to it that this boy was educated the same way his lawful
children were. And when the tutors came to the household, John was
also treated like the rest. There is no record of him being a slave and no
record of his being freed from slavery.

As is customary in the bad old days, slave owners and their assistants
from Europe always looked for attractive African slave girls to produce
a crossbreed of lighter complexioned children who would group up and
become house slaves. These would work among the Africans who were

working in the houses, learned the African languages, and so report to the masters if there was any insurrection planning going on. These half-breeds, who were called mulattoes, were mostly treated better than full Negroes. This was a way of controlling slave rebellions, and it worked well sometimes. But when these mulattoes are treated as harshly as the slaves were, this was where you got plots for rebellion. Most of the slave plots and rebellions in the West Indies and the Americas were carried out by half-breeds.

When John grew up, we are told, he became a part-time sailor and studied externally to become a clerk in holy orders. This is the title given to young men in the Anglican Church who want to become pastors. This was not a good calling for a mulatto in Jamaica, but it had been noted how fair his complexion was and that strangers thought he was white with a substantial tan from the tropical sun. As a clerk in holy orders, he was assigned to the Reverend William May, rector of Kingston. This William May was a very rich man and he owned slaves and a vast property with sugarcane as well as cattle. His property named May Pen was in the parish of Clarendon, and became the parish capital when Vere parish was combined with Clarendon in 1866 as one parish. The capital of Vere was Alley, and the capital of Clarendon was Chapleton. This dispute over which of these capitals should be the capital of the new parish was settled when they created May Pen as the new capital situated at the boundary of the two former parishes.

As John Tittle grew in stature and importance in the Anglican Church, the time came for him to be inducted as a full-fledged pastor, but he was a mulatto. The white churchgoers in Jamaica at that time would have none of it. It is still going on today. Nothing has changed. This did not deter his ambition to become a pastor, but when his father Edward Tittle Jr. died, he got the setback of his life. He was not mentioned in his father's will. His stepmother also when she died omitted his name from her will. We presume that his father gave him an education and so the family thought that was sufficient. John was still not considered poor because he owned property himself. We have no evidence that he owned slaves, so there will be no presumption. In those days, mulattoes of wealth who were given freedom from slavery and money to buy properties from their white fathers sometimes bought slaves to work the properties. Some bought their black mothers and other members of their own family to work on these farms and reduced the harsh treatment normally meted out to slaves. There is no evidence that John did this.

When John Tittle concluded his clerical studies, he wished that a position could be found for him in Jamaica. This was not to be, because his luck was in the island of St. Kitts. Sometime in 1730, he traveled by way of New York to Basseterre, the capital of St. Kitts, and there he was domiciled for quite a number of years, experiencing misfortunes and calamities from the white leaders who found out that he was either a mulatto or quadroon. The people there gave him a very hard time, and he bemoaned the disrespect of the planters and professionals in that island.

He also had many fortunes there because he came in contact with one Dr. George Strachan, a Scottish doctor of wealth. Dr. George Strachan had a daughter named Margaret and a son named George who also became a doctor and took over the practice of his father when he died. This daughter fell in love with John Tittle, who was now pastor of two parishes in St. Kitts. There were racial problems with this love affair because those Scottish doctors did not want to see their family marrying a mulatto, no matter how fair, for mulattoes were considered black by the majority of white people. Even in modern times, they are still considered black. However, John Tittle got married to one of the rich man's daughters in St. Kitts sometime around 1733. It seemed to have caused the death of her father a few months after she got married to John Tittle.

This was a common occurrence among white people when their children married black people. The chief thing they always do was disinherit them. Dr. George Strachan did not do this, because there is evidence that Margaret inherited some property from her father, which caused the poet's father, Robert Browning, to challenge his father as to who his mother was. Robert Sr. had nothing substantial to say except that she was a Creole from the West Indies and she was very pretty and attractive.

Now the term "Creole" as used then was interpreted to mean white people who were born in the western hemisphere. There are many notions of who Margaret Tittle was. There is no record of her being born. People have tried to find a birth certificate but have come up short. To all intents and purposes, she was born in Jamaica when John Tittle returned from St. Kitts. He had so many problems in St. Kitts, even from his brother-in-law, the young Dr. George Strachan Jr., who did not like the choice his sister made in choosing John as her husband. What John and Margaret did with their properties when they left St. Kitts is not known for sure, but they had them for years after they left until their grandson Robert Browning Jr. disposed of them. There is no evidence recorded that John resigned as pastor of the Anglican Church, and no record whether he pastured in Jamaica after leaving St. Kitts, but we do know he lived in Jamaica for a few years before he disappeared from history.

As to Margaret Tittle's beauty, one must be very careful when assessing it. She was so beautiful to Robert Browning Sr. that he did not fully check out who she was. But based on the answer he gave his son, she was very beautiful indeed. Apart from their being beautiful, the middle class and below did not care much about Caribbean girls' ancestry provided they were daughters of sugar planters in the West Indies.

Margaret Tittle was one of those girls, and she went to England to be educated. She was as educated as the elite Englishwomen were at that time, and being pretty, she was a prize to be desired by any English gentleman. Her culture was British all the way, and the touch of the tar brush she had could not be seen by the naked eye easily. It had long been the custom of Englishmen to get themselves attached to wealth, and in the days that sugar was king, wealth and sugar were synonymous, and racism was put on the backburner.

This goes to show that racism on a whole had plenty to do with economics. Even in Jamaica in the twenty-first century, any man of means is attracted to any woman of any race, and not only in Jamaica but in England also. During and shortly after the First World War, when West Indians went to England to help out the then British Empire, those black men who stayed on to study and graduate, especially law, came back home with white wives. This had been the custom from long ago. And these wives were not the poor, unfortunate women of Britain, some were the daughters of doctors, lawyers, and politicians.

So when Margaret graduated, she was ripe to be plucked by any ambitious young Englishman. It was not long after her graduation that her parents left the scene of the action. She got engaged to Robert Browning Sr., and her parents were either dead or kept themselves out of the fray. Shortly after marrying, they became the proud parents of a son whom they named Robert Browning Jr. The author is only referring to Margaret's husband as Robert Browning Sr. for the purpose of clarity in getting to Robert Browning the poet. There were many more before them.

As Robert Junior grew up, he was not conscious of the fact that his mother was a quadroon. She looked like any other beautiful English lady and no one ever hinted that she was a bit different from them all. Her son Robert grew up as any other young Englishman, and as time went by, he was named in the will of his mother, who gave him the properties she inherited in St. Kitts from her parents. There is no evidence of property in Jamaica when John and Margaret Tittle died, so it is supposed that they got rid of them when they left Jamaica to reside elsewhere. There is no evidence that Robert Junior ever visited Jamaica.

When Robert Junior grew to be an adult, he decided to take a trip to St. Kitts to look at the properties his mother left him. These were in the hands of attorneys (not necessarily lawyers) who acted for the absentee landlords, as was a common thing to do in those days. While there, Robert Junior paid a visit to a church that had been pastored by his grandfather John Tittle, and he had an episode in his life he would not forget up to the time of his death. This story is related best by Jeannette Marks in her book *The Family of the Barrett*. She said that when he went into the church and sat down in a pew, a white church warden came to him and said, "Sir, you are sitting in the wrong pew. These are the ones reserved for whites. Please go and sit over there"— pointing to certain other pews—"where they are reserved for Negroes and mulattoes." When he challenged the warden, the warden stood his ground, so Robert Junior got up and walked out.

We have no record of the complaints he made, but imagine a man born in England, brought up in England, being told that he was a Negro or mulatto. Just suppose what you would have done were you in the position of Robert Junior. Well, he went back to England, never to return to St. Kitts again, and the properties he had there were disposed of like hot potatoes. That man's blood pressure must have gone through the roof. Many supposed that he cursed the very ground on which he stood in St. Kitts, and we suppose that this encounter was passed on to his son, the poet, who in all his writings never mentioned the West Indies as far as is known.

Elizabeth Barrett also hated Jamaica because her beloved uncle Samuel Barrett Moulton-Barrett died there, as well as her brother Sam.

Also, her detested lawyer cousin Richard Barrett, three times Speaker of the House of Assembly, lived there, and was foremost in bringing the lawsuit against her father that almost ruined him. Even though most of her money came through Jamaica, she detested the island vehemently.

Robert Junior's anger was not left behind in St. Kitts. He went back home a very angry man and challenged his father about his mother's ancestry. He told his son that all he knew was that she was a Creole from the West Indies and that her beauty got to him, as well as knowing that she was the daughter of a sugar planter from there, so he married her. And if both of them wanted to find out about her, she was now dead and nothing could be done about it, so he better keep his ignorance and misbehavior to himself and get on with his life. He had a far way to go, and if he did not like what had happened to him, make sure he did not marry anyone from the western hemisphere.

The young son kept his cool after being chided by his father, and he listened to what his father said and made sure to marry a German who was always considered a Teuton of the aristocratic class. Little did he know that she was a Jew of German descent and could have also had a touch of the tar brush, which was prevalent among German Jews even though they looked 100 percent Teuton.

Before anything is said about Robert Junior's marriage to his German Jewish wife, let's go back to his grandfather, who was Thomas Browning, who lived 1721–1794. He was a member of the Fraternity of the Rosy Cross, which later became known as the Rosicrucian Order. According to Vivienne Browning in her book *My Browning Family Album*, "The cross was the symbol of the descent of spirit through matter and the Rosy Cross gave it an aura of Divine Love. Some held the rosy cross to be tinged with the blood of Christ. Traditionally, Rosicrucians revealed to no man who they were, as from Jesus Himself it is known that he who was ready to receive esoteric knowledge would seek and find and recognize himself in others. In the seventeenth century, the 'Fraternity of the Rosie Cross,' gave succor to the sick, resulting in miraculous cures. None of them should profess anything but to cure the sick, and that free of charge." The foregoing statement is significant since all the sons of these Brownings seemed to have continued in the tradition of Thomas Browning, and we find Robert Browning the poet doing something quite legendary with the illness of Elizabeth Barrett when he met her in 1846.

Based on the book quoted above, we find that Thomas Browning was the father of Robert Browning Sr., who married Margaret Tittle (1754–1789) of St. Kitts, West Indies. They had three children, Robert, Margaret, and William. He later married Jane Smith in 1794 and produced nine more children. Robert was born in 1782 and lived until 1866.

It was now time for the frustrated Robert Junior to make sure he did not marry anyone in whom the tar brush passed nearby. So he sought out Sarah Anne Wiedemann of German ancestry with the hope that he did not make the mistake of his father who married a Creole. What Robert Junior seemed not to have known was that Sarah also had Jewish ancestry. We are not sure he knew that the Jamaican Tittles were also Jewish. So on February 19, 1811, he married his beloved Sarah in Peckham, London. They produced two children, Robert the poet and Sarianna, in whose arms Robert Junior died in 1866. Robert the poet was also present at his bedside. We now come to the poet, who will be called from now on Robert Browning for the rest of the chapter.

Robert Browning was born on May 7, 1812, at 3 Southampton St., Peckham, in east London. Many historians called this place Camberwell, and for all intents and purposes they are one and the same place. Growing up, he was from middle class to poor but he was not in poverty. He had an uncle named Reuben who helped him out very well and took him on his first overseas trip. Some of his family were just able to make it and others were poor. No wonder Edward Moulton-Barrett said that they were too poor to marry Mr. Barrett's daughters.

This poorness did not deter Robert Browning from calling on unknown powers to overcome poverty and make him respectable even to some of his detractors. We know very little of his education, but since he was poor, his parents could not employ private tutors like Elizabeth Barrett's did, so it is presumed he went to public schools. However, he developed a superb mind, especially for poetry, and he followed in the family tradition that all males became Rosicrucians. How adept he was at this secret order, no one knows for sure, but just look at the result of his getting Elizabeth to recover enough from her illness and fall in love with him. People are free to say what they want, but there are some supernatural forces around, and those who know how to utilize them always succeed materially. They get what they want when they want it, but there is wonder and amazement in how some of these great men came to naught.

There is a story going around about a Rosicrucian sailor in World War II. Its veracity cannot be proven, but the scene took place in the Pacific Ocean during one of the great naval battles between the United States and Japan. It was in 1945 when the Allied powers had succeeded in defeating the U-boat menace of Hitler's Germany. Germany was reeling from the Russian attack from the Red Army headed by marshals Semyon Timoshenko and Georgi Zhukov. They were blasting their way on the eastern front, and the western front had British Field Marshal Bernard Montgomery and US generals Omar Bradley and George Patton under the overall command of Dwight Eisenhower. At that point, Britain sent a battle group to help out in the Pacific. No sooner had the group got there than disaster struck. The aircraft carrier *Ark Royal*, the pride of the group, was destroyed by the Japanese. At the same time, a sailor on the US fleet somewhere in the Pacific disobeyed his commander and was court martialed. He was a Rosicrucian. As the story goes, he was on trial for his life in the midst of raging war. The captain who brought the charges against him was a brilliant man, so there was no way that sailor would go free. The sailor knew how serious the charge was, so he mailed a letter to the headquarters of his order somewhere in California. How he mailed it we do not know, but the letter mysteriously got to its destination within three days. There was no mail ship around but the mail was delivered. The trial should have taken place aboard ship on a certain day. Two days before the trial, a helicopter landed on the deck of the sailor's ship with orders from the commander of the Pacific fleet with certain instructions. The same day the helicopter landed onboard, the sailor found a letter in his room from the scribe of his order saying, "Everything will be all right." As soon as he read it, the news was announced that the captain was miraculously promoted to rear admiral and had to leave immediately to take charge of a new battle group formed to replace the sinking of the British *Ark Royal*. The captain had to cancel everything, including the court martial, so the sailor was home free. If the story is true, then when Elizabeth was confronted by Robert Browning things had to happen.

The story all began when Robert Browning, before he knew her, wrote to her commenting on her poems he had just read, indicating that he loved her poems and even suggesting that he loved her too. This is a story that is hard to believe, but it is true. From this time onward, a flurry of letters between them both continued. The preponderance of

the letters bombarded the minds of the poets in such a way that they
were captivated by each other. On a daily basis, the letters began to
flow in superfluous numbers that they were like individual snowflakes
falling from the sky during a ten-inch-per-hour snowstorm. They were
like the vapors of an ice mountain that crashed into the sea off the coast
of Greenland and created numerous avalanches simultaneously. Books
have been compiled of these letters, and not all of them were located. It
is said that when Robert finally visited her at 50 Wimpole Street, when he
left her upstairs bedroom and got downstairs he wrote her a letter and
asked her sister Arabel to take it upstairs because he did not want to go
back upstairs and get engaged with her again. This might have been for
the purpose of getting away from meeting Edward, her father, since he
knew Edward did not like him. Sometimes they wrote each other three
times each day, and on many occasions the letters written last always got
to them before the previous ones. They had to rearrange letters in order
to get the correct sequences of thought.

Now, after hundreds of letters passed between them, Robert
Browning finally was given permission to visit 50 Wimpole Street. This
was on August 30, 1845, as suggested by Jeannette Marks in her book on
the Barrett family. On that eventful day, he used his power of persuasion
to its fullest when he got a sick woman to leave her bed and come to him
some distance away in the room. When she did, he had her from that
time onward.

When the suggestion was made that he was some kind of
psychoanalyst, it was not known that he was a Rosicrucian. With this
ability to do some form of healing, Robert was able to commandeer
some aspects of her life to the fullest extent. After Elizabeth was turned
down by her father on the Pisa, Italy, visit, Robert was the mastermind
behind all the planning for her to get to Italy no matter what. He knew
that her health depended upon getting away from the hostage situation
at Wimpole Street to a warmer climate than that of England. It was now
a battle of the minds between a sugar baron and a poor man who had
touches of the tar brush over who should control the mind and body of
a sick woman who also considered herself tainted with the same West
Indian tar brush.

No one knew at first who would win, but to the victor went the spoils,
and Elizabeth decided to break up the Barrett hegemony over her and
flee to warmer climes where her health would improve. And not only

that, her feminine hormones were activated and she needed a man to keep them in check. It was not only her health she was considering. She also considered some form of pleasure that her family, especially her father, was denying her. She needed a complete break from the bondage of Wimpole Street, and even if she had to give up family loyalty to do this, she was prepared to do so. With Robert behind her fully, she decided to have a full break from her family detractors. Losing her inheritance for the love of her life fully compensated her. She had enough of her own to live an ordinary economic life and with certain amount of pleasure attached, fully compensated for the loss of what her father would have given her. After all, life without a little pleasure is nothing more than slavery.

When months of planning by Elizabeth and her doctor to request her father to let her go to Pisa in Italy, where the climate would do her much good, came to naught, the master performer Robert Browning came up with another idea. He meant for her to go to Italy no matter what. In his mind, all along, he wanted to propose to her. He did not break the word until the Pisa affair flopped. The plan to get married and elope came to mind some months after.

In the midst of all this wishful thinking, Edward Moulton-Barrett became the catalyst that would push the idea of eloping much further. He had sent his barrister son George to find an alternative residence so that he could move the family for one month in order to carry out repair work on the house at 50 Wimpole Street. This plan to move, even if temporarily, would throw a monkey wrench into the poet's plan. So among other things, the idea of bringing forward the elopement took on accelerated urgency.

Elizabeth wanted to get away from the prison house of her father, and she also wanted to get away from the use of opium, which wreaked havoc with her brain cells. She had heard there was treatment in Italy that would make her better without her having to be a drug addict in a home tantamount to a prison. Even though she had a strong mind of her own, she acceded to every plan of Robert in order to escape.

As September 1846 began, Edward announced that the family would be moving on the twenty-second of the month to Little Bookham, where George had taken a house. Sometime before that date Robert and Elizabeth had to flee or else they would have to stay put until further plans could be made. Robert knew that once the move to this place was made it would be more difficult for him to see Elizabeth, so he put the plan in motion. Many letters were now passing between the two lovers, and soon after September began Robert secretly got a marriage license to carry out phase one of their project. Now Elizabeth had to start packing, and coincidentally, all the Barretts of Wimpole Street were packing too, so there was no suspicion, except Elizabeth's packing had another motive.

All went well throughout, and one now has to wonder if Robert used any of his Rosicrucian connections to enable things to run so smoothly. All her siblings seemed to have been hypnotized. Not even one suggested a hint, but it is presumed that her maid, whose only name was known as Wilson, was in on the various undertakings since she also would be kidnapped for the journey to Italy. Elizabeth, as far as is known, told only one person, a Mr. Boyd, who was her Greek mentor, that she was going to marry Robert Browning. Her poet cousin John Kenyon suspected something based upon the questions he asked her. He was also a rich Jamaican sugar planter and was a close friend of Robert Browning. When Robert fell into hard times, John Kenyon always bailed him out financially. It is believed that Robert told him of their plans. What John Kenyon wanted was that Elizabeth, his cousin, should confide in him enough to tell him the secret personally. She did not. No one at this time should be told anything. Robert did not tell her that he told John anything, but Elizabeth was sensible enough to know that something was let out to someone else. Since everything was secret, had Elizabeth asked Robert anything about telling John of their plan, it would cause a crisis of confidence in those crucial times. So the secret plans for the marriage went through, and when the press began to harass Robert about a secret wedding, it is understood that he told the inquiring newsman to hold off and he would get the full story in an interview. The newsmen at that time were much more decent than those we have today. Our present group would have splashed it all over the front page of their newspapers and television news, and the whole plan would have fallen through. After the marriage and the elopement were fully underway, Robert told them everything on the day of the elopement. The newspapers had a field day, and Edward Moulton-Barrett's blood pressure went up to stroke level. How he did not have a heart attack can only be left to one's imagination.

When all plans for the wedding were completed and the date set for September 12, 1846, the sun that was shining on Wimpole Street began to set. It did not finally set until some eight days after the wedding. Elizabeth took her maid Wilson while Robert took an unnamed cousin, and off they went to the Marylebone Church, not far from 50 Wimpole Street. It is not known how many others were present. So the two illustrious poets who had a common background in Jamaica tied the knot and became man and wife sometime around eleven o'clock in the forenoon, and most people did not know what had happened until one week later.

Now, after this secret marriage, Elizabeth returned to 50 Wimpole Street for one whole week without any of her siblings knowing what had taken place. Maybe her sisters Henrietta and Arabel suspected something but no one asked any questions. It seemed that the supreme power of the Rosicrucian Order was in operation at 50 Wimpole Street. For that whole week of anxiety, there is no record of Robert Browning visiting, even though letters came. One can just imagine what Edward Moulton-Barrett would have done had he known that his first daughter was apparently married to a poor man on whom the tar brush passed nearby. What a tragedy it would have been! To keep this a secret for a whole week must have had some supernatural power protecting the secret. The major thing that threw off the watchmen was the packing to leave on the twenty-second of September for Little Bookham. The boys, who were the spies for their father, were doing all the packing arrangements for their father and themselves and even for Elizabeth herself. This deflected any thought about any other movement. They were caught off guard, and the two lovers were not suspected.

On Saturday, the twentieth of September, Robert was at a place called Hodgson, where the plan was to meet Elizabeth there. Her maid Wilson had secretly moved some of Elizabeth's things to the home of a friend who knew about the plans. Some more things were already at the Vauxhall Station since Friday night. According to Jeannette Marks in her book *The Family of the Barrett*, "On Saturday afternoon about half after three, with Wilson and Flush (her dog) beside her, she walked down the two flights of stairs from her room and out the front door of 50 Wimpole Street. With Wilson and Flush in the 'fly' beside her, she reached Hodgson's and her lover. In this great hour of her life, Elizabeth Barrett left the known for the unknown as did her many ancestors before her."

The *fly* mentioned in the quotation above was a puzzle Elizabeth gave to her sister Arabel when she was planning the marriage and elopement with Robert Browning. What she meant by this was not fully explained, so let the imagination work.

As the plan was, Elizabeth and her group found Robert waiting at Hodgson, where it is presumed that he gave an interview to the press, and at five they took the train at Vauxhall Station to Southampton, where they took a ship for Havre, France. It was sometime after midnight on that eventful Saturday night, the twentieth of September 1846, that the people in 50 Wimpole Street knew what had really happened. New copies of most newspapers in London were reprinted. These were the evening newspapers. Shockwaves went through London and especially the literary communities. No one in these communities ever felt a shock like this. How a sick, almost invalid person got enough zest to marry a younger and stronger lover will ever go down in history as some kind of enigma.

When Edward Moulton-Barrett got the news, he became furious. He called all his children who were present to the living room, where he had a boisterous conference. He tried with the little bit of the intelligence left in him to find out from his children who knew what and when did they know it. After bullying his way around for over two hours, he got the report form his younger daughter Arabel that she only knew about it when Elizabeth was on her way out of Wimpole Street for the last time, and this was a few hours before he came in and there was no way for them to get to him with the news. She then went on to say that Elizabeth told her of a fly that was trapped in a net and suddenly it found a way out and flew away. That story was told to her two weeks before but she did not know that Elizabeth was talking about herself. She had a fondness for talking in parables about herself, some of which up to more than 150 years after her flight have not been deciphered.

Edward accepted this from Arabel but the other daughter Henrietta was only smiling with her head in her lap. She knew that she would be the next one to flee Wimpole Street in marriage to her long-time lover and cousin Capt. Surtees Cook. When Edward could not find anyone responsible for telling him something about this marriage and flight, he began to think that the sons he paid to watch Robert Browning were busily engaged in packing the things for the move two days later. These boys were also on the prowl with their girlfriends since they knew that they could not marry during his lifetime. They had no time to watch their sister when they had other people's sisters in their arms. They had, presumably, many girls calling on them at Wimpole Street, and there could have been a conspiracy among the siblings to circumvent the wishes of a tyrannic father. One would have to judge for themselves what went on in a large house with many adults pretending to be children. That house was nothing more than a meeting place for lovers who were being suppressed.

The next day, when Edward Moulton-Barrett calmed down, he called his son George Goodin Moulton-Barrett to revisit his will. George was his barrister-at-law. Anywhere that Elizabeth's name appeared, he had it removed and the assets reassigned. In fact, it was no codicil. It was a brand-new will George had to draft. Edward was to do this two more times when two other children married during his lifetime, and George was the recipient of most of the assets taken from the three. He got so much of his father's estate that he stopped working as a circuit court judge and sat home and lived off his inheritance until the time of his death.

Based on Elizabeth's inheritance from her grandmother Elizabeth Moulton, her father could do nothing but to continue the investment, which he had also inherited from his mother Elizabeth Moulton. Someone had to be in London on behalf of the elopers, so her friend, cousin, and also a poet John Kenyon took over for her. He had to deal with Edward on behalf of Elizabeth, and when dividend or interest was paid on the investment, John Kenyon would take her portion and send it to her in Italy. He also informed the Brownings that should they ever run into financial difficulties they should contact him for help. There is no record that they ever did, but this man, John Kenyon, was a sugar baron from Jamaica, and he had plenty of money and no children.

The travel from France to Italy was uneventful, and on their arrival, all seemed to have been well. They met many of their friends from England in Italy, and were introduced to many new American friends who thought that the climate in Italy was ideal. A great number of people from all over the world at that time made Italy the place of their vacation, especially Pisa and Florence. It was here in Italy that Robert and Elizabeth wrote most of their poetry and became more famous as their flight from England as elopers began to take on added importance. The literary world was blessed with a fairytale description of how two lovers had come together.

As they traveled through Italy, they decided to settle in Florence, where Elizabeth later died. This was one of the loveliest places on the continent of Europe and also one of the healthiest. It was here that she wrote her father nine letters, which the rascal did not open, not even one. But she got a letter from him disinheriting her and expelling her from the family of the Barrettts. None accepted this expulsion, because even though she married a Browning, through her the Barretts became more important and famous. She is the one who gave fame to the family.

One has to wonder whether Edward Moulton-Barrett knew that Elizabeth may not have been his real child since she was the only dark-complexioned one out of twelve. Since his wife Mary Graham-Clarke grew up among the four quadroon sons of George Goodin Barrett of Cinnamon Hill, Jamaica, and her father was caretaker and protector for them, could there be a possibility that Edward was not her father? The reader will have to decide. Elizabeth herself wrote that she was of dark complexion, and mentioned many times about the blood of slaves. And although she had inherited money produced by the blood and sweat of slaves, she was also an abolitionist.

Apart from poetry, her greatest achievement was to produce a son for Robert Browning. After three miscarriages, she finally came through and gave him the traditional name of Robert Wiedeman Barrett Browning. He was born on March 9, 1849, in Florence and died on July 8, 1912, in Asolo, Italy. He ended the sequential name of Robert Browning because he had no son, and it was rumored that he had two daughters in France by some unknown woman. No one knew their names and whereabouts, so they disappeared from history.

Elizabeth did not have long enough to see her son grow up, but she enjoyed twelve years of life with him. She also paid a trip with him to England, and her father saw him and inquired who he was, and when he was told, he snorted something and left the house without even greeting his grandson. This was still at 50 Wimpole Street, because even though they had left it for one month to do renovations, the family returned there even though Elizabeth had fled. It was at this same place in 1857 that the tyrant died.

Robert and Elizabeth lived together as man and wife successfully, and their lives are a reminder to most women who find themselves in a better financial position than the men. Robert treated Elizabeth as best he could, and as far as history will tell, there were no disputes over finances even though Elizabeth was much wealthier than Robert. He was barely eking out an existence with his poetry, while she was making much on hers and also getting money from her inheritance. Based upon what has been divulged, they were not as poor as some historians would suggest if one would look at the life of their only child after the death of his mother. He owned one of the most expensive places in Italy and lived a lavish lifestyle like the Barretts, and one wonders where he could have gotten so much money to buy that grand palace and several other places of business. I don't know if there is a will made by Elizabeth, but her son seemed to have inherited quite a lot.

After the death of his wife, Robert returned to England, where he lived and wrote several years. And with the help of his family as well as Elizabeth's, young Robert, who was commonly called Penn, grew up to be a man. Having been born in Italy, English became his second language, so he did not decide to make England his home. He went back to Italy, where he was a *de facto* Italian, and set up business there. Meanwhile, his father Robert was quite at home in England where his sister and sisters-in-law lived. He was accommodated by his two families, and Arabel Moulton Barrett was very close to him. In modern times, there would have been a rumor about his closeness to Arabel, his wife's younger sister. He was also honored by the British literary society and finally became the poet laureate of England. He lived in many places in and around London, especially at 19 Warwick Crescent, where he stayed for over twenty-five years with his sister Sarianna as housekeeper. This was not very far from Camberwell where he was born. His son Penn became a painter and sculptor and had several paintings exhibited at the Royal Academy of Art, London, as well as Paris and Brussels.

Robert went back to Italy for the last time to visit his son Penn, and on December 12, 1889, he died at Asolo, Italy, in the home of his son. His body was returned to England, and he was buried in Westminster Abbey at the section known as Poets' Corner. When this author visited Westminster Abbey in 1989, he did not know that it was the centenary of the death of Robert Browning. He was so amused at Westminster, having read so much about it that he had forgotten everything he learned about any one person. Since this chapter is not to detail history about Robert Browning, we now conclude it by saying that in those days, had the report of his connection with ancestors on whom the tar brush passed nearby or were fully tar drum, he might not have had so much glory passed on him, much less be buried in Westminster Abbey. Even now in the twenty-first century, the stigma of the tar brush is still playing havoc with the minds of underdeveloped people. It is a great credit to the brilliance and capabilities of a great poet and one should be judged by the character and intellect of a person rather than by this pseudomentality that one race is superior to the other. And being one of multiple race, one has to consider that all persons are created equal. Those who do not believe this are merely evolved from the lower class of animals.

CHAPTER 7

Peter Barrett Bonnick

It is with much reluctance that the name Peter Bonnick enters into this book because the family of the author is a secretive family and would not like such exposure to take place. However, the author found the characteristics of his grandfather identical to those of the Barretts. He looked like them and behaved like them in many respects. It was shocking to find out that the derogatory terms *tar brush* and *tar drum*, as well as *tar barrel*, were common terms used by him when in fact these were traditional terms used by the family from the eighteenth century. Since he was no literary person, it was important to communicate this fact to readers since the book is somehow describing some racial features of the Barrett family, which behaved from one extreme to the other in their love lives and attitudes. Most of the family treated black people much better than the normal English family did, but there were many who were just like the rest. Peter Bonnick, a descendant of the Barrett family, went from one extreme to the other simultaneously. His mother Ellen Barrett was born sometime after slavery was abolished in the British Empire in 1838, but her father owned slaves. He was John Staple Barrett Sr., and he was a descendant of one Thomas Barrett, who was given three hundred acres of land in the Santa Cruz Mountain in the parish of St. Elizabeth in the year 1751 by King George II.

Peter was born in 1875, at a district named Round Hill in close proximity to the village of Mountainside. Since there is another Round Hill district near the Pedro Crossing, the one where he was born was commonly called Mountainside Round Hill to differentiate it from the one near the Pedro Crossing. They were both in the same parish of St. Elizabeth, and tradition has it that these two places were owned by the same person and the districts developed from the property names, as was customary in the island of Jamaica.

Now Round Hill is the property name of the Bonnick family in Scotland, and most members of the family presumed that the two Round Hill properties were owned by Moses Bonnick who settled in St. Elizabeth. He came from Scotland sometime around 1831, just prior to the abolition of slavery. He had a brother with him by the name of Joseph who settled in the parish of Clarendon at a property he named Round Hill. This Round Hill is now Bray Head, near Crooked River and Frankfield in the just mentioned parish. These two brothers were Scottish Jews, but because of anti-Semitism they left for Jamaica and changed their religion to Anglican so as to prevent further discrimination. They only revealed to their descendants that they were Jews just prior to their deaths. All of their children and some grandchildren later found out their Jewish connection but never made much of their discovery.

Moses produced three children by a native Jamaican wife who was of mixed race. Their names were Henry, Peter, and Charlotte. The total descendants from this family in St. Elizabeth up to the beginning of the twenty-first century was not more than eighty-five. The Clarendon counterpart numbered in the hundreds, if not thousands.

Henry Bonnick became the second husband of Ellen Barrett when her first husband died. She previously married a Mr. Rodgers and had a boy and a girl. The boy's name was Thomas Rodgers, and he settled at Little Park district near the Pedro Crossing and had many children. The marriage between Henry Bonnick and Ellen Barrett produced five more children. The first boy's name was Peter, named after his uncle who lived at Bull Savannah in St. Elizabeth. It is Peter Bonnick, who is the author's grandfather, that is the topic of this chapter.

Since Ellen Barrett was white and Henry Bonnick a mulatto, their son Peter Bonnick was now classified as a quadroon, even though he passed for white among the people because he had blue eyes, straight hair, and a straight nose. He was not the only quadroon who passed for white. There were many others like him who pretended to be white.

Having attached himself to the Barrett family, Henry Bonnick produced children who were connected to famous British families such as the Scottish Falconer (pronounced Faulkner), Foster, Barrett, Palmer, and the French Montique family, who fled Haiti in 1803 to escape the revolution of Toussaint L'Ouverture. They settled in St. Elizabeth and produced a host of French descendants.

Peter grew up a boy common to the inhabitants around him, and since he was the first child of this new marriage, his father took him in confidence. And even before he came of age, he was receiving preferential treatment from Henry. He always told his descendants the joke of the bird he plucked. He said that his father and himself were going on a mule cart the family owned to the parish capital of Black River for the purpose of transporting goods and lumber back to the district of Round Hill. When they got to Fullerswood Park, a very large property near Black River, his father shot a large bird that was flying nearby. It was a bird that was edible. The time was about five in the morning and it was still partially dark. Henry told Peter to get off the cart and pick up the bird. On his arrival back on the cart, Peter was told to pluck the feathers from this bird because it would be cooked for dinner. When Peter completed the plucking of the bird, he said to his father, "Puppa, the bird is wiggling itself in my hand." Henry said, "Throw it away, boy! It could be a ghost or duppy!" Peter threw away the plucked bird, and he said he saw the naked bird pick up each feather that was scattered along the way, then fly back over the cart and flopped its wing as if to say it was alive and well.

These fantastic stories are what Peter Bonnick was good at telling his children and grandchildren. Even though he was good at telling stories like the one above, it was not always stories he was telling. He was very serious about life and his family. He gave us correctly some attitudes of his family and he was one of the chief actors when it came to racism. This man was dead serious, and wherever the Barrett family lived and worked, he knew. He always boasted about his family traditions. Growing up at the foot of the Santa Cruz Mountain, he always looked at the palm trees at Malvern, which was on the property of the Lawrences. Roy Lawrence, the famous Jamaican sport commentator, was born there, and Peter adored this mountain and did everything to live on top of this mountain.

It was difficult for people in other British countries to hear of a Santa Cruz mountain in Jamaica. One thing that should always be remembered is that Jamaica was a colony of Spain for 161, so the mountains and rivers were named by the Spaniards. Some were later anglicized by the British, but others remained Hispanic.

Now the Santa Cruz Mountain begins at Lovers Leap in the southern part of the parish of St. Elizabeth, and ends near Lacovia, the one-time cashew capital of Jamaica. Its name then was Cobie but was spelled Cobre. Santa Cruz Mountain was called by the Spaniards the health resort area of the island, and most of the rich men gravitated to this location. When the British took over in 1655, they also went to live on that mountain, and the remnant of the British people are still there because of its salubrious climate.

It was not very long before Peter Bonnick found a girl on that hilltop in a district named Stanmore. This district was at the next highest point on the mountain to Munro and was adjacent to the district of Elgin. These two districts were north of the town of Malvern and slightly to the west. This girl's name was Frances Whyte, with the pet name "Fanny." She was the daughter of Charles Whyte who hailed from the Pedro Plains and acquired much land in the mountain. Peter Bonnick's land at Round Hill climbed some distance up the mountainside to a point adjacent to the land owned by Charles Whyte.

There is a significant conjecture here since Peter was a quadroon and Fanny was totally African in complexion. The coming of these two together in friendship was an irony of the highest degree. Peter grew up in the Barrett tradition of not liking black men but had a fondness for black women. There are many cases in which the Barrett family members disinherited their children and even declared them dead when they crossed the racial line because they loved it so. The Peter and Fanny contradiction is still being felt and discussed within the family circle. Some believe that white men marry black women because the black women will almost worship them and do much more for them than their own white women. Some also believed that black women will act more as a servant class than as an equal partner. We do not know what Peter was thinking, but he publicly displayed his hatred for black men who were not working for him and showed exceptional love and favor to black women.

His love for Fanny ended in marriage, and something strange happened. When both sets of parents died, it seemed that the couple inherited most of their parents' land, and Peter found himself on the top of the Santa Cruz Mountain where he had looked with longing eyes to be eventually. The combination of the properties of Fanny and Peter made them one of the largest landowning families of the Stanmore, Round Hill area. With this amount of land, Peter was able to take care of his family handsomely. He was now the senior member of his family and he set out to help them greatly.

His brother's children were many, and at least four boys and four girls were dependent upon him for help. The Rodgers family could have passed for white and some of them were even prejudiced against some of their uncle Peter's children, since most of them came out dark and resembling the East Indian people. Some of them were called "Coolie," which is a derogatory name for poor East Indians. Even the rich ones were also called by that name, but the *Oxford Dictionary* also applies that name to the poor working-class Chinese. In Jamaica, the Chinese were never called "Coolie."

Peter was also involved in the courtship and marriage of his nieces, and most of them came to him as if he were their father, and requested permission to marry the man of their choice. Some did not abide by the instructions of their uncle, but some did. He also did not go against them fully, but handed down the St. Elizabeth instruction to them. In the old days, the St. Elizabeth instruction to girls by their father was that men they were going to marry should have houses, lands, cattle, and a job. Depending on how much of each asset they had, one could augment the other, but the four classifications were necessary.

I would like readers to note one of Peter's ironies. This was the case of Blossom Rodgers and her boyfriend Clinton Robertson. They both lived in Balaclava, some twenty miles from Stanmore in the said parish of St. Elizabeth. Blossom brought Clinton to Peter as if he were her father, and requested of him to give consent for her to marry this man. Peter took Clinton away from Blossom to a mango tree on the property and asked him the St. Elizabeth questions. Clinton replied that he not only owned one house but many. He also owned a store, many acres of land, dozens of cattle and horses, and ran a small bus company in the parish. Peter was flabbergasted at the wealth Clinton had, so he told him to rejoin Blossom while he and Fanny talked. Now Fanny is his wife, who had notable African complexion. He said to her, "Fanny, the man is black, but he has something much, so let us give her the consent she asked for." Fanny remained speechless because she was three times as black as Clinton. Peter then said to her, "Fanny, you not saying anything?" Fanny replied, "Peter, they live so far away, if we even say no, they are going to get married anyway and we will only hear about it, so tell them yes."

With the consent of his wife Fanny, Peter went to the couple and gave them his blessing. With this blessing in hand, Clinton and Blossom got married and the family prospered. So Peter sat back in his old chair with his pipe and for years was satisfied with himself for giving his blessing on a prosperous marriage that produced two sons and one daughter.

As the years went by and Peter's ten children grew up to manhood and their teens, he had a daughter whose name was Molly. She was of dark complexion but had a straight nose and long, flowing hair that reached her hips when let down. The family compared her hair to that of her grandmother Ellen Barrett, who made a ponytail with her hair and wrapped it around her thigh. She was over six feet tall, and it is said that the Bonnicks from St. Elizabeth got their height from her. Very few of the male Bonnicks are under six feet tall. Some even linger close to seven feet tall. As her hair was long, so was Molly beautiful. She did not always associate herself with handsome men. So one day, she misbehaved herself and the worst happened and the man was very black.

When Peter heard from Fanny that his daughter was pregnant, and of all persons a jet-black man, he went ballistic and took to the bottle for weeks. As all Barrett men loved to drink strong drink normally, when they came under pressure that drinking became abnormal. So one evening, Peter went to the village bar to quench his thirst and began drinking the notorious Jamaica white rum, which sometimes is brewed to 186 proof. He became tipsy and left the bar and sat on a stone wall nearby and started to cry. When people saw him crying, they went to him to find out what was wrong. He said, "My daughter Molly has got into a serious accident and I don't know how she is going to come out of it." The people then asked him what kind of accident and what they can do about it, he did not then reply. After about half an hour had passed, a brown-skinned man whom he admired came up and said, "Uncle Peter, what kind of accident did your daughter get into?" Peter got into a rage but answered him loudly so that everyone could hear. He said, "She got into an accident with a damned tar drum!"

Some days afterward the district got to find out that Molly was pregnant by a jet-black man. So the Barrett family phrases began to be played out in Peter Bonnick, and it is this issue that caused some of the spilling of the Barretts' secrets on racism. Sometime after this incident, Peter began to console himself with tales of his ancestors' actions in dealing with racism in the family.

Since the Barrett family was a close-knit one, in peace or in strife they all knew what the other section of the family was doing or had done, whether they lived in St. Ann, Trelawny, St. James, Westmoreland, or St. Elizabeth. They seemed to have spied on each other since the horse-and-buggy days. So the Barretts and other white people from England to Jamaica developed the derogatory phrases *tar brush*, *tar drum*, and *tar pan*, as well as *tar barrel*. Peter and other Barretts told their families of their ancestors at St. James and how when two of their sons slept with black women and mulattoes and had children with them, one father who outlived two of his sons knocked off the doors of two rooms at the great house at Cinnamon Hill in St. James and concreted them up. The old man said that not again will his family sleep in rooms that were occupied by Negro lovers. Those sons of his were never married and would not have any affairs with white women. He thought they were mentally deranged, and as executor to their wills, when they died he altered those wills to suit other grandchildren of his liking.

History has now come forth with the proof that this old man in the Barrett family was none other than Edward Barrett of Cinnamon Hill. He had two sons, George and Henry, who only fooled around women who had the tar brush all over them. When they died in 1794 and 1795, the doors of their rooms were taken off and the space concreted up, but historians could only surmise why. Now we have the evidence passed down through the family even though the family did not know for sure what happened. They only made statements they heard coming through the family grapevine.

The author, whose aunt was the Molly in question, tried to find out from the family whether she was allowed to stay at her father's house but they remained dormant. However, people from Stanmore district told him she had to flee to some other member of the family who took care of her. From his experience with his grandfather, the author knew that Molly had to go.

The existence of the rooms without doors continued until Johnny Cash bought the house with the eight acres of land that was left from the large property of over one thousand acres, and he kept it as a winter resort. He gave permission to the author to visit the house in 1987. The visit took place on April 27. On observation, he found where the two rooms were located, and when he looked through a window he saw one room empty with no entrance to anywhere. He then looked at the adjacent room through another window and it was like the first. Based upon his detective training, he could determine where the outside door for each room was located. These rooms were not a part of the old house that was completed in 1734, but they were a part of the great extension done by Edward Barrett sometime after 1768.

After the death of Johnny Cash, the house was sold, but the author does not know whether those two rooms are still there as they had

been in 1987. Other places of interest that the author visited were the
hurricane shelter, which people called "Cutwind." He went inside and
observed it very well but he felt uncomfortable inside after remembering
the great history of this place. After giving the caretaker a shocking
experience with his historical knowledge of the place for several hours,
he made a longing suggestion to the lady whether Johnny Cash would
like to keep it for posterity. She told him that the house belonged to the
Cash son and he would never sell it. It is now sold but no one knows why.

After spending a wonderful time in the hills of St. James, I will now
return to St. Elizabeth and my grandfather Peter Bonnick. He had an
abundance of land he got from his family and also from Fanny's family.
He was always planting something on the land, and when the Pedro
Plains became a desert because of drought, his family from there would
converge on Stanmore, where the rainfall was consistent because of
afforestation. He would willingly supply them with donkey-loads of food.
One will have to recognize that in those days there was an abundance of
food on the Santa Cruz Mountain. The family looked to him for survival
in times of drought. He had so much land cultivated that he could feed
a battalion.

It is very difficult to write about my grandfather but he was a person
with many minds. Not only did he not like black men (excepting those
working for him) but there is also no evidence that he ever dated a
woman of his complexion. It just came to my notice when I decided to
write about him that he was married first to a woman whose complexion
was similar to Fanny's, but her name was never mentioned. No one in
the family knew her name. The marriage ended in one year and no one
seemed to know what ended the marriage. This wife had no children. As
far as I know, he married Fanny as a man free of children. He also had
an affair with one of his workers whose name I will give Miriam. This is
not her correct name, and since Miriam had other children, I will have
to protect their privacy. Few people, if any, knew anything about this
affair, and most of his children are in denial.

After having ten children with my grandmother, he succumbed
to the flirtation of a younger woman. Both of them were working on a
large cassava plantation near Miriam's home where she lived with her
boyfriend and they had several children together. Shortly after a two-
week spell of work on Peter's farm, she became pregnant, but neither
she nor her boyfriend considered anything different because every night
they slept together.

Nine months after this pregnancy, the truth came to light. When the baby was born and the boyfriend was called in to see his newborn daughter, he came back outside the room and hollered in stentorian voice, "Lawd, people come yah, look what kind a pickney Miriam say a mine! This is a white man pickney! Lawd, help me! Wey mi a go do!" Soon after this a large crowd gathered at the house and had a look. Miriam was as black as a tar drum and so was he. The child was a white-looking child. Even though most people in the district suspected that it was Peter Bonnick's child, no one said anything funny about it. In those days, there was no DNA testing and the libel and slander law of Jamaica was so strict and stupid, even today at the time of writing, that one could be sued in court for just suggesting anything funny about someone else.

For years the family of Peter knew about this girl, who I will name Gloria for privacy purposes. Her parents are both dead but their children and grandchildren are around. None of my uncles and only one of my aunts ever admitted the truth about this girl. I never discussed this with my father, who died before I got the story. The truth came to my uncle George when he was about nineteen years old and went to live in the district where the girl grew up. How he did not see that the girl was identical to his youngest sister Lyn, who was one year her senior, remains a puzzle to this day. From information received from my cousin who knew Gloria, she was the alter ego of Lyn. Since Gloria had a different last name from all of us, George decided to have an affair with this girl. Before it came to fruition, other members of the Bonnick clan sent for Uncle Peter and told him that George was getting close to Gloria.

Now Peter found himself between a rock and a hard surface. He would have to admit for the first time what the relationship was between Gloria and himself. When Peter visited George, he was working in a cornfield. When George saw him, he was very surprised. It was about noon that day, and Peter was always a very busy man. For him to walk that two miles from the top of the Santa Cruz Mountain to the lowland had to be something very important. They greeted each other as usual, and Peter in his own undiplomatic way said, "George, I hear you are trying to have an affair with Gloria. Don't go there. It is very dangerous." George then said, "Compta, she is a very pretty girl. Why shouldn't I befriend her?"

Now, *Compta* is the name Fanny and all her ten children called Peter Bonnick. It is an abbreviation of *Cousin Peter.* Why should children call their father *cousin,* I don't know, but that is what it was. Peter was in no way related to his children as I am. My father and I are second cousins.

Peter then replied to George, "Boy, I tell you, don't do it and you will have to listen to me." George said, "Well, Compta, you have to tell me something more." Peter then said, "Well, the something more you want to hear is she is your sister. You can't fool around her!" With this statement, Peter turned around and headed back up the Santa Cruz Mountain and went home. He did not tell anyone his mission, so George the next week told some of his siblings. They all brushed it off as being sarcasm, and as far as I know only one sister believed the story.

George found himself confronted with a truth that he could not handle, so he went to Gloria and told her the story. She said to him, "I thought you knew long ago. I was just waiting for you to make the proposal then I would deal with you. Don't you see how much I look like your sister Lyn? I thought you were just being friendly like an elder brother. You ought to be ashamed of yourself. I am your sister." George thought he had a good catch but was greatly disappointed. He then set out for other dates, and when the girls found out that he could not go with Gloria, there were many who tried unsuccessfully. George did not marry until many years later.

The escapades of Peter and his way of looking down on black men is a total history by itself. Every time a real black man does something wrong, he magnifies it with his disingenuous remarks. A real black person is one who is so black that according to Peter he can be classified as a tar drum. On a daily basis, when he is not cutting down trees and sawing them into lumber, he was always on the go talking about black men and duppy. Let me repeat, a *duppy* is what other people call an apparition or a ghost. His nephews, who went by the last name of Rodgers, behave in a similar fashion but to a lesser degree. The nieces by that same name defied all of the tar-drum insinuations and married black men because they said it would give their children a better color. These women call themselves red-skinned and they were grandchildren of a Barrett.

As has been said, some Barrett men had children with dark-complexioned women and were ostracized for doing that. On a whole, some Barrett families believed in mixture while others did not. Some believed in racism while others didn't. But whatever way these ideas went, they reflected the Jamaican popular attitudes. In Peter's family—black, white, or brown skinned—from time to time they would call one another by some of the derogatory racial descriptions.

Even though most of the Rodgers women came to Uncle Peter and requested his permission to get married to a man, the men did not ask any permission as far as can be remembered. They married any woman of their choice and Peter found out only when they took their wives and introduced them to him. He did not care about the color of any woman. His only concern was that of the men marrying his daughters and his nieces. The practice of Barrett men marrying their cousins was something that many Barrett men hated. There were so many cousins marrying among themselves that some of the wealthy ones disinherited their children for doing so. Peter did not say a word when some of his close relatives did so; there is no opinion one could attribute to him about this.

As his children grew up, they defied his philosophy about black men, and most of his East-Indian-looking daughters married men who were very black. Some of these marriages sent up his blood pressure and most of them stopped visiting him because of their very black husbands. Many nieces and grandnieces who married against the wishes of Peter also stayed away. It got to a point where his attitude made him lonesome, and some of his grandchildren mocked him when he became ill and could not move around as he used to do.

Because of his last name, which is Scottish Jew, members of the family started to inquire what name Bonnick is, and he would say it was Jewish but when his grandfather came from Scotland they became Anglican for fear of religious discrimination, which was rampant in Britain at that time. Another check with his Clarendon namesake and it was also declared to be the same, and for the said purpose.

As time went by and Peter's descendants proliferated, he reminded his family that all Bonnicks were related and that they should keep in touch with one another as his side of the Barrett family did. He was always telling ghost stories that would scare the daylight out of anyone who was a coward, and he told of many encounters between him and other people. When he was not talking about these, he spoke about his Barrett family, how they were rich and prosperous, and how some did not get along with certain kinds of people. His famous story was about the Barrett from Cinnamon Hill who removed those doors and had them concreted up. He gave this man all the right because those boys who had children whereon the tar brush passed should not be honored as those who abided by the Barrett doctrine. What my grandfather did not know was that the most famous of the Barretts considered herself of dark complexion. He died in 1960 without knowing this. He would have been surprised to see who some of his tar-brush descendants became.

Chapter 8

Some Other Barretts

There are many other Barretts who are worth mentioning in any book that describes any part of the family. The most important name that comes to mind, and which few authors ever wrote about, is that of Samuel Barrett Moulton-Barrett, the one who seemed to have saved the Moulton-Barrett side of the great estate for many more years before the properties and fortunes of that side of the family went into decline and fell. Few people will remember him as the one who saved and secured the inheritance of Elizabeth Barrett Browning when her father disinherited her. She had shares with her father in investments run by him, and only the help of her uncle Samuel and a brother named George helped her out. When her investments, which she inherited from her grandmother Elizabeth Barrett Moulton, faltered, it was her uncle Samuel that bailed her out financially while she was living in Florence, Italy. This Samuel was very important in the life of the Barretts, so he had to be included here.

He was born Samuel Barrett Moulton on March 31, 1787, at Cinnamon Hill estate in the parish of St. James, in the county of Cornwall, Jamaica, West Indies. He was the second son born to Elizabeth Barrett during her ill-fated marriage to Capt. Charles Moulton of Middlesex, England. Samuel was born to fortune. He was the grandson of Edward Barrett of Cinnamon Hill, and that was enough. In order for his brother Edward and himself to inherit some of the wealth of his grandfather, they both had to change their last name to Barrett. So on the second day of January 1798, he, along with his brother, took by license the name and coat of arms of Barrett so that all the Moulton boys ended up with a funny name, with two Barretts in each name. So Samuel became, after

1798, Samuel Barrett Moulton-Barrett. I suppose he loved the name because of the wealth that was always attached to it.

One could say that shortly after the nineteenth century had begun most of the Barretts were Wesleyan Methodists, and Samuel Moulton-Barrett was one of them. He moved to Yorkshire and became a member of Parliament. Being the heir to sugar, it is not clearly known whether he represented a rotten borough or constituency. In those days, the idea was that in order to protect the evil of the slave trade, one had to be at the seat of power. The sugar barons always bought a seat in the House of Commons to protect their goods and chattel. This was another name for African slaves. The sole reason why slavery existed so long in the British Empire was that seats in Parliament were being sold by the powers that be and they were being purchased by the sugar barons who were absentee landlords to properties in the West Indies, especially the island of Jamaica where the Barretts held sway.

The sale of the seat went like this. John Brown is a sugar baron. He owns a large manor house with over five hundred acres. He has two hundred workers on the property. He applies to the electoral office to make his manor house and property a constituency, with the two hundred workers as voters. These are his constituents. Whoever does not vote for him has no job. He is their only employer. This condition is paid for by the property owner. On election day, he wins 100 percent of the vote and is sent to the House of Commons as MP for his property. This was called the rotten borough system. The other constituencies adjoining his property had an aggregate total vote of over five thousand. And this was so in the days of slavery. Most of the members of Parliament were not sugar barons but they benefited much from them. The antislavery movement in Parliament was started by people who where not in the sugar circle, such as William Wilberforce, Fowell Buxton, and Granville Sharpe.

It was not until the Reform Act of 1832 that the rotten boroughs were dismantled and each constituency had to be numerically as close as possible. The election after 1832 saw many sugar barons losing their seats and the Abolition Act was finally passed in the House of Commons around 1834, which led to the abolition of slavery in 1838.

This was not the reason, however, why Samuel gave up his seat in 1828. There were problems with the properties in Jamaica and one of the brothers had to go. Edward had twelve children to attend to, so therefore Samuel decided to go. There was a great lawsuit between the

Goodin-Barretts and the Moulton-Barretts. It came to the point where Samuel Moulton Barrett had to pay to the Goodin-Barretts over £30,000 between 1822 and 1828. This was only half of the court settlement for the illegal use of slaves and steers. The other half was paid by his brother Edward Moulton-Barrett. To bring the properties, slaves, and cattle to productive use was the reason why Samuel had to depart. When he left England for Jamaica in 1827, on seeing the situation, he did not return. He resigned his seat in February of the next year, and until he died on December 23, 1837, one year before emancipation, he did everything to bring back prosperity to the Moulton-Barretts and succeeded in doing so.

When the missionaries were on the go in Jamaica for the proper treatment of slaves, it was Samuel who got Hope Waddell, a Scottish Presbyterian, to be chaplain on all the estates of the Moulton-Barretts. He gave the missionary full support, and his new wife Mary Cay-Adams set up schools to teach the slaves to read. As a result of this connection, whipping of slaves stopped on the Moulton-Barrett estates. Samuel Moulton-Barrett then did something that was a revolt to slave owners. Within a few years after Waddell became a fixture on his properties, the first black overseer (*busha*) was appointed in Jamaica and was given the name Edward Barrett. Also, the first black schoolteacher was appointed on his properties to teach slaves to read. This was so revolutionary that when the Sam Sharpe rebellion of 1831 came, most of the planters of the north coast of Jamaica blamed Samuel for being the instigator. Even though it turned out that this was not so, people wanted to know why not even one root of his sugarcane was destroyed. The Moulton-Barretts had at that time more than thirty thousand acres of sugarcane. With all the abuse that Edward Moulton-Barrett got later on in life, he was the chief instigator in teaching slaves to read and letting them go to church. So much for a tyrant.

When the Colonial Church Union was organized, it was much worse than the KKK of the United States. The members of the Church Union would invade the courts of Jamaica and remove members of the church who where on trial for treating slaves right, and beat and lynch them right there in the courthouse. When Samuel Moulton-Barrett became custos of St. Ann in 1833, he tried and freed several missionaries who were later found beaten to death. He himself was threatened, and on many occasions had to flee with the prisoner through the back door of the courthouse. A famous pastor that Samuel saved from lynching was Morris Knibb. The Church Union people then burned his house to the ground. It was actions like these helped fuel the Sam Sharpe Uprising of 1831.

Another famous preacher Samuel protected was John Greenwood. He had to hide him in a back room and he escaped through a window. When the Colonial Church Union members heard that the missionary had escaped, they broke up and thrashed the courthouse and nothing that could be broken was left intact. These people, who went to church every Sunday and owned slaves, destroyed the king's courthouse. They did not touch Samuel Moulton-Barrett because he could have called out the militia to shoot them down. They dared not touch the king's magistrate.

The news got to Spanish Town, the capital, and the governor sent for Samuel to tell him what happened. When he gave the evidence before the privy council presided over by the governor, they all concluded that something had to be done to this Colonial Church Union. The governor then invoked the Toleration Act # 52 of George III and legal prosecutions and persecutions of missionaries were made null and void. Only lynching of missionaries at a slower pace continued, but the burning of the preacher's house continued. Not until the abolition of slavery in 1838 did the Colonial Church Union (CCU) go out of existence but formed other groups (KKK) to persecute and rob the emancipated slaves.

Samuel Moulton-Barrett died in 1837, the year before emancipation but what he did on his properties prior to emancipation laid the foundation for all decent men to follow in their treatment of their African brothers who happened to have been slaves. It is to the praise of this man that the Barrett family stood head and shoulder above all other slave owners in their partially decent treatment of those unfortunate slaves. No member of the Barrett family at present, even though some of them are black, have any reason to be ashamed of the name; and the person foremost among that name is none other than Samuel Moulton-Barrett.

The other Barrett of note is Richard Barrett of Greenwood Great House, which is still in existence near Barrett Town in the parish of St. James, somewhere along the Queen's Highway. This great house was built by him in 1809, and his cousin Philip Morris was architect and chief builder. When this author visited the great house, he discovered something looking rather funny. Standing by the center post of the verandah that faces north and looks out over the sea near Montego Bay, he observed that the side of the house resembled a part of the diameter of a circle, which showed the curvature of the sky where it touches the horizon. He inquired of the attendants whether the house was built according to astronomy. None of them knew; however, one of them said, "If you were here on the twenty-first day of June at twelve o'clock, when you look up, the sun would be right on top of this upright. It appears as if it was exactly over it, so you can think about this."

The name Richard in the Barrett family is associated with tragedy. The last famous three by that name died under suspicious circumstances. This Richard was three times speaker of the House of Assembly, the governing body of Jamaica at that time. He was a prodigy, and was one of the many Barretts who matriculated at Oxford University between the ages of fourteen and fifteen. They all graduated before nineteen, and at twenty years, they were full-fledged lawyers practicing before the British Supreme Court.

Richard Barrett of Greenwood owned many properties and slaves. He was the grandson of Edward Barrett of Cinnamon Hill, and was first cousin to Edward Moulton-Barrett, the father of Elizabeth Barrett Browning. Something went on suspiciously over the probating of the will of Edward Barrett of Cinnamon Hill, and Richard Barrett was one of the litigants in a lawsuit that lasted over twenty years. Richard and others were successful in the case, and the Moulton-Barretts had to sell properties to pay up. Both Moulton-Barretts got too much from their grandfather, who illegally transferred slaves and cattle from the estates of his son George Goodin Barrett, who preceded his father and left him to properly administer his will. Because George Goodin Barrett had black children who would benefit handsomely, his father, who hated black people, misappropriated the will to benefit the white grandchildren, the Moulton-Barretts. Other white grandchildren were also robbed, and Richard was one of them. When both black and white grandchildren recovered what was rightly theirs, the court made Richard the receiver and collector on behalf of the others, and from that time forward the Moulton-Barretts hated the Goodin Barretts, especially Richard. Only Samuel, the MP, spoke to Richard. Elizabeth Barrett Browning disdained him, and even in some of her letters to friends she very much derided him for causing financial problems for her father. Be that as it may, Richard did what he was supposed to do.

He privately derided slavery even though most of his earnings came out of it, but he put in what was right for him during the period he was in control. While Samuel Moulton-Barrett had black overseers at his properties, Richard also had them at Barrett Hall property. He also used Hope Waddell on his properties to teach and educate his slaves, as well as to establish churches on his properties. The rapport that Richard and his cousin Samuel had with slaves on their properties surpassed that of all the other slave owners in the West Indies.

Richard, as speaker of the House of Assembly, was one of the most respected planters in Jamaica. After the uprising in 1831, he was selected by the government of Jamaica as one of two representatives should an Emancipation Bill be introduced in the House of Commons. So in 1832, he set sail to London and effectively represented Jamaica in the major question of what would the planters get if all the slaves were freed. He was not one of those planters who opposed the abolition, but wanted compensation for doing so. Richard knew that cheap labor was better economics, and even though his family had more slaves than any other in the West Indies, the Barretts were in favor of abolition. Even Elizabeth Barrett Browning was on the side of the abolitionists and she wrote many letters supporting them, even though her father was a major owner of slaves. The Emancipation Bill went through, and how much was given the planters can be seen in the effectiveness of Richard Barrett. Twenty-three million pounds in those days was a very large sum of money, and thanks to the Reform Act of 1832, when the rotten boroughs were outlawed, a new set of members of Parliament came in and destroyed slavery throughout the British Empire. Slavery in the world would have continued for another fifty years or maybe another civil war would have to be fought.

Many people thought Richard Barrett was born in Jamaica. His father Samuel Goodin Barrett was. He came to Jamaica as a young man, and when he saw slavery in its fullest extent, he was bent on its destruction from that time. He also stated that he wanted equality for the freemen of color who bought their freedom from the white men. Most of these colored folks were quadroon and mulatto sons of the white sugar barons, most of whom were sent to England to be educated and returned with college degrees. These were not poor people. They also had plenty of land and many slaves. Some of the white people disdained them, and Richard Barrett, as speaker of the House of Assembly, would not agree to such treatment. These colored people had votes because they paid property taxes. So Richard embarked on his ambition for equality and was partially successful. He, for one, was bent on the complete emancipation of both slaves and freemen. He was a diplomat, however, and that's why he was sent to the House of Commons to represent the plantocracy of Jamaica in 1833.

He got fed up with life at Greenwood Great House in St. James, and went and bought properties in St. Ann. These were the Albion and Rio Hoja (now known as Moneague Lake) properties, which may still be owned by members of the Barrett family. He gave as his reason for leaving St. James harassment from the then governor, the Marquis of Sligo, who accused him and some other agents of destroying his north coast properties. We don't know if any of these allegations are correct, but in those days agents always robbed their absentee landlords. Whatever happened, Richard still kept ownership of Greenwood and Barrett Hall.

Shortly after slavery was abolished in 1838, Richard Barrett became one of the wealthiest landowners in Jamaica. As emancipation took root, the law of diminishing returns set in, and many of the planters sold out and fled. The recipient of this economic confusion was Richard Barrett. He had more money than he ever had, more land than he could properly oversee. He was many times a member of the House of Assembly, custos and judge of St. James parish, three times speaker of the House of Assembly—apparently one of the most powerful men in the island of Jamaica. Yet with all this power, he was still one of the Barretts' wineheads. He was a slave to alcohol, and this could be seen in his contemporary Barrett family, as well as many before him and many after him, right down to the present-day generation of Barretts even in the twenty-first century. This dirty practice of alcoholism was the thing that did him in.

According to Jeannette Marks in her book *The Family of the Barrett*, on a Saturday morning, May 8, 1839, shortly after having breakfast, he went to Montego Bay to transact business at a store owned by one DeWar. He became very ill and was carried upstairs to the lodgings of Catherine Shaw, where he died a few hours later. Family tradition passed it down to our present generation that he had been drinking and someone slipped cyanide into his drink. No one really knows for sure what happened since no formal autopsy took place, and it seemed that no one forced the issue. The body was taken to Cinnamon Hill, and finally laid to rest in the Barrett cemetery adjacent to Rose Hall Great House. No mark was placed on his grave, and when this author visited, he did not see a headstone with the name of Richard Barrett. Thus ended the life of one of Jamaica's great sons.

As far as can be seen, Richard had many enemies. Some were his family and others were his colleagues in politics, and even some governors did not like him. What he was hated mostly for was his secret hatred for slavery, which came out after the abolition and his fight for colored people. He was the Barrett who fought members of his own family so that the quadroon children of his uncle George Goodin Barrett could inherit their father's estate, which was willed to other white members of his family. He won the case and the quadroon children inherited, so he was hated by the Moulton-Barretts, and even Elizabeth Barrett Browning in some of her letters to her friends disdained and derided him for such a great fight. Whenever people try to help the poor, they were always destroyed by the rich.

In 1840, tragedies struck the house of Edward Moulton-Barrett, the so-called tyrant of 50 Wimpole Street. In 1837, his brother and coheir to most of the Barrett estates died, but his son with the exact same name as his brother, Samuel Barrett Moulton-Barrett, took over the operations of the Moulton-Barrett properties. The first son and heir of the so-called tyrant of Wimpole Street had the same identical name as his father, Edward Barrett Moulton-Barrett. He was sent to take care of his sister Elizabeth Barrett Barrett, who later became Elizabeth Barrett Browning, where she was recuperating from her illness at Torquay. Shortly after being sent there by a reluctant father, he died in a drowning accident somewhere near Babbacome Bay in the area of Torquay on July 11, 1840. The family was still mourning the death of Samuel Barrett Moulton-Barrett, who died earlier in Jamaica on the seventeeth of February 1840 at Cinnamon Hill, Jamaica. He succumbed to the deadly yellow fever, which every European feared. Now there was a vacuum in the management of the Moulton-Barrett estate, and had it not been for the honesty of their lawyer Matthew Farquharson of Font Hill Estate, in the parish of St. Elizabeth, who took over the reins of running the properties, maybe the so-called tyrant would have died a pauper.

It was at that crucial time that Charles John Barrett Moulton-Barrett was called to go to Jamaica. He reluctantly did so, but he was the pick of his father and the rest of the family. Elizabeth, the poetess, never wanted him to go even though her inheritance was involved in the operation of the estates. Her inheritance came from her father's mother also named Elizabeth Barrett of Cinnamon Hill. Charles took over possession of the properties and brought them back to production as they had been. So the Moulton-Barretts profited and prospered until a brother of Charles named Septimus came to Jamaica with him and began the decline and fall of the Moulton-Barrett empire.

Charles bore in mind the threat made to the family by the so-called tyrant that none of his children should get married during his lifetime, so Charles kept several mistresses, two of whom produced quadroon children. The only one who became prominent in Jamaica was a daughter by the name of Arabel Moulton-Barrett. She was named after one of her aunts, her father's sister, and the reason why she is mentioned is that she was a writer and wrote a newspaper article defending her grandfather as a decent man and not as a tyrant. Rudolph Besier had just written a novel entitled *The Barretts of Wimpole Street* in which he depicted Edward Moulton-Barrett as a tyrant. It was a novel of course.

Arabel could not have defended her grandfather because she did not know him. All the information she used was what she got from her father, and had she, being a quadroon, been born when her grandfather was alive, that same grandfather would have turned against her father for producing a child whereby the tar brush passed nearby. Little did she know that one of the reasons why her grandfather treated Elizabeth so unfairly was because she married a man who had the tar brush passing nearby.

When Charles' father died in 1857, he decided that the time had come for him to get married. He had many mistresses, and no one knew whether he would marry a mulatto or quadroon. So one day in 1865, he decided to marry Anne Margaret Young, the daughter of John Young of St. Ann parish. The wedding took place on the first day of August. This was done to celebrate the abolition of slavery, but why he did it on that date is still a puzzle. However, the wedding was rushed because she lied to him that she was pregnant. He fell for the lie because he did not want her father to disinherit her, because this was the custom of the time. After the wedding took place and three months had passed, there was no sign of pregnancy. This annoyed Charles to the point that the wedding almost became a travesty. They did not divorce, but Charles did not display the true behavior of a husband, and most of the time they lived in the same house as strangers. He had no more children except the previous two before his marriage.

As time went by and the will of his father was probated, the black sheep of the Moulton-Barrett family appeared on the scene in Jamaica. His name was Septimus Barrett Moulton-Barrett. He was the greatest winehead of the Barrett family. He would sit by the great house and drink himself to a stupor. How he became custos of Trelawny, no one knows. How a man who was always drunk had become the chief lay magistrate for a parish goes beyond understanding. But he was a Barrett. He started to run up debts by the thousands of pounds, and Charles had to sell property after property to keep the custos out of debtor's jail. The situation had become so bad that the family's fortune was almost ruined. This was the decline and fall of the Moulton-Barrett estate, and if Charles was not a very wise leader, he would have gone to the grave a pauper. After less than ten years, Septimus destroyed the family's wealth. And when he died on the seventeenth of March 1870, Charles breathed a sigh of relief. Even after the death of this winehead, Charles had to sell the most famous of the Barretts' properties to pay off the debt of Septimus.

It was a good thing that Charles had bought other small properties whereby he could earn a living for himself, and lived for a good time after the death of Septimus. So after a peaceful life thirty-five years after the death of his brother Septimus, Charles died at a property called Clifton in the parish of Trelawny on January 21, 1905, at the good old age of ninety-one. So after spending over fifty years in Jamaica, only returning once to his native land, this stalwart of a Barrett survived many tragedies and presided over the decline and fall of the Moulton-Barrett empire.

Not since the time of the *Mona Lisa* have the world come upon a greater portrait painting than that of Pinkie. Her portrait has gone to the ends of the earth. The Woolworth Company and many others have used her on postcards all over the world. They have repainted portraits of her that are better looking than the *Mona Lisa*. Many people did not and still don't know her name or who she was. My duty as a member of the same family of Barretts is to expose her so that all may know who she was and that she was a real person.

She was the daughter of Elizabeth Barrett of Cinnamon Hill in the parish of St. James, Jamaica, West Indies. She was the granddaughter of the famous Edward Barrett of Cinnamon Hill whose only surviving daughter Elizabeth married Capt. Charles Moulton of London and produced four children. Pinkie was the first and was born about 1783. Her full name was Sarah Goodin Barrett Moulton. The author is the one who put the name Barrett in the middle since most girls in those days did not get their mother's maiden name in the middle of theirs. She was also the sister of Edward Barrett Moulton-Barrett, the father of Elizabeth Barrett Browning. Sarah (Pinkie) Moulton died very young, so she did not know her famous niece and Robert Browning.

When her two brothers, Edward and Samuel, left Cinnamon Hill for England in 1795, they were accompanied by their mother Elizabeth, grandmother Judith Goodin Barrett, and grandfather Edward Barrett of Cinnamon Hill. She also joined the group and bade farewell to Jamaica, the land of her birth, for another place euphemistically called home, since home to most people of English descent was England. They instilled in their children that England was home.

On their arrival in England, the boys were placed in schools all over London. The Barrett families lived in the West End of London at a place called Portman Square. Most of the Cinnamon Hill Barretts lived there and it was here in 1795 that the great portrait painter Thomas Lawrence was commissioned to paint a portrait of Sarah Goodin Barrett Moulton and to ship it back to Cinnamon Hill when completed. The grandparents had only come for a short stay, so they went back to Jamaica to await the arrival of the painting. This was not to be. When the painting was completed and before it was sent to Jamaica, Thomas Lawrence requested permission to put the painting on display with his other works. This painting of Pinkie was so lovely that he won many prizes with it, and this was what catapulted him to receiving a knighthood. Before he concluded the exhibit, Pinkie died on April 23, 1795, and the death created such an uproar in the family that Judith Goodin Barrett, her grandmother, told Sir Thomas Lawrence to do what he wanted with the portrait. She did not want to see it. What Lawrence did with it, no one knows for sure, but it never got to Jamaica.

The painting of Pinkie was such a success that she became more popular in death than in life. The portrait took many prizes all over the world wherever it was displayed. Many companies bought out the rights to use it in postcards for many years. It became so famous that people were standing in line all over the world to get a copy of the painting. And based upon how many copies of it are all over the world, it is apparent that numerous persons were granted permission to duplicate it, so many members of the Barrett family and houses at the present time have a copy of the Barrett *Mona Lisa*.

There are many people who would like to get a copy of *Pinkie* and her brother *Blue Boy*. The so-called tyrant of Wimpole Street appears in a classic painting but this author does not know the painter. Be that as it may, the painting still looks very good.

One thing about Sarah Goodin Barrett Moulton (Pinkie) is this, there is only one original painting of her by Sir Thomas Lawrence. All the others are copies, whether authorized or not. The original is now worth millions, and the last place it was seen, up to the time of writing, was in the Colis P. Huntington Museum, San Marino, California. It is my hope that millions will go to have a look at the Jamaican *Mona Lisa* and remember that the person whose portrait they are admiring was born on the beautiful island of Jamaica, at a place called Cinnamon Hill, which juxtaposes the famous Rose Hall property near Montego Bay in the parish of St. James. It is my hope that the government of Jamaica or a historical society will purchase Cinnamon Hill and preserve it as a museum for future generations. This place is too important for private individuals to have and for the public to have no right to see. This may sound a little arrogant since I am descended from this great family, but when a statement is true, despite it appearing as self-praise, it is not arrogance.

CHAPTER 9

Rose Hall

It would be a great disservice to any book elaborating on Cinnamon Hill Great House not to mention something about Rose Hall Great House. These two great houses are in juxtaposition to each other, and although they are about three miles apart, the two properties adjoin each other for miles. Although Cinnamon Hill is a little older, they both were finished in the earlier part of the eighteenth century, with Rose Hall being the more fabulous in style, quality, and material, and had a more luxuriant view of the Caribbean Sea. Yet Cinnamon Hill produced the great intellectuals of that era, and the most popular gentleman with riches and political clout more than any other of his time. His name was Edward Barrett of Cinnamon Hill, whose granddaughter was England's greatest poetess and had the most fabulous love letters in the world when she corresponded with Robert Browning. It was Cinnamon Hill that produced the inimitable Elizabeth Barrett Browning.

Rose Hall was not to be overshadowed by Cinnamon Hill's intellectual greatness, for it produced some characters that have made Rose Hall most famous even in modern times. The unusual deaths of its first female owner's husbands and the appearance of a white witch later on have taken on a new mystical quality that can only be considered as ultranatural. There are many views from various historians about the existence of these two famous women. Some people think that the two women were one and the same person. What is most annoying is that some so-called historians are denying the fact that there was a white witch by the name of Annie Palmer. They claimed that she was only a character in the novel *The White Witch of Rose Hall* written by Herbert George DeLisser. Had they done their homework, they would have found out that Annie Palmer did exist, as her marriage certificate would show, which can still be found in the Island Record Office in Spanish Town, Jamaica. Many of us as historians know that it is there unless it has been recently destroyed, and I don't believe it has.

My job as a historian is to debunk the idea that Annie Palmer is all fiction. She was Annie Marie Patterson, a person of Scottish-Irish descent, who was brought up in her young life by a voodoo nanny from whom she learned the trade very well. Many of what has passed down to us as legend is in fact correct history, but since most of the people involved could not read or write, they passed it on as verbal history or tradition. I would not use the word *illiterate*. Take for example my grandmother, who is descended from the Ashantis. She helped teach me to read but she could not write. She did not go to school in those days shortly after the abolition of slavery, but even when I was in the third grade she corrected my reading and she was correct. As children, we could not ask her why she couldn't write. It would have been most impertinent for us to do so. She would personally ask me to write letters to her many sons who did not live in the same parish, and when she got the replies, with money in most of the letters, she would read the letters to the family but never mentioned how much money she got. She skipped over that part. I would then have to write the reply to say thanks. Sometimes my other brothers did the writing. Now when people like my grandmother handed down historical data as tradition, the so-called educated disregarded these as facts even though they were true. When I read and write history, I discovered for myself that many things written as facts were just the opposite. History is not a science. Don't say that things aren't true because they seem improbable.

So we now return to Rose Hall and some of its fantastic history. As a man from St. Elizabeth, I am very excited that the founder of Rose Hall Great House had something to do with St. Elizabeth. Her name was Rosa Kelly, the daughter of the Anglican rector of St. Elizabeth, John Kelly. My historians did not record when he became rector of St. Elizabeth, so we do not know whether Rosa was born in that parish or in St. James parish where John had also been rector for some time. The younger generations can find this out. However, around 1746 she married one Henry Fanning of the parish of St. Catherine, and the two began to build this great house the same year.

There is very little known of Fanning, so the question is where all this money, £30,000, came from. Rectors do not make much money, not even in those days, but some were overseers of large properties owned by absentee landlords. Some rectors themselves owned many slaves and properties, so Rosa Kelly could have been the daughter of a slave-owning rector who had plenty of money. One notable rector who was very rich was a man by the name of William May, who was rector of Kingston in the latter part of the eighteenth century. So vast were his estates in the parish of Clarendon that the present capital of this parish was named after his property, May Pen. That's exactly what it was. So John Kelly could have been one of those rich rectors.

We are also acquainted with the fact that the Anglican Church owned many slaves and that their rectors in many parts of the West Indies were merely chief operating officers of the church's properties, masquerading as ministers of religion. They had control over much of the sugar money, and some diverted large portions to their families while sending a paltry sum to their benefactors. So Rosa Kelly could have had that large sum of money. Henry Fanning could also have had a large sum of money, but to expend so much on a dwelling suggests that there was much more money left where that £30,000 originated.

Construction at Rose Hall Great House started at a time when a genius builder was living at Cinnamon Hill Great House, which was completed some twelve years earlier. He was Edward Barrett of Cinnamon Hill, and he had to agree to allow Rose Hall to use a spring that originated on Cinnamon Hill property as their only source of water. So whatever happened to Rose Hall, the Barretts had a part to play in it. Both Rose Hall and Cinnamon Hill estates occupied the same hillside overlooking the Caribbean Sea and the city of Montego Bay. The two adjacent properties are no longer in existence as they were, and many changes have taken place. The spring from Cinnamon Hill no longer exists, but a copy of the small aqueduct remains, with a standpipe draining water that leads to the duck pond at present. This was the water tank that supplied the Great House years ago.

This author had a fascinating time when he visited Rose Hall in 1987. He spoke to a number of guides, about eight in all, and asked whether they knew of the aqueduct system that brought water from Cinnamon Hill to Rose Hall during the occupancy of the Palmers. No one knew about it, so they consulted with the workers all over the property until they brought the chief guide, who inquired who was this person asking such a difficult question. She took me to the standpipe and pointed

to the hillside nearby and showed me that the present aqueduct is a
replica of the old one. She had not told her guides about this because
she did not think anyone would ask that question. She still insisted that
she wanted to know how I came by the information. The author then
told her he was a descendant of the Barretts and he'd studied his family
and Rose Hall came up in his research, so that's why he knew all these
things. She shook her head and said, "I will have to find out some more
about this place and teach it to my guides."

Now we return to Rosa Kelly and Henry Fanning. However they came
by the money, the house was started in 1746 and continued to be built
by the specifications Rosa wanted. Some three years after work started
and the house began to take shape, Henry Fanning died mysteriously.
In those days, the British criminal law had not yet been developed.
There was no police force in Jamaica, nor in Britain for that matter.
No postmortem was done, nor did they know how to perform one.
The marriage seemed to have been happy, although in those days if a
married woman did not get pregnant the marriage would be considered
a disaster. Rumors went flying all over the place, and her father, who was
now the Rector of St. James, had to quell some of the dirty things being
said about his daughter. When all was said and done, Fanning's death
passed on as if nothing happened, and Rosa Kelly was free to marry
again if some brave fellow would come along.

With this mysterious death, accompanied by others, many people
mistakenly believe Rosa Kelly to be the same person as Annie Palmer
the white witch. It must be recognized that these two women of Rose
Hall did not even exist together in the same century. Rosa lived in the
eighteenth century, and Annie in the nineteenth. More than fifty years
separated them. Rosa died in 1777, and Annie came to Rose Hall in 1820
and died there in 1832.

It was not many years after the suspicious death of her first husband
that a Casanova came calling. No one knows for sure why she was so
fortunate. She was the most educated female in Jamaica at that time, and
many people in those days wondered why John Kelly gave his daughter
such a high education. Maybe it was because she was the only child he
had. History is not kind to her mother. No one ever heard of her. Was
she the child of a mistress and John Kelly was the father of some funny
romance? This we do not know. But it is said that Rosa was too educated
for a woman, and many men avoided her because of this. Many men now

tried to get to her because of the great house she was building. It was more than half completed when Henry Fanning died. Then along came George Ash as an eligible suitor, and Rosa Kelly Fanning accepted him.

George Ash set to work on the great house, and in about three years it was completed to great fanfare. No house on the north coast of Jamaica was as fabulous as Rose Hall. The carpets were from Persia, and the mahogany was from South and Central America. After this great accomplishment, all were looking forward to a happy life between George and Rosa, but the sword of Damocles was hanging precariously over the head of George. Some people who saw how Rosa's father was treating her so gloriously began suspecting all kinds of evil thoughts. According to Jeannette Marks in her book *The Family of the Barrett*, on page 178, "The rector had given his daughter an education beyond the usual and a friendship deeper than is custom of most fathers. Sixty years after her education had been begun by her father, the education he had given her was still a matter of comment." Most people thought the rector was a man of integrity and nothing funny went on. The question is whether something funny really was going on or it was all mere coincidence. People will have to think for themselves.

Three years was sufficient time for any man to live with Rosa Kelly. Only those who survived knew this. George Ash didn't. He also died mysteriously shortly after three years had elapsed, so the Jamaican fairy queen was at her tricks again. No investigation took place as was customary. No postmortem. No cause of death. So Rosa Kelly got off again. Maybe it was just yellow fever, which was a brutal killer in those days. Many of the Barrett family also died from this malady.

Now, the third marriage would soon to be upon a frightened people in the parish of St. James. The year was 1753 when the notorious bastard Norwood Witter became engaged to the man-killer Rosa Kelly. What she saw in him, no one knows, but she had other things up her sleeve. Could it be that her father was also involved in these secret deaths? We have no evidence, but the author, who was trained by men from Scotland Yard in murder investigation, suspects Rosa had some help. The manner in which her two husbands died and the closeness she had with her father would cause a good detective to wonder whether there were other accomplices. From extrapolations, deductions, and conclusive presumptions, it is clear that a single woman may have had some help either physically or mentally. There are some ancient ministers of religion who have been guilty of genocide.

Norwood Witter had the evil reputation of brutalizing slaves and keeping them under subjection. Those whom he could not control, he would break up families and acquaintances by selling them off to other owners far away, especially to those in faraway St. Thomas and Portland so they could not in any way walk back to St. James. He also devised a system of flogging and control that many American slave owners came to Jamaica to study and enforce in America. As a result of the Jamaican method of controlling slaves being introduced to America, we had more slaves committing suicide than at any other time in the history of slavery in America. And Norwood Witter was one of the architects of this kind of punishment. He was also a conniver and a dishonest person. He had few friends and was considered antisocial.

When he married Rosa Kelly in 1753, the guest list for Rose Hall dried up. No one wanted to be in his company except Rosa Kelly, but soon he found out that she too did not want him around. Within a few years, this notorious rascal was dead. His death was under the same mysterious circumstances as the other two husbands. This time, no one cried foul because most people were happy to get rid of him, and Rosa Kelly succeeded where most people had failed. As time went on, no man was brave enough to propose to this rich widow ever again. They were as scared as when a lightning bolt strikes a cat under a pear tree but does not kill it. The news went far and wide, and got to Europe by the time the second husband died. The local white men took cover when they saw her coming, and only her father was her friend and confidant. But things had to change.

At last, in the year 1767, her father died, possibly of old age. No one attached any significance to his death, but some old people in the eyes of their children are very expendable. No one here is thinking of foul play, but don't rule anything out. Rosa at that time became very lonely, so she developed a plot. She knew that the Honorable John Palmer, the custos of St. James, was a widower living alone. He had two grown sons who were domiciled in England with no intention of returning to Jamaica. She put out a bait on a hook and positioned it where he always went, and the custos took and swallowed the bait hook, line, and sinker.

When the news got out, the first man to challenge him was his cousin, Edward Barrett of Cinnamon Hill, who'd lived beside Rosa Kelly since 1746. Cinnamon Hill property juxtaposed Rose Hall. The entire Barrett family and people of goodwill came down on John Palmer and told him to back off. He refused, and to the disapproval of everyone in

St. James, he married Rosa Kelly and became her fourth husband in twenty-one years. Most of his family did not attend the wedding, and the great house at Rose Hall became an enchanted castle. Her three husbands were buried on the property, with a palm tree planted beside each grave. The present palm trees that can be seen at Rose Hall today are not necessarily the ones that Rosa planted by the graves. No test has been made to prove the ages of the palm trees, so no one can be sure about them.

It was very strange that life went on as usual at Rose Hall, because after five years John Palmer was still alive and even his cousin Edward Barrett paid him visits. This Edward Barrett wanted to be in friendship with people of power, and John Palmer was the custos. He had several properties and many slaves. When he combined his properties to Rosa's, it was great wealth. Rosa had just inherited her father's estates. John Palmer's properties extended outside of St. James to St. Elizabeth, where Rosa Kelly's father also had property, being the rector of St. Elizabeth for some time.

The prosperity of this strange marriage continued for ten years, and to the surprise of all except the couple, there was peace and happiness most of the time, because no one heard anything unusual that took place during this period. Had there been any untoward behavior, Edward Barrett of Cinnamon Hill would have heard, he being the adjacent neighbor and first cousin to the custos. Also, the Barretts' slaves were in direct communication with the other slaves on Rose Hall property, and these slaves had permission to be on Cinnamon Hill property from whence the spring flowed to supply water to Rose Hall. The two cousins dominated the properties on the entire hillside overlooking Montego Bay, and this amounted to many square miles. These properties created and formed a part of the Jamaican culture from the early eighteenth century down to the present time. The landscape of Rose Hall and Cinnamon Hill is still the talk of today, especially by people from Europe, Japan, Latin America, and most of all, those in the United States of America. The land, as in those days, is still the most expensive in the parish of St. James.

Contrary things began to occur at Rose Hall Great House. Early on, it was the husbands who got sick and died mysteriously. In 1777, there was no mysterious illness, but Rosa Kelly Palmer, the notorious killer of husbands, took sick. She then wrote her will, and since she had no children and no relatives left behind, she willed everything she owned to her beloved husband John Palmer, stating explicitly that he rightly deserved it. What made this Jamaican Lucrezia Borgia so generous to her fourth husband? One can only surmise. Maybe he was very strong and could satisfy her extraordinary desires of lust. It could also be that she became first lady of the parish and all important functions in the parish had her on a pedestal of fame and importance. Also, the popularity the husband gave her for ten years had removed the stigma from her being a suspected killer. No one knows for sure what happened, but we know for sure that she died in 1777, leaving behind the next wealthiest man in St. James parish, second only to Edward Barrett of Cinnamon Hill.

When the will was probated and people got to know what it said, they began to think that John Palmer was a superhuman. No man ever survived the onslaught of Rosa Kelly Palmer for ten years. How could he have done it? Many thought he was a mystic or was protected by angels of unknown strength and power, but John Palmer lived on a few years longer, and we have no record of his will. It was said that he had two sons by a previous marriage and they both lived in England and no one knows of any correspondence between them. It was not until 1820 that a man came from England and took over the estates of John Palmer and was purported to be the grandson of John Palmer or his grandnephew, as some historians believe. It was this newcomer who caused all hell to break loose at the Rose Hall Great House.

The notoriety of Rose Hall Great House was enhanced in 1820 when John Rose Palmer married Annie Marie Paterson, a young woman from Haiti who was of Scottish descent and brought up by a maidservant who was a voodoo nanny. Annie Marie picked up these diabolical traits from her caretaker and developed them further since she was educated as a white child in those days. She became adept at this culture and practice far beyond her nanny's teaching. There are some educated people who do not believe in witchcraft, voodoo, and obeah, but this author got to find out that those who are publicly in denial of these are the ones who indulge in these satanic practices the most. If you should go to the bars in the country parts and just stand by to hear those men declare some preposterous things, you would be shocked. Many of those who declared that such evils never existed were the ones who most frequently visited the places where spells can be cast upon other people for good or for evil.

This writer, as a former detective of the Jamaica Police Force, had many experiences with these obeah men and obeah women during the time he served. He has arrested quite a few of them, for it is illegal to practice obeah or witchcraft or voodoo. The discussion will have to rest here, but just this one basic fact should be said. Hitler, Napoleon, kings of Europe, people at the top of some religions also practice the art. Presidents and prime ministers and rulers from the times of the pharaohs of Egypt in the fourth millennium BC also practiced witchcraft and other demonic engagements.

On the sixth year after the marriage, which was registered at the Island Record Office at Spanish Town in 1820, John Rose Palmer disappeared from the scene, and he has not been heard from since. This mysterious disappearance caused people to wonder whether another Rosa Palmer had come into existence. As people came to know who Annie Palmer was, no white man would work for her on her properties of Palmyra and Rose Hall. She had to import overseers and bookkeepers from England, and it is said that those who came had to sleep with her at the Great House. Those who refused were ignominiously terminated and sent back to England, and some of them mysteriously lost their lives. She would never marry again because no man was brave enough to try. Since her sexual orgies could be satisfied by those who worked for her, she did not care, nor did anyone care.

As she practiced her witchcraft, so did she practice her sadistic affairs with her slaves. She would stand on the ledge of her bedroom on the upper floor and looked down on her overseers beating the slaves mercilessly. When she did not see any beatings for a few days, she would order the overseers to bring one or two slaves and tie them up so that she could personally beat them herself. These slaves did not have to misbehave. She only liked to beat them because in her mind they were not real human beings. She was not alone in thinking along these lines because heads of churches in those days believed the same thing. All one has got to do is read the Dred Scott Decision handed down by the United States Chief Justice Roger B. Taney in 1857. He said that black people were monkeys and not real human beings. He must have belonged to that church that believed as he did.

So when she got her sadistic satisfaction, she ordered them loose and sent them back to their huts bruised and humiliated in the presence of their women and children. After practicing these inhumane activities on

God's creation, she would go back to her room to engage in debauchery with one or two of her English employees for her pleasure. This evil continued for about ten years, when in 1831 a slave uprising took place under Sam Sharpe, and Rose Hall and Palmyra estates were put to the torch by her own slaves. At that time, she was at the property house at Palmyra, and a few days after the rebellion she was found strangled in the house. It is said that her slaves heard screams coming from the house but did nothing to find out what had happened.

Days passed by until vultures started to hover around and a stench covered the entire area. It was then that Samuel Barrett Moulton-Barrett, MP, now at Cinnamon Hill ordered his slaves to find out what had happened, because the slaves of the white witch refused to find out since in earlier times she would play dead, and when they came to see if it were true, she would suddenly get up and beat them mercilessly. He got his own slaves to carry the dead body of the white witch back to Rose Hall for burial. They agreed to do so provided he gave them a prize steer he had at Cinnamon Hill property for them to kill and do an obeah ritual. While the grave was being dug and the body lay in state at Rose Hall Great House, the steer was killed and the chief obeah man among the Barrett slaves used the blood of the steer to perform some sort of African ritual. When this was done, then and only then would the mason of Cinnamon Hill who built something like a vault allowed the men to put the body into the grave. After this, the mason (whose name was Downer), as well as the chief obeah man, allowed the body to be placed into the grave and said, "Earth to earth, fire for fire, and blood for blood." While he was chanting this, he sprinkled some of the steer's blood all over the place, and those who had to handle the body had their hands all washed in the blood. When the body was let down into the grave, the mason gave the order to cook some of the steer for a feast and to distribute the rest to the family members. So Samuel Barrett Moulton-Barrett, MP, gave most of the slaves on Cinnamon Hill a day off and a steer in order to get the white witch buried. He was happy to do so for the rest of the planters and himself, and many white planters hailed him as the hero of St. James because he removed a great problem from the neighborhood.

Rose Hall Great House lay in ruins from that time onward, 1832, until it was classified as a haunted house. What happened to the heirs of the Palmers is not clear, but when people died intestate as the white witch did the properties fell directly to the administrator general of Jamaica. This is the method of the old British system so it appeared that's what happened to Rose Hall. There are many stories of apparitions, ghosts, or duppies traversing the old properties, and many obeah men had gone there and set up apparatus trying to catch the ghost of the white witch or the first owner, Rosa Kelly Palmer. Some of them claimed success, but most of them claimed failure. Those who claimed failure said that the white witch was too strong for them, so they had to go back and train better in order to catch her. Those who claimed success came up with all kinds of cock and bull stories that did not make any sense. Over one hundred years passed and no one came to the rescue of Rose Hall until Johnny Rollins, former governor and Congressman from Delaware, USA, came and bought out many old properties, including Cinnamon Hill and Rose Hall, and refurbished the great houses, and is still making plenty of money from tourists and many Jamaicans, especially returning residents.

John Rollins has done a fine job on both houses. He tried to restore Rose Hall as closely as possible to its 1746 structure. He reintroduced the mahogany stairway that led to the white witch's bedroom, and it is now a museum making a lot of money for the Rollins family. John is now dead, but his son has carried on his work and has lately acquired thousands of acres of the hillside overlooking Montego Bay. He also owns several hotels and guest houses all over St. James, and it is a disgrace for the government of Jamaica to be selling off all the historic landscape of Jamaica to foreigners. The Jamaican government should be making all this money by owning all these properties, and use them as museums and places where people can go to relive their history. It is a sad note when a country has to sell its legacy to foreigners. However, be that as it may, Rose Hall is drawing a crowd even though Rosa Kelly Palmer is gone and so is the white witch Annie Patterson Palmer. I hope Jamaican historians will do their homework and find out that there existed a white witch with the name Annie Marie Paterson Palmer.

Chapter 10

Newspaper Articles

It is unpredictable what people will say or think about the same situation at any given time. People are just different no matter how others think of a certain object or topic. In this case, Arabel Moulton Barrett wrote an article in the *Jamaica Daily Gleaner* defending her grandfather whom she did not know. Some people called him a tyrant, and some said he was a gentleman. She was the daughter of Charles John Barrett Moulton-Barrett, and he was the seventh child of Edward Barrett Moulton-Barrett, who was called the tyrant of 50 Wimpole Street, and the father of Elizabeth Barrett Browning.

The reason why Arabel came out defending her grandfather was the publication of a book by author Rudolf Besier entitled *The Barretts of Wimpole Street*. This book did great injustice to her grandfather, some of which were lies and guesswork. The book became a movie in which derogatory insinuations were concocted by both the author and the movie company. It so annoyed her when the movie was shown in Jamaica, West Indies, around 1938, that she went back to some old letters her father had left and what she could remember of some stories he had told her about his sister Elizabeth, who died in Italy, June 29, 1861, and was buried in the English cemetery in Florence. Her father died in Jamaica on January 21, 1905, and was buried at Retreat property in the parish of St. Ann, Jamaica, West Indies. She was just over twenty when he died. Apart from letters she might quote in the article she wrote, the rest of the story is hearsay. No one must doubt the sincerity of the article because of this.

She was a prolific writer in Jamaica when this movie came out, and as one can suppose, she was buffeted with questions about her family and she was glad that she could somehow protect her grandfather by explaining why some things were done. There could be no doubt that her father Charles told her many things about the family, and such an explosive situation as the elopement of her aunt with Robert Browning had to have been told to her. As we all know, Charles agreed with the action of his father to save his inheritance. We do not know if he would have taken another course.

Historians knew why Besier wrote the book the way he did. There is evidence that he went to a grandson of Edward Barrett Moulton-Barrett, Lt. Col. Harry Peyton Moulton-Barrett, and asked him about the nine letters that Elizabeth wrote to her father from Italy asking for forgiveness for what she had done. This request, or these requests, are only presumptions since her father never opened any of them. Based upon other letters she wrote to her brother George Goodin Moulton-Barrett requesting compassion and forgiveness, many people, including this author, have concluded that the letters to her father were of similar nature. Nothing is wrong with a good guess. Harry, being a lieutenant colonel in charge of Argyll and Sutherland Highlanders in the British military, thought it was not wise to expose the family's dirty linen. Upon hearing at the same time that Elizabeth's son Penn Browning had sold the love letters of his parents, it is understood that he burned Elizabeth's letters in his fireplace the same day he was asked about them. We do not know how Harry came in possession of these letters. We suppose his father gave them to him since he was in good graces with his father Edward Barrett Moulton-Barrett.

Many historians believe that the treatment meted out to Rudolph Besier by the lieutenant colonel made him manufacture some of the comments in the play. However it was done, the book got rave reviews and many reveled in the movie for its supposed clarity, whether it was true or not. The movie has a new name. It is now *The Forbidden Alliance*, and can be found in some video stores all over America and Britain.

Arabel was annoyed at the book and the movie, so on June 12, 1938, she wrote an article published in the *Daily Gleaner* outlining her defense of her grandfather. The following is her article as printed in the *Daily Gleaner*, Jamaica's only newspaper at that time. The article is entitled "The Barretts of Wimpole Street" and Arabel began her article thus. This is a word for word quote from the *Gleaner* article.

In these ultra-modern days, when custom gives only a playful tolerance to fathers and mothers, and uncles and aunts—accepting them merely as pegs whereon to hang a name, a roof, or a doctor's bill—it may create a smile to read a woman's defense of her grandfather. The honorable man needs no defense; yet occasion arises when, through the greed and callousness of an inferior mind, vile aspersions are cast on the dead; and when this is done, then even a modern girl might find time between drink and drink to cram the lie down the throat of the traducer.

In the notice given of the "Barretts Of Wimpole Street" which is now being shown at the Carib Theatre, there are many adjectives applied to my grandfather, Edward Moulton-Barrett, which would provoke me to laughter were he here to laugh with me. "Grim." "Cunning." "Demonical."

What else is needed to stain a man's character? Yet the children of Edward Moulton-Barrett loved and reverenced him. His son Charles (my father) never spoke of him save with love and reverence.

"He was an indulgent father," so said his son to me. And in the man's own letters to his children we read his faithful and ardent thoughts for their comfort and happiness. He was a wealthy man, possessing as he did a good bit of Jamaica; but, with the abolition of slavery came diminished income, and thenceforth his circumstances were greatly changed. (May I be allowed to squeeze in here just one small truth? The light of Truth is far reaching; and even at a distance of nearly a century, an illuminating ray may reach the man I write of, revealing him as he was and not as he is portrayed by Adolph [it should be Rudolph] Besier, the dramatist. [The correction in bracket is that of the author.] It is this I wish to say. In the annals of Jamaica, the name Barrett has never been linked with the word "demonical." Peace and order ever reigned on the Barrett estates. The slaves loved the Barretts for this reason; they were treated as human beings possessed of equal rights to life and liberty. In the management of his Jamaican properties, as well as the regulating of his own household in England, Edward Moulton Barrett showed himself to be a man of high principles; just, kind, loving and strictly honorable. Are there any to deny this?

Loyal Devotion
To return now to the fact of Edward's reduced circumstances. He never permitted the real state of affairs to be made known to his wife. She lived her usual life, surrounded by every luxury love could devise; and when Mary died she was still unconscious of her husband's selflessness and loyal devotion. But, following it and because of it, Edward's own material future was greatly crippled and it never recovered from the strain put upon it at that time. Tell me, was that act of his "demonical?"

Edward's income being much reduced, it was found necessary to leave the lovely home in Herefordshire. He writes from London to his brother Sam in Jamaica: "I expect soon to return into Herefordshire, although it will be for a distressing object—the packing up of all my things for removing thence; God only knows where, but He knows best. I dread much the effect on my dear children in tearing them away from all their most happy associations. Again I say, He who has afflicted the chastisement will so temper it as to enable them to bear it. Say nothing on the subject of removal to the girls. They must forget it."

Tell me, is there anything of the "demonical" in this letter? And now I give an extract from another letter to his brother Sam in Jamaica. It is dated November 7, 1833.

"You will be surprised to hear and I trust pleased that, when this reaches you, my beloved Bro (Note: his son Edward was so named in the home) will be at no very great distance from Jamaica. I have thought much upon it, and chiefly through your earnest desire have at length been led to a step that I trust will turn out of advantage to us all. Our beloved Ba, (Note: Elizabeth was so named in the home) namely as being profitable to Bro's interest, has consented in a spirit that has, if possible, raised her still higher in my estimation. I need not ask you to take care of him, under Providence; when you know him you will, I doubt not, love him as much as all do who know him. I fear that he will be too willing to expose and exert himself over much, but you will be a kind guardian and advise and restrain him from all excesses. He is sound in principle and everyway trustworthy, and I hope will be useful to you. Bro will tell you all the news and may the Lord bless and keep you my beloved Sam. Yours very affectionately, E.M. Barrett."

Tell me; is there anything "demonical" in this letter?

Another Extract
Again I give another extract from Edward to his brother Sam. It is dated August 8, 1834 and is written from Sidmouth:

"You will perhaps have heard through Bro, that I went to London, on or about the time Selby was expected, and that after two fruitless visits to Gravesend in order to intercept him on his way up the river, I was fortunate enough to fall in with him on the third expedition, and truly happy was I to hear his report of you all, and gratified not a little at the account he gave me, of you and approbation of my dear Boy; indeed it is the only circumstance that can afford me the least compensation for his absence, and in such a climate and such society around him. May the Lord keep him from the evil effects of both, and restore him uninjured in body and mind in his good time. Upon the subject of climate, I scratched him a line, or two, in a spare corner Ba left me in her letter to him by this packet, wherein I begged him to be more guarded than I am given to understand he is in exposing himself to it. I do not like to hear of his long rides in the broiling sun, and perhaps subjecting himself also to the Evening Dews unnecessarily, by which I mean he might, at a little cost, get a gig, or Phaeton to convey him. I beg you to procure such a conveyance for him immediately, and let me see it in my account. I think I wrote you before, indeed I am sure of it, to supply him with what money he may require, and although his wants in this particular may not be much, still there must be occasioned demands upon him; as he may feel some delicacy about this, I hope you have or will speedily anticipate his application to you."

Tell me, does the foregoing letter reveal anything of "spleen" or "cunning?" Is it even "grim"?

Elizabeth, in her early girlhood, was strong and active, and was often to be seen riding down Herefordshire lanes on her black pony, Moses. But the fatal day came when, whilst saddling Moses, she fell and strained her back. From thence on, she drifted into invalidism—an invalidism made endurable through a father's unwearying care and devotion. Amongst the many efforts for her comfort he had a carriage especially built for her ease when traveling. From this apparently helpless condition, Elizabeth was roused by her love for Robert Browning. Eventually, she left her home, married Browning, returning immediately after the wedding to her father's house.

Path of Immortality
A week later, she, the invalid, fled with her husband to Italy, there to "climb hills and drink Chanti." So writes one of her many admirers. In her father's home, Elizabeth had accepted and had skillfully played the part of invalid. The role was congenial to her. It gave her leisure to dream, to write, to climb the Path of Immortality. But it was to a father's unremitting devotion and whole-hearted sympathy she owed her happiness as poet, wife and mother. For nearly thirty years he had never failed her in care and selfless solicitude.

At the time of her marriage, Elizabeth was not the "fragile girl" of romance; she was a woman of forty, and she had already published some of her finest work. Miss Mitford, a famous writer and a close friend of the Barrett family, wrote that, Elizabeth married "with one foot in the grave" to which doleful statement let me cheerfully add that, the poet's other foot, taking with it its fellow was very soon trampling the hills of Italy.

One word more. Edward Moulton-Barrett never met Robert Browning. He knew of the friendship between his daughter and Browning but believed it to be friendliness and nothing more. Meetings between the lovers were arranged with skill and cunning. (Quite recently I have seen the word "cunning" applied to Elizabeth's father. I now attach it to the daughter herself and to her lover, and I think the result rather a happy one—don't you?)

Just at this time Edward's business affairs took him much into the city; and it was during his absence the lovers met. There followed conversation and laughter. But when the father returned home he found only an invalid daughter lying on a couch and swathed into Indian shawls. And then there came for him the last tragic day when there was only an empty room – an empty home.

Edward Moulton-Barrett was never reconciled to his daughter, though she strove hard to obtain his forgiveness. Her letters to him were returned unopened. There will be many who read this, if they chance to read it at all; and I hope they will read it, who will acknowledge that, after so ugly a return for years of care and tenderness there could never be desire for reconciliation. Trust was forever dead.

Rudolph Besier, in his desire to produce a popular play was attracted by the Browning love story. But though quite a pleasant romance, there was still something wanted in it. Why, a villain, of course. All dramas house a villain. Without a scoundrel of some kind, a drama would be absolutely cold. The public would not accept it. So the dramatist carefully thought out the character of Edward the Tyrant, the Ogre, the Hypocrite; and then he built it into the ruins of Wimpole Street. And the public applauded. They threw stones at the dead man, though he had been dead nearly a hundred years. But stones flung by human hands cannot reach into the spiritual world. So Edward Moulton-Barrett is, and ever will be untouched, unscarred by calumnies spoken of him. If the living standing between him and the stones, receive a few bruises—does it matter?

This ends the article of Arabel Moulton-Barrett. That was a good attempt to defend her grandfather, and people are very fortunate that so much had been divulged to another family member. It is quite clear that she relied on her father very much in coming up with a defense like this. It took me many years to get from my family that my grandfather Peter Bonnick was descended from Scottish Jews. I am trying to find out whether he was a direct descendant of Abraham or David, or whether he was just another white man converted to Judaism. There may be many Jews who were only converted to this religion, but there are many who are Jews by race as well as religion, and can trace their ancestry back to the children of Israel. This is not a comment on Judaism. It is a critique on Arabel's article defending her grandfather.

First of all, Edward acted in such a manner because he knew that Robert Browning came out of black ancestry. His great-great-grandfather John Tittle was the son of a slave on a farm at Half Way Tree in the parish of St. Andrew, and this farm was owned by Edward Tittle, cordwainer of Half Way Tree. Edward employed the services of Dr. Frederick Fumival, a genealogist, to investigate Robert, and he came up with a slogan in his report to Edward Moulton-Barrett that the "tar brush" passed nearby. So racism had a part to play.

Next, Edward threatened all his children to not marry during his lifetime or lose their inheritance. Three children did and lost their inheritance, including Elizabeth. The tender loving care he gave to Elizabeth was not his own money. She inherited quite a lot from his mother Elizabeth Barrett Moulton, and he looked after her inheritance until she fled to Italy. After that, his barrister son looked after her assets.

With all his misfortunes, he was not poor. When slavery was abolished in the British Empire in 1838, the government gave £22,000,000 to be shared among slave owners based upon how many they had. Edward and his brother Sam had over two thousand slaves. The share of the handout made both brothers super rich. When Edward got his share and made his will, his son George the barrister-at-law gave up his practice. He got sufficient money from his father's estate and stopped working.

One other comment: Elizabeth was sick when Robert came to 50 Wimpole Street. He is the one who got her well enough for the elopement. One must not forget that Robert Browning, in the full-fledged tradition of many Robert Brownings before him, was a Rosicrucian. They have a system whereby they can heal people of some kind of illness, whether we want to believe it or not. Vivienne Browning, a cousin who wrote the book *My Browning Family Album*, said so precisely. So Elizabeth was not relieved until her lover Robert came along. Nothing was hidden from Edward Moulton-Barrett. He had a home filled with spies, but Robert and Elizabeth outdid them. He always said to his family that such and such a one was too poor to marry Mr. Barrett's daughter, and Robert was one of them.

We also gather from many other letters that Arabel did not get that Edward sent instructions to Jamaica to treat his slaves much more humanely than the other planters did. But what Arabel said in her article about treating slaves with liberty and humaneness is not necessarily true. Treating slaves better than others is not freedom. The only good way to treat a slave is to set him free and give him some kind of economic start, such as land and a mule in those days. A slave is a slave no matter how well you treat him. And this is the sum total of treating slaves with dignity.

I have also examined Rudolph Besier's book. Arabel calls him Adolph, but since I have his book, I know his correct name. He was somewhat zealous because he did not get the information he wanted from the Barrett family, so he went and wrote quite a number of things that are incorrect. I have much the same problem with the family too. Even being a member of this family, they hide many local things from me because they say I am going to write about it. This is exactly correct. I am not critiquing Bessier's book, so I will just mention one thing that is wrong. Elizabeth's dog Flush was not killed at the instruction of Edward Moulton-Barrett. She took the dog to Italy and I have letters to prove this. However, it was a very good thing that Bessier called it a novel, because that is what it truly is. The rest of Arabel's letter is better left to the imagination of the readers.

It is not the aim of this writer to defend the deeds of Edward Barrett Moulton-Barrett. Nor am I going to totally condemn him. The agony he had been through up to the time of Elizabeth's elopement could have acted upon his mind to cause such obnoxious and unsavory behaviors.

People ought to recognize that some people will do the ideal thing but when under stress, some people will break and do unseemly things. I would rather, at this time, have a qualified psychiatrist examine the evidence and come up with some professional analysis of the entire situation as to whether such behaviors can be exonerated. The whole situation seemed somewhat funny to me, and immediately the Dr. Jekyll and Mr. Hyde scenarios come into play. One thing that I cannot tolerate in his behavior, from a born-again-Christian standpoint, was his being so unforgiving. The key points in any Christian experience are that of forgiveness and loving our enemies.

There is reference, if not proof, that Elizabeth wrote her father nine letters and he did not open one of them. When Robert Browning paid one of his impromptu visits to London from Florence, he went to 50 Wimpole Street and confronted Edward, his father-in-law, and gave him a Rosicrucian scolding, and told him to stop the foolishness and reply to his daughter's letters. Edward walked away from Robert, went to a mahogany chest, and pulled out nine sealed letters from Elizabeth to him and handed them to Robert Browning, saying, "You can give these back to her." He left Robert standing alone in the living room and went back to his study without saying another word.

Robert took the letters, and historians are not sure what he did with them. It is not clear, but we have no evidence whether they were taken back to Italy, but we know they ended up in the hands of Lt. Col. Harry Peyton Moulton-Barrett, who destroyed them. He was the nephew of Elizabeth. We do not know whether he read them but when Penn Browning, Elizabeth's son, published some of his parents' love letters, it angered Harry, who liked to have Barrett secrets remain secret, and that is the reason we guessed that he burned them.

Many people would love to know what were in those letters. There are many guesses but one can only conjecture that they were similar to other letters that she wrote to other people whom she thought she had wronged. Some of these letters have been published, and based upon these, it can be extrapolated that her letters to her father were asking for forgiveness and to let bygones be bygones. In some of her other letters, she stated that she would like to make amends for the wrong she did, and would like to have a family relationship again. These indications were made quite clear in her letters to George Goodin Moulton-Barrett. He was the one to whom her father handed over all the shares of Elizabeth

Barrett Browning inherited from her grandmother, Elizabeth Barrett Moulton. These shares were part of the same companies operated by her father. When Elizabeth fled, he made George the caretaker of Elizabeth's shares. George corresponded with her frequently and sent her dividend to her each time, so there was a frequent interfacing going on.

Now George became the closest person to his father since Charles was in Jamaica overseeing the operations of the properties there. George was the barrister-at-law, and he finally gave up the practice of law to help run his father's business. Arabel Moulton Barrett in her article said that because of his losses he became just an ordinary man financially but the evidence seemed otherwise. Even though George got most of his father's wealth when he died, those who were not disinherited got a substantial amount. None of the family was considered poor, and George got so much that he gave up working altogether and lived happily off his inheritance. There was still plenty of wealth to go around, and George gave a substantial handout to some of those who'd been disinherited.

There were three children who were disinherited because they married before their father's demise. Two married their second cousins and Edward Moulton-Barrett did not like family marrying family. His son Alfred Price Moulton-Barrett married his rich cousin Elizabeth Georgina, the daughter of George Goodin Barrett, first cousin of Edward Moulton-Barrett. It is confusing how all the Barretts' first names are reused throughout all their generations. We have more Edwards, Samuels, Elizabeths, and Georges than any other family in English history.

So since Alfred married during his father's lifetime, he was disinherited. He also annoyed his father more by marrying his cousin. The other marriage that annoyed Edward Moulton-Barrett very much was that of his daughter Henrietta. She was told that her boyfriend Capt. Surtees Cook was too poor to marry Mr. Barrett's daughter. She also knew that Surtees was her second cousin, and she married during her father's lifetime, so there were three strikes against her and her father was home plate umpire. So he gave the signal and she was struck out. Regardless of what her father thought, this marriage brought some prominent offspring under the name of Altham, and many were knighted by Queen Victoria, one of whom was Sir Edward Altham, and we still have the familiar name Edward again.

Elizabeth has been mentioned so many times, it may be absurd to mention her here again, but that old Barrett cliché "the tar brush passed nearby" is still ringing in the author's ears since he grew up knowing a grandfather who loved the cliché "tar drum."

We have now come to the point where a glimpse into the idiosyncrasies of the Barrett family has been partially exposed, and there are plenty more to be seen. But since there are many descendants of the Barrett family, each writer from that group will only touch on a small fraction of the activities of this great family. Many people only see Elizabeth and her father Edward Moulton-Barrett as the hinges on which this noble family swings. This is not so. There are more generals than poets. There are more governors than tyrants. There are more lawyers than criminals, and there are more politicians than slave owners. With this vast amalgam of professionals, no wonder the Barrett family is considered an intellectual family, and to crown it all, we have more prodigies than paupers. It is of significant note that for one year there were at least four Barretts, all close cousins from Cinnamon Hill in the parish of St. James, Jamaica, West Indies, matriculated and entered Oxford University at the age of fourteen, and all graduated before their eighteenth birthday. When all famous Barretts in the world are checked out, most of them have their roots coming from Jamaica, West Indies.

CHAPTER 11

The Author's Family

My family is not unique among the cosmopolitan families of the parish of St. Elizabeth, Jamaica, West Indies. Many of my family members asked me to tell them about the family they hardly know, and many others are withholding information about the family because they are fearful that I may write some secrets that they would like to keep. It took me many years to gather the information here because they are trying to withhold it. As a trained detective, I used this qualification to get even more than I had asked. Those who wanted to know would like to have their correct names available (just in case) so that they may not marry close relatives, and also, those who came, their location in Jamaica and their specific country of origin. Most wanted the ancestral part.

I am now giving all, the puzzle of my immediate family.

My father and I are second cousins. My paternal grandmother and my mother are first cousins. They are the daughters of two brothers, Charles and Robert (Bobby) Whyte. My paternal great-grandfather is my maternal granduncle, Charles. My maternal grandfather Robert (Bobby) Whyte is also my paternal great-granduncle. So I have a great-grandfather and a great-great-grandfather who is one and the same person, Thomas Whyte.

I will now begin with my maternal connection. My mother's name is Beatrice Whyte, commonly called Aunt Bea. She was born in the district of Beacon, located on the beautiful Pedro Plains overlooking the town of Treasure Beach in the parish of St. Elizabeth, Cornwall County, on the island of Jamaica, West Indies. This county of Cornwall was named after the county in England from where the Barretts came, and the Barrett family was instrumental in having it named after their own in

the mother country. Aunt Bea's mother's name was Grace Whyte, nee
Williams, born in St. Mary's District on top of the Santa Cruz Mountain,
adjacent to Munro College, to Sarah Miller and Joseph Williams. Sarah
Miller is a direct descendant of the Maroons of Accompong, after whom
the Maroon Town is named. These were two brothers and one sister, and
they were Ashantis from Ghana who claimed to be descended from the
royal family of Queen Ya Ashantewa of Ghana. It was this queen who
fought the British to the death when trying to prevent the British from
capturing her people as slaves. All the Miller families of St. Elizabeth
and Manchester claim a common heritage. Joseph Williams, her father,
is a direct descendant of an Englishman by the same name. He owned a
property in St. Elizabeth by the name of Big Wood, near Newell, which is
now a progressive district by the same name. There is also a Joe Williams
Big Wood in the parish of Westmoreland, and was owned by the same
Joe Williams.

This Joe Williams was a prolific child producer and seemed to have
owned machines to do so. As a slave owner, he produced children by
his slaves, which made him a multiplier of illegitimate children in the
parishes of Westmoreland and St. Elizabeth. By conclusive presumptions,
all Williams in the southern part of St. Elizabeth are related.

Grace Whyte (Auntie Gracie) had a brother by the name of Banga
Williams who lived in the district of Newell, St. Elizabeth. He married
one Mileeva from Treasure Beach, and had one son whose name is
unknown, but he went to live in Kingston, the capital of Jamaica. Banga
Williams' famous quote was, "Everybody is doing it, except me and
Mileeva."

Auntie Gracie also had many sisters. I only knew one of them. Her
name was Edith Williams. She married Panton (Bully) Ebanks. Their
children were Dinah, William (Bill), Stevlin, Edwin, Arnold, and Nellie.
All of them had "Bully" as their last name, even though their official
name was Ebanks. Panton had a sister whose name was Molly and she
and all her children were also called Bully. I don't know the reason why.
Panton was also first cousin to Auntie Gracie's husband, Robert (Bobby)
Whyte.

I will continue to call my maternal grandmother Auntie Gracie.
That is the name most people in St. Elizabeth called her by. She also
had a sister (name unknown to me) whose daughter married a tailor
from Flagaman district, whose last name was McLean. His son, whom

I knew as Septrian McLean, was a schoolteacher. He taught school in Westmoreland, and had at least two daughters by his wife. Septrian's sister, whom I saw once, was married to a preacher who lived and preached in Brooklyn, New York, USA.

Some of Auntie Gracie's family are all over St. Elizabeth. Her famous cousins include Bamboo Joe Williams of Williamsfield in St. Elizabeth, who is rumored to have had over 127 children by a multitude of women. At one time, I personally knew about forty of them. Another famous cousin was Edmond Williams of Bluntas district. He also had many children. Two of his children are married to two grandchildren of his cousin Auntie Gracie. Also, Sam Williams, who married Mahala Moxam of Bluntas, and lived at Beacon district. There is another of her cousins by the same name, Grace Williams. She married Willie Campbell, and produced some of the Campbell clan of Beacon district. There is also a Dovie Williams, sister of Sam Williams, who married a man by the name of Montique. He was a descendant of French refugees from Haiti, who fled the country in 1803 and came to Jamaica when Toussaint L'Overture took possession of the country and freed the slaves after beating the best military expedition that Napoleon sent there. I am also related to these French Montiques on my father's side. Richard Williams of Newcombe Valley is another cousin of Auntie Gracie. His two sons were Stamah and Wilbert Williams. Richard also had a sister who is responsible for a branch of the Channer family from Newcombe Valley. Almando Channer and Yoney Dobbs were two of these children.

There's also a Charles Stewart of Little Park district in St. Elizabeth. He married a lady named Silvera and had many children. There was also a Rosa Stewart of Newlands district in St. Catherine parish, and she has a daughter by the name of Vickie who also had children. All of these are Auntie Gracie's family and they all have practiced royalty by intermarriage, which is a common practice in south St. Elizabeth. There will be no book that can contain my family in full.

My mother's father is Robert (Bobby) Whyte. He was born to a Thomas Whyte and a Ms. Abrams (commonly called Mother Hanson). I have no information whether she was married to Thomas Whyte or a Mr. Hanson, but the fact that she was called by the Hanson name suggested she was subsequently married to this Hanson. She had no children by the name of Hanson. She was sister to Joe Abrams of Beacon, who married one Martha of the same district and had one daughter named

Agnes. She had a very distinct voice and could be heard up to half a mile away when she became irate. She had about five children with the last name of Bernard, and after having all those children, she became a Christian and was a member of about six different churches until finally she ended up at the Williamsfield SDA Church, where she remained a member until her death.

Thomas Whyte (Grandpa Tom) was six years old in 1838 and was prepared to go to the field as a slave when Queen Victoria caused slavery to be abolished throughout the British Empire. She had the right to do so, having been descended from the African Moors, coming through the Portuguese royal family by way of marriage to her German ancestors of Saxe-Coburg-Gotha. The author's paternal white ancestors were the Barretts, who as a family was the largest slave-owning family in the British West Indies.

Grandpa Tom produced many sons apart from Robert (Bobby) Whyte, my maternal grandfather. I will now give a sketch on the other brothers' families and then come back to Bobby.

One brother was Charles Whyte, who produced Frances, Ellen, and Kennen Whyte, who had a son named Ivan Whyte and lived all his life at Stanmore district. Frances is the author's paternal grandmother who married Peter Bonnick and produced ten children. The details will be later mentioned.

Ellen Whyte produced Cynthia (Tina) and Ivy Thompson. Tina's two daughters were Barbara and Daphne. Their last name was Newland, and they were both nurses. Daphne married a man named Clacken and produced two children, Michael and Sharon. Daphne migrated to London, where she remarried to Dr. Ben Acqua from Ghana and produced two children, Joy and Benjamin. They all lived in London. Barbara migrated to the United States and married Orville Harrison and produced three children, Debbie, Camille, and Charles.

Ellen Whyte's other daughter Ivy Thompson married one Claude Hall and lived in Retirement district on the outskirts of Malvern. She had several children, such as Shiela Doctor of Santa Cruz, St. Elizabeth; and Fay (Bibbs) Robinson of Toronto, Canada.

Another of Grandpa Tom's sons was Frederick. He lived at a place commonly called Whyte Town. It is an enclave of Beacon district. It was so called because of the preponderance of the Whyte family. Frederick produced two sons known to the author. They are Nathaniel Whyte, father of Police Inspector Alberto (Allie) Whyte, and two daughters, Lahomie and Meredith. Frederick's other son went by the name of Man-Man Whyte. No one seemed to know his right name. He was married to a lady named Esther. Information here is very scant. The one daughter I know was called Dee Dee Whyte and she was a revivalist who preached and had visions. She died at the early age of about forty-five.

James is another son of Grandpa Tom. He was the author's mother's favorite uncle, as well as his paternal grandmother's favorite uncle. The explanation to this conflict will be explained later on. James had a son that he named after himself. To differentiate the two persons, the younger was commonly called Jimbo, and most people knew him by that name. He married a woman named Hilda and produced many children. His most famous son was Alonso. Jimbo was a tobacco farmer and so were all the Whytes who lived at Whyte Town. James Senior also had a daughter by the name Roslyn. She married a man by the last name Banton. Roslyn Banton had three children, Charles, Goppy, and a daughter whose name is not remembered. They all lived at Naggo's Head district in the parish of St. Catherine.

Robert (Bobby) Whyte is another son of Grandpa Tom. Bobby married Grace Williams and produced seventeen children, some of whom died in infancy. Only those who survived to adulthood will be mentioned here, but before doing this, a comment on Bobby's relatives is important. There were some funny names that will be mentioned and there is no way at this time to locate the correct names. Many people will enjoy reading some of these names.

Bobby's father has already been named as Grandpa Tom. I am specifically being repetitious for the sake of emphasis, and no change or correction is to be made. Bobby's mother came from a place called Pedro, precisely Sandy Bank, sometimes Calabash Bay, but since 1932 the name Treasure Beach appeared, and the whole area is now called Treasure Beach. The people of the nearby fishing beach at Great Bay are vehemently resisting calling their Great Bay Treasure Beach. They claimed the Great Pedro Bluff makes their district more important. All the places named are in the parish of St. Elizabeth. The only name we have for Bobby's mother is Mother Hanson but she was born with the last name Abrams. Her father descended from English Jews who migrated from England to the colony of Jamaica to avoid anti-Semitism. They were persecuting Jews in England at that time. Her brother Joe Abrams has already been described, but she has two sisters that the author knows about. The names of the two sisters are so funny only people from St. Elizabeth parish can appreciate them.

One sister's name is Auntie Gamm. No other name can be located. She was the mother of one Ellen, who married a Mr. Moxam from Bluntas district. Ellen Moxam produced many children known to the author. Bertie Moxam married his second cousin Olga Dennis and produced many children. Another son, Stephen, married one Julia and produced some of the most beautiful girls in Bluntas. Two of them also married their cousins. Daphne married Kenneth Dennis, and Olive married Reken Dennis. They were brothers. Another son, Alfred, married his cousin Doris Dennis and produced a son named Gladry Moxam. Ellen Moxam's daughter Julie had a daughter named Atlin Dennis. Her father Norman was brother to Olga, Doris, Kenneth, and Reken. Atlin married the author's brother Adonijah Bonnick and they are domiciled in London, England. Everyone named in this paragraph is either a second or third cousin. All are descended from the one Jew named Abrams, from Treasure Beach. Is this royalty?

The other sister of Auntie Gamm and Mother Hanson was Auntie Yayah. Fortunately, there is a name here. She was Sarah Abrams and she married a man with the last name Dennis. She had three known sons. They were David, Charlie, and Cy. Cy migrated to Costa Rica and the family heard very little about him. Maybe he had children there by the name of Dennis. Who knows? Charlie married one Rosie Simms from Watchwell district and produced many children, including two sons, one named Desmond, the other Vivian. Some of the girls were Gladys, Lillian, and Gwendolyn.

I willfully omitted the names of David's children but I will name a few who married mostly Moxam men and women, or had children by them. Foremost among these is Norman, who had children named Hamlin, Mervin, and Atlin. Kenneth and Reken married Moxam girls. Olga and Doris married Moxam men. Mabel married a Mr. Black, and Estelle married Savly Channer. They all had many children all over the world. It is too difficult to go in detail here except to notify future generations of their family connections so that they avoid practicing royalty, because science has proven that it is not very good to do so, and St. Elizabeth is the leading parish in Jamaica that practices this. The whole history of St. Elizabeth could be anchored on royalty.

Another cousin of Robert (Bobby) Whyte is Panton (Bully) Ebanks, who was mentioned earlier as the husband of Edith Williams, who was sister to Bobby's wife, Grace Williams (Auntie Gracie). Panton had two sisters. One lived at Naggo's Head in St. Catherine parish and the only name we have for her is Sister Bully. The other sister is Molly Bully, who lived all her life in St. Elizabeth parish. She had three known children named Ethlyn, Faddie, and Basil. Both Molly and her children go by the last name Ebanks but were all called by the pet name Bully.

Bobby Whyte's children are many. The author's immediate family requested that he name them, which will not be by order of birth. Whenever the pronoun "I" appears and is not in quotation marks, it refers to the author.

The names of the children of Bobby Whyte and Auntie Gracie are as follows: Leithe, Lindsay, Annie, Thomas, Beatrice, Wilfred, Eustace, Irene, Rosalind, and Arthur. The others died as infants and numbered seven. This couple was very prolific.

Some form of description here is necessary. Thomas (Tom) and Eustace (Jimpy) are the most famous. In his day as a carpenter, Thomas was known as the carpenter of south St. Elizabeth, and there was not a day ever when he was out of work. People had to book him months in advance if they wanted him to work. Eustace (Jimpy) was a policeman in Kingston and became famous when he arrested a gunman for stealing cigars from Machado Tobacco Factory on Vitoria Avenue in Kingston. The gunman shot at him while they were fighting for the shotgun but he was not hit. When he left the police force, he became a lay Bible teacher of the Seventh-Day Adventist Church on North Street in Kingston.

Leithe married a man with the last name Lummine. They lived at Pear Tree River in the parish of St. Thomas, and had no children. Lindsay was married, and had a son named Stephen. Annie had one daughter named Lucille Muirhead, and she was the sister of famous barrister-at-law David Muirhead. Beatrice (Aunt Bea) had five boys, all the sons of David Bonnick of Stanmore district near Malvern, St. Elizabeth. The sons in order of birth are: Adonijah (Jack), George, Ronald (the author), Winston, and Lambert. Wilfred, who was commonly called "Blanco," went to Cuba around 1928, and got the name, which is Spanish for Whyte. He married one Iris of the Balaclava area and had two girls, Ella and Dulcie. Irene had two children, Ivy Lindo and Levi Lawrence. She later married Lofton Ebanks, and both lived for many years at Naggo's Head, St. Catherine. Rosalind was unmarried and had no children. Arthur married Violet Spence of Rose Hall district in St. Elizabeth parish and had over six children, and they all lived in Port Morant in St. Thomas parish.

Additional comments on Thomas (Tom) and Eustace (Jimpy). Jimpy had one daughter named Beverly, who lived in the Fort Lauderdale area of Florida. He was the first in the immediate family to become a policeman, the first to be a full-fledged vegetarian. During his last days he never ate or drank anything that came from the animal kingdom. Thomas decided that he was going to outshine his parents in the production of children. I personally heard him say that. We spoke closely about family matters when I was a teenager, and he gave me most of the information about my maternal ancestors. He was married to one Mary Lewis and these are his children as I remember them: Obadiah (Obie), Constantine (Connie), Aditha (Ena), Rachel (Ruth), Robert, Grace, Austin, Estella, Annie, Purcell, Cleveland, and Alfred (Buyer). I will not comment on any of these names except to say that they all made their places in society. Tom Whyte will go down in the history of St. Elizabeth as one of the best carpenters and builders of his time, and was one of the most knowledgeable on current and foreign affairs in the neighborhood.

I forgot to mention that Grandpa Tom also had a son named William. He had a daughter named Titta Whyte, and she had a son name Darrell (Moxie) Lawrence. His father was a white man from the parish of St. James. Darrell died young, in his early thirties; was never married, and had no children. The William Whyte side of the family disappeared at this point.

For the benefit of posterity, the following names should be examined so that those who want to avoid royalty will have enough material to make a choice and avoid these interrelational marriages. Scattered all over the world are descendants of these people. Robert (Bobby) Whyte and some of his brothers mentioned before are first cousins to David Dennis, Charlie Dennis of Beacon district, CY Dennis of Costa Rica, Ellen Moxam of Bluntas, and Agnes Abrams of Beacon. All of these are children of Joe Abrams and his three sisters, Sarah Abrams (Auntie Yayah), Mother Hanson, and Auntie Gamm. Sarah Abrams produced the Dennises, Mother Hanson produced the Whytes, Auntie Gamm produced the Moxams, and Joe Abrams produced Agnes Abrams.

Panton (Bully) Ebanks, Molly Bully, and Sister Bully of Naggo's Head district are also first cousins of Robert (Bobby) Whyte. All the descendants of the Bullys mentioned above bear that nickname, irrespective of what last names they have.

Auntie Gracie Whyte's family connections must also be noted. These are a few of her cousins located on the Pedro Plains and other parts of St. Elizabeth parish: Sam Williams, Gracie Williams Campbell, Richard Williams, Dovie Williams Montique, Edmond Williams, Bamboo Joe Williams, and most of the Williams family from St. Elizabeth parish. She also had many sisters and brothers that are not known to the author. The two that are known are Banga Williams of Newell district and Edith Williams of Beacon who married Panton (Bully) Ebanks. Her niece married into the McLean family of Flagaman, and produced Septrian McLean a schoolteacher, and one Mrs. Johnson, who was married to a preacher by that name, and was last seen in Brooklyn, New York, USA. Her other relatives are the Stewart family from Little Park district, Charles being the most famous one, the Miller family from St. Mary's district near the great Munro College on top of the Santa Cruz Mountain, and the Rowe Clan of Accompong in the parish of St. Elizabeth. These are just a few of Auntie Gracie's relatives.

I now switch to my paternal side of my family, which is an enigma in itself. This puzzle may finally work out as the family unfolds. If people cannot unravel this riddle, then maybe, it could be none of their problem. I have already said that my father and I are second cousins. My father is David Bonnick, and he is the son of Peter Bonnick and Frances Whyte. Peter Bonnick is the son of Henry Bonnick and Ellen Barrett. They lived at a district called Round Hill between Mountainside and Knoxwood. There is also another Round Hill district not many miles away. This one is located near the Pedro Cross Roads. Both were named after the Bonnick property in Scotland near Bannockburn. The two brothers who came from Scotland named their properties Round Hill. There is also another Round Hill in Clarendon parish, and was owned by the brother who settled there. This Round Hill is now called Bray Head. There are many Round Hills in the island of Jamaica, as well as in Scotland, but we have no evidence of any Round Hill in Jamaica until the Scottish settled there in 1700. When people are talking about the two Round Hills in St. Elizabeth, they refer to one as Mountainside Round Hill and the other as Cross Roads Round Hill.

Frances Whyte's mother was Mary Whyte, who married Charles Whyte and united the two Whyte families of St. Elizabeth and brought the families into royalty because it was presumed they were related in the first place. The author does not know any family ancestry of Mary Whyte except that she has a nephew by the name of Sam Bramwell who had many children on the Santa Cruz Mountain, mostly in the district of Stanmore and its environs. My grandmother Frances always said that she is related to the Bramwells of St. Elizabeth.

Let me see if I can explain part of the puzzle mentioned before. Frances Whyte's father is Charles Whyte and he is brother to Robert (Bobby) Whyte. This Charles is the uncle of the author's mother Beatrice Whyte. He is also grandfather of the author's father, David Bonnick, who is the son of Frances Whyte. Charles Whyte's other children include sons Ken, Henry, and Will. Ken has a son named Ivan who lived at Stanmore in St. Elizabeth parish. Very little or nothing is known about Henry. He just disappeared from the family. Will went to live in Clarendon and he was not heard from again. Charles also had four daughters. They were Ellen, Charlotte, Ann, and Julia. Ellen had two daughters; they were Ivy Thompson and Cynthia Thompson. Ivy married Claude Hall and produced many children, two of whom are Sheila Hall Doctor and Fay (Bibbs) Hall Robinson. Cynthia, who is called Tina, had two girls, Barbara and Daphne. They were Newlands, and were the nieces of Linden (Honeyboy) Newland, mayor of Kingston and later minister of labor for the island of Jamaica. Barbara married Orville Harrison and both lived in Brooklyn, New York. Daphne married Guy Clacken and then Dr. Ben Acqua of Ghana. They both lived in London where they all died. Barbara had three children, and Daphne four. Charlotte Whyte lived in Burnt Savannah and was a centenarian when she died. Nothing is known to the author of Ann and Julia Whyte. These two also disappeared from the family. Frances Whyte is the one left to be commented upon.

Frances (Fannie) Whyte married Peter Bonnick of Mountainside Round Hill, and shortly after they both settled on top of the Santa Cruz Mountain at a district called Stanmore, near the town of Malvern. She produced ten children, all known to the author, her grandson. There were five boys and five girls. The order of birth may not be sequential but this is as accurate as I can put them. They were first David (my father), Mollie, Winnifred, Alice (Agnes) George, James, Cleveland, Alfonso, Cynthia, and Lynvaris (Lyn).

David's children are Ruby, Adonijah (Jack), George, Ronald (the author of this book), Winston, Lambert, Herman, and Carmen. Mollie's children are Hermine, Astley, and Gordon. Their last name is Tucker. Winnifred's children: Pat, Victor, Vanette, Madge, Fay, Carrol, and Dahlia. They all have last name Rose. Alice has Hope Harrison and Winsome Stennett. George has Millicent, now Perry. James has Peter and Richard. Cleveland has five girls. They are Bridgett, Angela, Patricia, Sharon, and Sheila. Alfonso has three girls: Evereen, Fay, and Sandra. Cynthia has no children. Lynvaris married Norman Lynch and produced three girls. They are Jean Kerr, Leonie Bailey, and Andrea Fobbs. They all live in Laurel, Maryland, USA.

Peter Bonnick was the son of Henry Bonnick. Henry's father was a Scottish Jew who came to Jamaica just prior to the abolition of slavery in the British Empire in 1838. Tradition has it that the year was 1826 when he left Scotland with his brother and came to Jamaica because of anti-Semitism. They were Moses and Joseph Bonnick. Moses lived on the Carpenters Mountain (now in Manchester). It was St. Elizabeth until 1814. Moses lived in both parishes but lastly at the Bull Savannah area of St. Elizabeth. Joseph settled at Bray Head (Round Hill) and Frankfield in Clarendon. Apart from Henry, Moses had another son named Peter and a daughter named Charlotte. They lived somewhere between Alligator Pond and Bull Savannah. The author's grandfather Peter Bonnick was named after this uncle. Peter Bonnick of Bull Savannah had a daughter who married a man named Mr. Reid, and this Mr. Reid had a son who lived in Queens, New York, and later in Florida.

Moses also had a daughter by the name of Charlotte. She had a daughter named Sarah Creed. Sarah married a man by the last name Channer, who lived in the Watchwell-Williamsfield area of St. Elizabeth. They had some children, three of whom were Aubrey, Eugene, and Willel. It is not known whether Aubrey had any children but Eugene has several. Willel had two boys named Fenn and Tittin Roache. His mother later married a man with the last name Watson, and Tittin later took the name Albert Watson after his stepfather.

The children of Moses Bonnick came out of the Montique family who lived in the Southfield-Queensbury area of St. Elizabeth. This family of Montiques were refugees from Haiti and Santa Domingo. They came in 1803 with other families as the Desnoes, Escofferys, Deslandes, and many more. These were the French living in and operating plantations with slaves. During the Toussaint L'Ouverture uprising, they fled the

island of St. Dominique (Hispaniola) and took refuge in Jamaica. Peter
Bonnick told his descendants that all the Montiques from St. Elizabeth
were his relatives; and his popular cousins were Thomas Montique,
Aston Montique, and Hardie Montique.

Henry Bonnick had another son William who lived in the district
of Winchester, and later Pondside near Parrottee in the parish of St.
Elizabeth. He had a son by the name of John Bonnick, who later became
blind and lived in the Stony Hill area of St. Andrew. John had a son
named George and a daughter named Meeva, who married a man with
the last name Gentles. They lived off Mountain View Avenue, near the
National Stadium in the parish of St. Andrew. They had four children
when the author last saw them around 1962.

Henry had a daughter named Sarah. She worked in the parish of
St. James and had a daughter named Maud Levy who was sister to Mrs.
Duncan Clacken of Stanmore Hill in St. Elizabeth. She later married
a man from Round Hill district named Ledgister. She had several
children, two of whom are Stanford and Agnes Ledgister. Stanford had
a son named Willie who went to England, where he married a Spanish
lady. They had two sons. Willie returned to Jamaica with his family and
bought the famous Stanmore Hill property. He lived there with his
family for a few years and they all left for an unknown destination. Agnes
Ledgister married a beekeeper named Brown, who operated an apiary
in the Village of Mountainside at the intersection of the main roads that
lead from Mountainside to Malvern and the other to Treasure Beach.
They had several children and these were commonly called the children
of Bees Brown. That was a common nickname for their father.

Peter Bonnick from Round Hill, the son of Henry Bonnick, the
grandson of Moses Bonnick from Scotland, was a descendant of the
famous English family of Barretts. His mother was Ellen Barrett, a
cousin of famed English poetess Elizabeth Barrett Browning. Ellen is
also related to the Scottish family of Falconer (pronounced Faulkner)
who settled in St. Elizabeth during the nineteenth century, and it is said
that the Barretts and Falconers of St. Elizabeth are all related. Noel
(Large White) Falconer from Queensbury was Peter's favorite cousin
in that family. Noel was a carpenter by trade, and during their lifetime,
Peter and Noel visited each other annually.

Ellen Barrett's father was John, and he also had a son named
after him. John Junior had many children, three of whom are Edward

(Eddie), George, and Charlie. They all lived on the Pedro Plain area of St. Elizabeth. There are records showing that all Barretts of Jamaica are related, and they all came from Hersey Barrett, who came with the expeditionary forces of Admiral Penn and General Venables in 1655. Hersey Barrett was the officer in the British Army who personally executed King Charles I when he was found guilty of treason by court martial. No one was brave enough to chop off the king's head except Hersey, so he did it, and fled to Jamaica with the expedition. Also, among those fleeing with the Barrett family were members of the court martial, such as Henry Waite, John Bradshaw, and Daniel Blagrove. More will be said about these in another book.

The girls of the Barrett family in St. Elizabeth were so beautiful and attractive that rich men from all over the island came and married them. Even two Germans came and married two sisters, the daughters of George Barrett. Ronald Gilpin, Gladstone Ford of Great Bay, and Llewelyn Blair of Pedro Plains all married Barrett girls and had many children. Since the Barretts came from Cornwall in England, they made sure that a part of Jamaica was called by that name. We now have Cornwall Mountain in Westmoreland, and Cornwall is one of the three counties of Jamaica. All this was done by the influence of the Barrett family in Jamaica.

Ellen Barrett first married a man by the name of Rodgers and he produced a son by the name of Thomas (Tommy) Rodgers. He died in Cuba at a young age after having many children. Before going to Cuba, he lived in the district of Little Park. All districts and place names mentioned hereafter, when not specifically identified, are in the parish of St. Elizabeth. Thomas Rodgers' father also died young, so his mother remarried to Henry Bonnick, as aforementioned. The following are the nine children of Thomas Rodgers, who all lived at Little Park and paid frequent monthly visits to Peter Bonnick, their uncle, at Stanmore district: Joan, Hazel, Blossom, Daisy, Cordon, Tell, Coolie, Maurice, and Elaphilet. Hazel married one Mr. Nunes but had no children. Blossom married one Clinton Robertson of Balaclava and they had three children, Clinton Jr., Garth, and a daughter who became a nurse. The irony in the marriage of Blossom and Clinton is so glaring it had to be mentioned.

Blossom took Clinton, her boyfriend, to her uncle Peter Bonnnick at Stanmore (he being the *de facto* overseer of his brother's children) and sought his permission to marry Clinton. Peter questioned Clinton after the St. Elizabeth manner to find out what material possessions he had, and was very satisfied. This man was richer than himself. Peter sought the opinion of his wife Fanny by saying to her, "Fanny, the man black but he has something substantial, and if we say no, they are still going to get married, since they both live far away. So let us tell them yes." Fanny agreed, so they told them yes. Both Clinton and Blossom were pleased. Peter did not like black men, but he adored black women, and his wife Fanny was as black as anyone could be. And it was she Peter was talking to about Clinton, who was much lighter complexioned than her. What an irony.

Daisy had a daughter named Hazel Logan whose father was Corporal Diego Logan of the Jamaica Police Force. She also had a son named Thomas (Booker) Rodgers who was a schoolteacher. It is not necessary to go into much more detail except to mention another form of royalty at this point. Cordon, one of old Thomas Rodgers' children, married one Vera Williamson (Muss). She was the granddaughter of Ella Bonnick, his aunt from Round Hill. This marriage produced two boys, one of whom was a corporal of police in the Jamaica Constabulary Force, and the other, Pervis Rodgers, was an architect in the parish of St. Andrew.

Ella Bonnick's other children are Cleveland Braham, last heard of in Clarendon parish; Joseph Braham, Sam Graham, Willel (Pum) Graham (whose daughter Vera Williamson married her cousin Cordon Rodgers), and Madelyn Robinson.

In closing this book, it should be noted that Peter Bonnick is also related to the Foster families of Southfield and Munro, some of the Bromfields on the Santa Cruz Mountain, as well as the Barretts of St. Ann, Trelawny, St. James, Westmoreland, St. Elizabeth, Clarendon, and Manchester. These are the places where the Barrett family established themselves in the eighteenth century when they spread out from Jamaica's capital after the conquest of 1655–1661 to Santiago De La Vega. Some of these Barretts were called the Northside Barretts, with ancestral great houses at Cinnamon Hill and Greenwood in St. James. The Southside Barretts had ancestral homes at Alley in the parish of Vere (now Clarendon) and Mile Gully in St. Elizabeth (now Manchester). All of these Barretts came from a place in the county of Cornwall, England, by the name of Tregarne.

It is of significant note that when Governor Trelawny came to Jamaica in 1771, when he visited the north coast of Jamaica, he stopped for a few days at the house of Edward Barrett of Cinnamon Hill. It was later found out that he was from the county of Cornwall in England, the same county from whence the Barretts came. When a parish was named after him in 1773, it was Edward Barrett who told him where to put the boundary on the St. James side to include his wharf at Falmouth, and 431 lots became the nucleus of the town of Falmouth, as well as the commercial center of the new parish. It was this Edward Barrett whose great-granddaughter Elizabeth eloped with Robert Browning and made the Barrett name so famous, even though some members of the family thought it made them infamous.

This is not the last time the world is going to hear something about my family. There are plenty more materials in my possession about them, but there is one thing for sure, no one can precede Hersey Barrett in the execution of a king of England.

Overview: Rooms without Doors

From the beginning of the earth's existence, mankind has been intermixed by race, color, and surname. The fact that members of the Barrett family had other names when their last name should be Barrett is not something that happened only to this family. All over the world, we have this problem with tribe, clan, color, and name. So when Elizabeth Barrett Browning bemoaned her impure racial make-up, she was not alone. Europeans are nothing more than fair-complexioned Africans, and so are the Chinese, Japanese, East Indians, and Persians. European scientists have now determined that all races of people came out of Africa. I am not personally saying so, but I believe it based upon my knowledge of history. For example, I have sixteen great-great-grandparents, and fourteen are from Europe, one from Africa, and one from the Hebrews. Other races, mostly from Africa, are interwoven in my ancestral lineage. The closer it came to me, the more mixed up it became. Scottish Jewish Bonnick, English Jewish Abrams, Scottish Falconer, English Barrett, Welsh Williams, Irish Foster, English Staple, Scottish Whyte, French Montique, and African Ashanti, Ibo, and many others from Africa that I cannot identify, as well as other races of native Western hemisphere Indians.

Since I am writing about the Barrett family, it is wise to stick closer to them, but I will be mixing it up all over, because people should know some of the silent history that has been known to me. In my younger days when I played dominoes on a regular basis, whenever my partner heard me say, "The Vikings strike again," he knew that I had the game tied up and was sure to win. Little did I know that I was talking about my family and ancestral lineage. I read history most of my life, and from age twelve up to the time of writing, I have been looking from one end of the earth to the other, even though a round earth has no end. Every time I read that the Vikings struck some part of Europe (they also came to North America, but that is another story), I wondered why. I later found out that they were tired of the cold, so they were looking for warmer lands, such as England and France. These countries were warm in comparison to theirs in Scandinavia. The Gulf Stream current was then very effective, and lower western Europe and the British Isles benefited from this tropical air the current brought. I don't know what happened to that current in the twenty-first century. Norway and Sweden were the two countries in those days that sent Vikings southward. They were vicious people when they met resistance. They were peaceful people when they got what they wanted. They took over parts of lower Europe and created their new country. They took over England and ruled it for some time. They captured parts of France and called it land of the Northmen. King Francis of France signed a peace treaty with them in the year 911. The land they occupied was given to them provided they left Paris alone. They abided by the terms of this treaty, and the land of the Northmen became Normandy. They sent back word to their country and brought many more people to populate their new country. Many countries of Europe through the years recognized Normandy as a separate country, and through the Viking royal family in Britain, a prince by the name of William became the Duke of Normandy. He said he was the grandnephew of Queen Emma of Britain, and no one disputed his claim.

The year 1066 was an eventful year for Europe. It was that year that the duke made plans to invade England. There was a king by the name of Harold who acceded to the throne of England under dubious claims, just as William did. These two pretenders had no just claim to the throne of England, but since Harold lived in England, he grabbed the throne and started to rule. William, upon hearing this, went ballistic. He got a mighty army, and the pope gave him his blessing, so he led his troops in Viking fashion to take the throne of England. War started between Harold and William, two inept rascals, but each with truculent attitudes. At the Battle of Hastings in 1066, William destroyed Harold. Accompanying William in this battle was a man named Ensign Barrett. We have no clue where he was from except Scandinavia. Danish people joined the Swedish and Norwegians, and from these three countries over many years came the Normans. Since these Vikings were men, the people of Normandy over the years had to be very much French. Miscegenation between Viking men and French women had to be the order of the day. Viking blood only ran to a lesser degree in the veins of the Normans.

So who was Ensign Barrett racially? We can only guess. Whoever he was, he was held in high esteem by William, who since his latest victory became known as the Conqueror. When he took control of England, Ensign Barrett was handsomely rewarded. Based on my biased analogy, Ensign Barrett was one of the chief organizers who arranged and carried out operations at the Battle of Hastings. He got the county of Cornwall as his reward, and he settled there at places called Tregarne and Salt Marsh. No wonder that in later years his ancestors would name the county of Cornwall in Jamaica, and had properties by that name, as well as Salt Marsh and other Cornish names. My conclusion is that this ensign was more of a Frenchman than anything else. I have discovered Frenchmen with the name Barrette, having an E at the end, and presumably it was dropped by the English. We now have a few people in Jamaica who prefer the E at the end of their names the French way. For hundreds of years, the English Barretts spelled their names without the extra E.

We have the name Barrett taking centerstage again during the English Civil War, 1642–1649. It seems that the entire family from Cornwall sided with Oliver Cromwell in his fight against King Charles I. When the war ended and Cromwell became lord protector of England, he called a court martial into action and put the king on trial. This is the first time in English history that a monarch was put on trial. The doctrine of divine rights of kings came to an end. The king was convicted of treason and sentenced to die. This was a contradictory verdict, but the Parliament accepted it. I cannot say how many people sat on this court martial, neither can I say whether any Barrett sat on it, but Hersey Barrett carried out the final verdict by executing the king using an old-time axe.

There were at least nine persons on the court martial tribunal, but what I am interested in is some of the people who took part in it. Heading up the trial was the president of the court martial, whose name was Bradshaw. I am still trying to find his first name. Daniel Blagrove and Henry Waite, were other members. All of them, in 1655, came to Jamaica with the expeditionary forces of Adm. William Penn and Gen. Robert Venables. This expedition was for the purpose of capturing Catholic lands in the West Indies, especially the large island of Hispaniola, which now comprises the two countries of Haiti and Santo Domingo. This William is the father of William Penn, the founder of Pennsylvania.

When they got to Hispaniola, the cowardice of General Venables prevented the success of the British. He thought they were too well fortified for him to succeed, so he refused to land his army when the Spaniards blockaded the island. Later, Spanish historians said that the island could not have defended itself had the British landed. The two commanders then decided to go to Jamaica, which was the fiefdom of the Columbus family and was not well protected by the Spanish crown. The failure to take Hispaniola landed Penn and Venables in the tower of London, and only Penn was released after an enquiry.

Many other people went on this expedition for the purpose of escaping vengeance by Prince Charles, who was in protective custody of the king of Spain and who they thought would one day return to England as king. They were right. In 1660, at the restoration, he was crowned Charles II and those who killed his father had to go into hiding for fear of retribution. For all intents and purposes, retribution took place. I was very surprised to discover that King Charles II gave to Hersey Barrett hundreds of acres of land in Jamaica free of cost for his services to the British Crown, not knowing that he was the man who took off his father's head. Based upon this fact, I don't think he ever tried to find out, nor do we have any evidence that he found out. My interest in these regicides is that they have left behind in present-day Jamaica a vast number of descendants who know nothing about their ancestors. These children of the regicides now make up every nation on earth that is endemic of the Jamaican population.

It is correct for me to mention one name here who was not a regicide, nor was he British. His first name eludes me. He was a Portuguese Jew with the last name DaCosta, and he was employed in the service of Spain as a cartographer. He made several trips to the West Indies with the Spanish explorers for the purpose of producing maps of the various countries and islands, as well as the sea channels and ship routes. He had a quarrel with the authorities in Spain, and he went to England and sold this information to Oliver Cromwell, now lord protector. Having this information, Cromwell organized the 1655 expedition to take retributive justice against King Phillip for holding Prince Charles and not handing him over to the forces of Parliament. So when the British forces got to the West Indies, they knew firsthand how to make their attack and where to strike first. All one has to do is study the British attack on Jamaica to see that the British knew exactly what they were doing.

When Jamaica was taken over by the British, land was given to Bradshaw in what is now the parish of Portland, and while his family migrated to other parts of Jamaica, most Bradshaws at the present moment trace their ancestry back to Portland.

Daniel Blagrove got land in St. Ann, at a place known as Cardiff Hall, not far from St. Ann's Bay, and later Kenilworth in Hanover; and this family traces their ancestry to these places. Henry Wayte settled first in Port Royal, and after the disastrous earthquake of 1692, his family went to St. Elizabeth, and later Manchester, which was cut from St. Elizabeth in 1814 by the governor William, Duke of Manchester. More will be said about him.

Hersey Barrett, the executioner, got land everywhere. His family covered the whole island. This family intermarried with the Wayte family, and a host of new descendants emerged. Everywhere one went there were Barrett-Wayte cousin intermarriages. It even caused a rift in both families because there were too many family marriages. Right now in Jamaica, almost every Wayte (Waite) is related to some Barrett.

I now return to the DaCosta who gave maps to Cromwell. He is the ancestor of Sir Alfred DaCosta who owned properties in St. Ann parish. Foremost among these properties is the one called Lydford. In the early forties, he tried to grow Irish potatoes on this farm. At the early stages, the potatoes bloomed as if he was going to reap a great harvest, then suddenly they withered and died. Agricultural experts told him he should have the soil tested, and he did so. When the test returned from Florida where the soil samples were sent, the results came back that it was bauxite, hence the Reynolds Bauxite Company came, did more tests, and the bauxite industry in Jamaica was born. So Sir Alfred DaCosta is considered by many as the father of the Jamaica bauxite industry. So from the cartographer of the 1655 British expedition came the founder of the Jamaica bauxite development.

Among the regicides, the Barretts became the most prolific multipliers of legitimate and illegitimate children in Jamaica. The more children they produced, the more crown land they got from the king. The family had plenty of land everywhere. They occupied properties in St. Andrew (Liguanea), St. Cathereine, St. Ann, and St. James, as well as Westmoreland, St. Elizabeth, Cambridge, and Trelawny. At one time there were twenty-two parishes, and these were reduced to fourteen by the governor, Sir John Peter Grant, who was governor from 1866 to 1870.

Famous properties of the Barretts were Moneague, with that beautiful lake in St. Ann parish, and Withywood in the parish of Vere. This Withywood property included what is now known as Paradise Estate, and a large portion of Monymusk Estate. Later descendants of Hersey Barrett acquired properties in St. Ann and St. James prior to the creation of the parish of Trelawny in 1773. There were Hersey Junior and Samuel, sons of the regicide Hersey Senior. These had children, plantations, and cattle and horses all over the island but they were not the only people with wealth. Others were equally wealthy and had many properties.

Since Elizabeth Barrett Browning was complaining about her dark complexion, the blood of slaves and wished she was from a purer race, I will mention first a few English barons who also complicated the racial picture. John Gladstone, who owned Holland Estate in the parish of St. Elizabeth and was the father of William Gladstone, was four-time prime minister of Britain under Queen Victoria and had many children. They all went by the surname of their mothers and could not inherit any property belonging to their father. Should these children come out looking more white than black, they were sent to England to be educated and lose themselves in the white English population. These were not to return to Jamaica. A few did, and came back as white overseers and landlords, and became agents of many properties for absentee landlords.

Other prominent figures included Jordan Spencer, son of the Duke of Marlborough. He had royalty in him, and he settled on properties in Lacovia and Newton. He is the person buried at Tombstone, Lacovia, with his horse. If the tombs are still intact, the one without a name is that of his horse. The other had his name and at one time the coat of arms of the Duke of Marlborough. This man is the granduncle of Sir Winston Churchill, who is also a son of a Duke of Marlborough. The first Duke of Marlborough was the illegitimate son of Henry VII and brother to King Henry VIII. He was given the duchy of Marlborough to keep him politically quiet. Jordan Spencer was also the third great-uncle of Princess Diana Spencer who married Prince Charles of England. One should not be surprised that many prominent English persons got their wealth from sugar and cotton produced by slave labor. There are a host of people in St. Elizabeth with the last name Spencer, and it is my guess that these are all related to the Duke of Marlborough.

Another prolific producer of mixed-race children was William, Duke of Manchester. He came to Jamaica sometime around 1813. It is said that he served twelve years as governor of Jamaica. He had a liking for mulatto women, and when he left Jamaica, it was rumored that he left behind twenty-two children of every shade, hue, and complexion. They had many different last names, but the foremost name was Powell, and most of them had relatives with last names Lord and Clarke. Many lived

in the new parish of Manchester, which he cut from the large parish of
St. Elizabeth and named after himself. The town of Mile Gully was his
country place for many carnal activities when he got tired of Spanish
Town. I supposed there were too many mosquitoes there during the
months of April and May when crabs were running wild during the rainy
season. The climate of Mile Gully is very pleasant, and it reminded him
of Manchester in England, where he held his duchy.

While hanging out with the big boys of Mile Gully, Cottage, and
Greenvale properties, they complained to him about the long distance
they had to go to pay their taxes. They had to go to Black River to pay
land taxes to the collector for St. Elizabeth. It was these complaints that
gave him the idea to create a new parish with his name. In the year
1814, he decided to cut a new parish from St. Elizabeth and named it
Manchester. He then went to the owner of the Caledonia Estate, a Scot
by the name of Robert Crawford, and asked him to sell to the Vestry one
square mile of his estate where William could set up a courthouse and
an Anglican Church and a post office as the capital of the new parish.
Crawford agreed, and the parish capital was named after the governor's
first son, Mandeville. So a new parish with its capital was named after
the governor and his son.

One of the famous taxpayers who made the request was someone
from the author's family. His name was Thomas Hearcy Barrett, and he
was the owner of the Mile Gully property. At this very moment of writing,
the town of Mile Gully has three names. The post office is Mile Gully.
The police station is Cottage. The railway station is Greenvale. These
were the names of the three properties converging at the same place.

There are many descendants of the Duke of Manchester who became
prominent people in Britain, Jamaica, and the United States. These
made up the middle class after slavery was abolished in 1838, and many
went back to England as white Negroes to take their position among
the people as white Creoles, and were accepted as equals because the
English people thought they were descendants of sugar barons. Those
who remained in Jamaica became lawyers and educators. One famous
lawyer was a Judge Clarke who lived at a village called Perth, about two
miles south of Mandeville, opposite the Bulldead property owned by one
Ms. Nightingale of Britain. She lived at this property most of her life.
Both these persons are known by this author.

Another prominent descendant was the great educator Wesley
Powell, also known by this author, who founded the Excelsior College

on Mountain View Avenue in St. Andrew. There are many other famous people, too numerous to mention in this book. The most famous of all the Powells is Gen. Colin Powell of the United States. He became the first black chairman of the Joint Chiefs of Staff of the United States military, and also the first black secretary of state for that country. Even though he was born in the United States, his parents are Jamaicans. I saw an interview with him and Barbara Walters, and I know he was reluctant to say anything about his ancestral lineage. So after reading his book entitled *My American Journey*, I will not be saying much about him here except that I am very proud of him because he has done very well. I did not know his parents, but I know his aunt, Mrs. Meikle, who lived at Spur Tree in the parish of Manchester. His two first cousins Vernon and Trevor Meikle were schoolmates of mine at Hatfield Elementary School under the leadership of that bearded lady who was principal. She shaved like a man, but was one of the best teachers I ever encountered.

I am only trying to show that no matter how a family considers itself to be of high moral quality, funny things do happen. We had a man by the name of Sir Thomas Roxborough who lived in the parish of St. Ann. No one knew where his ancestors lived or from whence they came, but he looked very much the same like some world-famous people. One thing I personally know is any time a member of the British royal Family visited Jamaica, most of them paid a visit to Sir Thomas Roxborough in St. Ann parish. I always asked why. Nobody was brave enough to tell me, but some people said he looked like them. I never saw him, so I cannot say this. The royal family always visited Sir Harold Mitchell of Prospect property in St. Mary parish. I know him very well. He did not look like any of the royal family, but royalty always visited him and stayed at his beach house known as Frankfort Beach House. This cottage was by a beautiful beach on Jamaica's north coast between Ocho Rios and Tower Isle.

In 1960, when I was a policeman at the Oracabessa Police Station in St. Mary parish, I was one of the military-police duo that provided security for the Princess Royal. She was the sister of King George VI. On her arrival in Jamaica, she left Kings House in St. Andrew parish for the Frankfort Beach House as the guest of Sir Harold Mitchell for about three days. Now, Sir Harold was one of the world's ten richest men at that time. He owned wheat fields in Australia that were about the same in square mileage as the area of Jamaica. I spoke with him during the course of one day at the beach house, and heard him speak about his wheat production in Australia. I was, and still am, very inquisitive, because I wanted to learn how some people were so rich while I was very poor. He had some interesting tales to tell, which I heard, even though he was not talking directly to me. But I was there as one of the many policemen protecting the Princess Royal. It was at this time that Sir Harold made it known to us that he was taking her to see Sir Thomas Roxborough. Shortly after this, his Rolls-Royce pulled up, and he beckoned her to join Lady Mitchell and his lone daughter to get into the car. Inside the car were some secret service police from the Special Branch Department. Sir Harold got in with them, but the three security men got out and joined a military vehicle, and they both sped off to the home of Sir Thomas Roxborough. They all returned about four hours afterward, and the twenty-four-hour watch around the beach house continued.

During the night, at about two in the morning, while I was among the coconut trees on the western side of the property, I saw a figure moving toward me in the dark. I recognized the figure as one of the Jamaica Defence Force personnel, but my call, "Who goes there?" was unanswered. I had my loaded Mark 7 rifle with ten bullets in the magazine but none in the breach. On not getting an answer, I loosed the rifle bolt and had a bullet in the breach ready to go. Upon hearing the rifle bolt movement, a shout came out of the dark, "Colonel Mignon! Colonel Mignon!" He knew I had the authority to shoot anything that moves without an identity. He came up to me and said, "I knew someone was at this point, but I did not see you, so I was just checking to find out." He then left and went elsewhere. I still kept that bullet in the breach until I was relieved later on. Only then did I remove it and place it back in the magazine.

We are now back to the visit to Sir Thomas Roxborough. I overheard the secret service men discussing the resemblance of this man to King George VI. They said he was the stamping image of the king, and since so many of the royal visitors paid him a visit when they came to Jamaica, there must be some relationship. I am sorry I did not get to see this man, because I would have certainly made some family connection. It has always been rumored that there were members of the British Royal Family living in Jamaica under different names. One name that belonged to the British Royal Family is the last name of Cambridge. When Queen Victoria gave the last name Windsor to her family who could succeed to the throne, those who could not should not go by the name of Cambridge. There are some people who were businessmen in St. Elizabeth parish, at a place called Newell, who had the last name Cambridge. Could it be that these people were related to the British royal family?

My reason for digging up these tidbits about some families is that Elizabeth Barrett Browning had made many comments about her being of dark complexion, and with no family trace that she had the blood of slaves, I am only trying to show how this could have been. Maybe she was not her father's child. She could be one of many Barretts who were white Negroes. There were many in England before and after her time. She wished that she was from a purer race, but there is none. We are all a mixture from wherever we emerge. There was, and still is, a mixed race in the House of Commons. I caused a stir one night when I visited a hotel on Ruthven Road in St. Andrew parish in 1965. A robbery had just taken place there, and as a detective at Halfway Tree Police Station, I got the call and went. After doing my investigation, there were five British guests there, some of whom were robbed, and the nightly news came on the television about 11:00 PM. The headline news was Prime Minister Ian Smith declaring a unilateral declaration of independence from Britain, and the British Prime Minister Harold Wilson making a reply. A discussion took place shortly afterward and I participated. I told the English people that I did not see why there should be such a furor over this race issue in that England's greatest wartime prime minister was colored. This turned these English people upside down. They hurriedly wanted me to identify this man. I hesitated, but continued the discussion for some time until I told them it was Sir Winston Churchill. They wanted proof, which I had in my cranium. I told them that his mother was Jennie Jerome from Brooklyn, New York, and his mother was a Sioux Indian and her father British. She married Lord Randolph Churchill, the Duke of Marlborough, and produced Winston Spencer Churchill. They looked up to the ceiling in wonder and amazement and then I knew it was time to leave. They were robbed of their property as well as their ignorance. The Sioux Indians of New York were the ones who did not consider it a problem to crossbreed with other races.

The Robertson clan of Scotland is another case in point. They traveled all over the world, and the rule in that clan was a succession instruction that could not deny any person the position of chief of the clan provided he had proof that he was connected and should be the chief. There was a man living in St. Elizabeth parish and his name was Robertson. He was in direct line to be chieftain. He married a colored woman and produced a white Negro. Quadroons are now called white Negroes. It happened that the father died and and so did the clan chief. This was sometime in the 1950s. There was no leader of this clan, because the one who should have succeeded died. When the clan in Scotland found out that there was no Scottish successor, they summoned the ancient council of the clan and inquired what to do. The council voted, and told the Robertson clan that a quadroon in Jamaica was its leader and they could do nothing about it. They called this quadroon from Jamaica and he accepted the leadership of the clan until he died some years ago. From the information I received, the rules have been changed and only those born in Scotland can be installed as chief. They did not rule out colored people but they believed no black Robertson would be born in Scotland. They can't be too sure about this.

Many members of the Scottish clan are still in St. Elizabeth, and many of the younger generations of Robertson have migrated to the Kingston area and are not dedicated to their parish of origin. They all falsely believe that being born in Kingston or St. Andrew will make them more modern. This is why I boast to the contrary about St. Elizabeth. A great many of these people also migrated to Britain shortly after the last world war, and many Robertsons are now being born in Britain who have direct lineage to the original clan.

Shortly after the English Civil War, Oliver Cromwell sent thousands of people to Ireland to colonize it, and a vast mixture of the British population went there, and the descendants of these British people who were colonizers became Irish. There are now many Irish people with English last names. To make them appear Irish, many changed their names by adding an "Mc" before their names. They also changed the Scottish "Mac" to "Mc" before the names. My Scottish family told me that these two prefixes mean "son of." I presume that some Celtic sympathizers will say otherwise, but I grew up with many of them in St. Elizabeth and I am related to many. I will never forget when I came to the United States in 1970 and an old Irish lady identified me as having her Gaelic accent, as well as identifying some of her relatives who were sent to Jamaica during the potato famine around 1854–1860. There were two shiploads of them, and they at first settled in southwestern Jamaica, the place from whence I came, and many of their descendants are still domiciled in the parish of St. Elizabeth. Whenever you miss the Irish in Ireland, come to St. Elizabeth and you will find them.

The Germans also came from about 1835 onward due to the potato famine in Europe. They were scattered around the parishes of Westmoreland and St. Elizabeth. The greatest influx of Germans came as a result of a request made by Dr. William Lemonius of German origin, and between 1835 and 1845 he brought in over eight hundred and settled them on his property in Seaford Town, in Westmoreland parish. John Myers, a St. Ann penkeeper, also brought in many others, and over one thousand were scattered all over Jamaica prior to the abolition of slavery. Many districts and properties now have German names. Contrary to common belief, Seaford Town was not owned by Dr. Lemonius. It was owned by an Englishman who owned large tracts of land on Montpelier Mountain, and a large portion was made into Seaford Town in honor of the donor of the land, Lord Seaford. There were many other Germans than just in Seaford Town, and a great many of them settled around Montego Bay, St. Ann's Bay, Black River, Lacovia, and Spauldings. Some other Germans were Jewish who hid their religion in order to succeed. The Myers were Jewish families who settled on the Santa Cruz Mountain, and the place Myersville was named after them. So St. Elizabeth got a great many Germans who now make up an endemic portion of that parish's population, and Jamaica has benefited much from names such as Eldemire, Stockhausen, Eberle, and Schlieffer. There are also other prominent German names all over the island, and even my own family, the Barretts, got involved. My grandfather's first cousin George Barrett had two daughters who married into the Bunnyman German family of Seaford Town, so we have a whole set of European crossbreeds all over the country.

One of the most famous groups of people to arrive in Jamaica were the Scottish people. My Irish friends told me that they were formerly Irish. There were a group of Irish who left their country for various reasons and did not return. They ended up on the northern portion of the British Isles and established a country for themselves. Somehow it became Scotland, from the Gaelic word "Scottia," meaning those who left. This has always been a boast of the Irish people. Even though there could have been others, the earliest record of the Scots in Jamaica date back to the year 1700.

A Scotsman by the name of Col. John Campbell went with a group to establish some form of colony on the Isthmus of Panama at a place called Darien in 1699. Yellow fever mosquitoes told him otherwise, so he fled to Jamaica in 1700 and domiciled himself in the parish of St. Elizabeth. He found a rich woman there, and they were married. He produced the first group of Campbells known in Jamaica by his wife and several mistresses. Since the mistresses were not slave women, they all went by the name of Campbell. It was not very long before the name Campbell became a household name in St. Elizabeth. They spread out from there, and Campbell is now one of the most common surnames in Jamaica. He became everything important to St. Elizabeth. Every known political office was held by him, and he dominated the parish for the next forty years. When he died in 1740, he was buried at a property called Hodges Pen, just west of Black River, and at the time of writing, the property still goes by that name. He was not totally responsible for all the Campbells in Jamaica, but they are all related to him.

The same approach he had when he went to Panama, which ended in failure, was to establish a place where he could send back to Scotland for a large group of his family. They were under pressure from their constant war with the MacDonald family, and if he could relocate and establish a place for his family and become a sugar baron, then he would win the bragging rights for his clan. This was not to be so. He sent for hundreds of his family back home, and many MacDonalds came with the groups who came to find this land of milk and honey, and mosquitoes, to get enough to enrich their families back home.

Following the pioneer John Campbell, thousands of Scots came until they became one-third the population of white Jamaica, second only to the English. They were so numerous that St. Elizabeth could not contain them, so they went all over the country. There are many places that were named after the Scottish settlements, such as Aberdeen, Culloden, Anchindown, Kilmarnoch, Crawford, and many others. All these names are in the parishes of Westmoreland and St. Elizabeth. These Scots were prolific child producers, and very soon they became a large part of the white population. Not only did the Campbells and MacDonalds find peace in Jamaica, they intermarried and broke down the walls of prejudice between them.

The Campbells were descended from an old family in Scotland named Auchenbreck. During one of the battles between themselves and the MacDonalds, there was a famous warrior among the Campbell clan with a twisted mouth. The group who followed this man was called Twisted Mouth Clan, so after a time the story went that in old Scots language their name was Campbell or a derivative of it. I personally thought that the name meant *camp bell*, but some member of my Scottish family told me that the first part of the name, "cam," means twisted, and the other part comes from the word for mouth. This is very much amusing to me since a cam shaft in a motor car engine is also twisted. I presume that some Scot is going to attack me for this, especially members of the Campbell family. I am also related to them from St. Elizabeth. Some of these Campbells have returned to Britain since World War Two, and they have run into their white counterparts who looked down upon them as not being full human beings. These people will soon find out how irrelevant their thinking is. With the same opportunities, all mankind are the same.

With the migration of these Europeans to Jamaica, many of them with skills and qualifications to produce sugar and other exports, using the Africans to do the brutal labor, these Britons exploited the markets back home and made themselves very rich. The results were the island became economically wealthy and its influence was felt even in the British House of Commons, because in those days, prior to 1832, money bought seats in the parliament.

We now look at the people who left Jamaica for other countries and did well. They are willing to return to the homeland with the skills and money but cannot do so because of the criminal elements in the country. Those returning residents could shore up the economy in Jamaica to the point that the island could become a real paradise, but criminals have taken over the island from around 1977. In every class of people, there is a criminal group. You cannot do business in the country without bribery or extortion. The politicians and policemen who are to preserve law and order are themselves the foremost lawbreakers in the country, so the people who would like to return are scared and go elsewhere. If the slaves were as vicious as these types of criminals, all the white men would have been killed, and there would have been no plantation around. Get crime under control and economic development will take place without any effort. It was Adam Smith who said in his book *Wealth of Nations* that if the government would let people feel secure and safe in their property and wellbeing, then economic activity would take off. When people are insecure, they will hide their assets and do nothing to employ anyone. This is the condition of most countries in the West Indies today.

Let me return from my digression and deal with real people and history. My reason for mentioning the people in this chapter is to show that the Barretts are no different from the other Englishmen of their time. They engaged in miscegenation of every kind. Man is man, and woman is woman. Sexual activity is not something to be taught. It is an innate disposition. If you take a boy baby and brought him up by himself without teaching him to read or write, and do the same thing with a girl, let them loose on a strange island after their fourteenth birthday and within a short period the girl will become pregnant without ever hearing the word *sex*. So when people get together, black or white, red or yellow, something is going to happen. When the Barretts began having many slaves and many children, something contrary to common European belief happened.

Now Edward Barrett of Cinnamon Hill did not want any of his children to cohabit with slaves, and he set that example himself. He was not cruel to slaves like the other planters, but he did not tolerate companionship with them. Even though black nannies looked after his children and prepared meals for his family, he did not want anything close to occur between slaves and his offspring. When his son George Goodin Barrett became a prodigy and matriculated for Oxford at age fourteen and went on to the Inns of Court to read law, which he did in two years, he returned to Jamaica a full-fledged barrister-at-law and became his father's confidant and advisor. The only problem was he would not get married. He roamed the plantations, even those now owned by his father, and produced many quadroon children. These are who the author calls white Negroes.

In the tropics, with such high temperatures all year round, there could not be seen any differences in color between those born in Europe and the quadroons born in the West Indies provided the Europeans lived in the tropics for more than six months. What really happened in those cases was the owner would quickly make the white Negro a supervisor on the farm or a house servant. If the two slave owners were friends, on finding out that his friend or his children sired siblings on his farm, a sale or exchange would be made. If these exchanges were not made, then special care would be taken of his friend's quadroon or mulatto descendants. This was one way the peace was kept between slave masters. The number of children born to George was not definite. Sometimes the number seven appeared, and sometimes nine. Whichever number is correct, that's a great many. Henry had less than his brother George, but George is the one of importance here since Elizabeth Barrett Browning is discussed in the foregoing. As can be seen in the beginning of this chapter, the Barretts were not the only family that practiced miscegenation. It was commonplace among most British families, and some were sorry they did it, because these crossbreeds were the ones who created most of the slave revolts, not because they were more intelligent, but because they did not consider themselves slaves. Many of them thought they should be treated as equals of the whites and not as equal of Negroes.

Edward Barrett of Cinnamon Hill believed that as long as the tar brush passed nearby, that person was not an equal, and so did his grandson Edward Barrett Moulton-Barrett, the legal father of Elizabeth Barrett Browning.

George Goodin Barrett made his will, and his father was executor along with John Graham-Clarke of Newcastle-upon-Tyne. These two men were to shape the history of the Barrett family for a very long time. These men were much older than George who died before them. As executors of his will, they should have seen to it that the provisions of his will were carried out. Unknown to Clarke, Edward changed some aspect of the will by transferring ownership of some ninety odd slaves from George to himself, and later willed these slaves to Edward Barrett Moulton-Barrett and his brother Samuel. It was these slaves and other properties illegally removed from George's will that were to bring about one of the longest civil lawsuits in British history. It lasted more than twenty years. John Graham-Clarke did not object to the change in the will because he had long-term ulterior motives in mind. As Edward of Cinnamon Hill grew older, he had to manufacture his own will to include assets illegally removed from his son George. When Edward finally died four years later, John was also an executor of Edward's will. What a coincidence!

As a reminder to the readers, George's will stated, among other things, that all his slave children who were either quadroons or mulattoes should be bought out of slavery with their mothers, and they should be sent to England with a one-way ticket. They were to be sent to school and educated or trained as artisans or for any other kind of trade. The four children that I will be dealing with here are the sons of Elissa Peters, and these all have the last names Peters, even though they are the sons of George Goodin Barrett. Customs of the British made it so that children born out of wedlock would not have the last names of their fathers, only that of their mothers. These four boys were more Barrett than may of the other Barretts.

The responsibility to carry out the wishes of George Goodin Barrett toward his sons fell on none other than John Graham-Clarke. He had these boys living for many years on his large property at Newcastle-upon-Tyne. They all grew up with his children. And when Edward Barrett-Moulton and his brother Samuel came to England, they too lived with the same family for some time. These two boys had Moulton as their surname, being the children of Capt. Charles Moulton and his wife Elizabeth Barrett Moulton of Cinnamon Hill. It was John's duty to have these Moulton boys' last name changed to Barrett in order for them to carry the coat of arms of the Barretts and inherit properties from their grandfather, Edward Barrett of Cinnamon Hill. John did just that, so their grandfather adjusted his will and bequeathed to them most of his estates and slaves, including some taken from the estate of George Goodin Barrett, which caused the great lawsuit.

This is just a reminder to let the readers know that George Goodin Barrett was one of the first Barrett prodigies who matriculated at Oxford University at age fourteen, graduated at eighteen, barrister-at-law at twenty, and a practicing legal scholar when he wrote his will. It was as airtight as any legal brain could imagine. So when his nephew Richard Barrett, whose father Samuel Barrett of Portman Street in London was an heir in his brother George's will, looked through Edward's will and saw what he did, he sued him on behalf of his father Samuel. Richard Barrett himself was no legal chicken. He was also a prodigy and followed in the footsteps of his uncle George Goodin Barrett.

Prior to the lawsuit, John Graham-Clarke sent these four boys of George to school and trade. The one who came out brilliantly was the eldest one named Thomas Peters. We know that he had the title "Esquire" after his name. This is the title commonly used by lawyers. Now these four boys were a little older than Edward Barrett Moulton-Barrett. These boys were sons of a West Indian sugar baron, and those who knew them were convinced they had money, so they were called white Negroes. From all the evidence available, these boys married white

girls and produced white children, even though their complexion could
have been a little more robust. Money was more important in those days
than the color of the skin, and racism is something that is taught.

John Graham-Clarke had the trump card in his hand. When Edward
Barrett of Cinnamon Hill died, he was the chief executor of his will.
He studied it inside out. He saw that the two Moulton grandsons whose
names he had changed by deed poll were the richest of the Barretts, he
grabbed the elder of the two and married his daughter Mary off to him
despite her being four years his senior. Edward Barrett Moulton-Barrett
dropped out of college for this purpose, and it is believed that John
encouraged him to do so because he was very rich and John wanted a
rich son-in-law. John was still Edward's protector when he got married
to his daughter Mary. Edward could not inherit until he was twenty-one,
but John could not wait. Mary was about the same age or younger than
Thomas Peters, who lived in her father's household. Were Mary and
Thomas in the friendship mode when John hurriedly married her to
Edward? There were many people who thought so. Now Thomas Peters
looked like a Barrett, talked like a Barrett, thought like a Barrett, and
he was really a Barrett. This author did not guess that Elizabeth Barrett
Browning was Negroid. She herself wrote about it. If she was of dark
complexion, she was the only one that said it in her writings. Her friends
who made statements about her complexion were only repeating what
she said. None of them who saw her said she was dark. She repeatedly
attacked herself as having the blood of slaves, and wished she was from
a purer race. She also attributed the hard times on her family as a
result of miscegenation. No one ever thought of it. Even though she
was born nine months, twenty days after her parents got married, the
Barrett boys named Peters were still around and in close proximity.
The several statements Elizabeth made have caused many inquiring
minds to wonder how she came to this conclusion. As a member of this
ancient family and being aware of the many cases of infidelity among
the family, ancient and modern, I can make a good guess as to what
took place. My deductions are that John Graham-Clarke saw something
going on between the boys he was caring for and his children, and
having the authority to do many things with several wills of which he was
executor, before anything could go bad financially against his family,
he used his power of attorney to carry out a marriage between Edward
Barrett Moulton-Barrett, who was not of responsible age, and his elder

daughter Mary. He also knew that of all the boys under his control Edward would become the wealthiest at age twenty-one based upon his grandfather's will, which John controlled, so he took Edward out of college and married him off to his daughter Mary. She was four years his senior.

Having said all this, no one knew whether there was any suspected relationship going on between Mary and one of the Peters boys her age. And as such, John did not want a connection between a quadroon and his daughter. Even though we know that racism was real in the household of the Barretts and the Clarkes, John did not want anyone with the tar brush to be his son-in-law. Other white people did, because there is information that the Peters boys all married white girls because there was little prejudice against the sons of sugar barons from the West Indies. I am emphasizing this to let English people know that there is Negroid blood running in their veins, no matter to what degree or quantity. Too many Europeans are hiding this fact.

In those days of the early nineteenth century, there was no genetic engineering, and even if there had been, the blood of slaves, as spoken by Elizabeth to be running in her veins, could not be detected differently from that of the Barretts. If indeed she had this blood, the best guess would be it was from one of the Peters boys. Now these boys were Barrett all over. Everything they were was Barrett. Maybe Elizabeth knew something others did not know. She was the confidant of her mother, and maybe, just maybe, her mother told her something unknown to the other children. Many people would like to know why after age twenty-one she began writing about her complexion and the blood of slaves when she'd begun publishing at age fourteen and never mentioned it before. I know that her father loved her very much, but did she love him that much?

When she came of age, she would not sign the name Moulton as part of her name. She signed her name as Elizabeth Barrett Barrett, and used the acronym EBB. Was this a coincidence? Historians will have to look into this. It is my intention to do so, because I think some evidence is around somewhere. I have some doubts whether my family would ever allow these records to survive. They like to burn family documents. They also like to hide information. When I was doing the investigation of the Barrett family, my cousins and uncles who knew quite a lot about the family ridiculed me and withheld vital information from me, believing I was going to write about it, which all already knew. I also had difficulty with the College of Arms at Queen Victoria Street in London. Since I was not a white Negro, the Red Dragon did not want to discuss anything with me, and so it is with most black writers. There is much information there, but since I am black, it is difficult for me to retrieve them.

Some black writers will have to depend on the goodness of white friends in order to get the necessary information. I personally found that out when I went to the College of Arms in 1989. The clerk at the desk looked up my name and found out that I had previous business there, and was shocked when I presented an American passport with a picture on it looking like me. She then went to the rear and I heard the discussion about who I was, then the instruction for her to tell me the Red Dragon had no time to see me. I then requested an appointment within the ten days I was in London, and that was unceremoniously turned down. I don't want to go any further with this because I know that the Red Dragon died long ago, and I have not yet checked again to see if I can find a reasonable person there.

Many persons who grew up in the British West Indies thought that the Englishmen who worked among them were the same as the people who lived in England. Unfortunately, this is not so. I worked under several English officers in the Jamaica Police Force prior to Independence and these were gentlemen. I later found out that they had to act as ambassadors to give England a good name, so they were handpicked for the job and were not the common Englishmen walking around the streets of London.

Elizabeth Barrett Browning is my target, so I have to be repetitious about her. The statements she made about herself are rather suspicious. She wrote her friends about how she looked, especially to one Ms. Mary Mitford. I have in my possession most of these letters. As I read them many times, the only conclusion I can arrive at is that she was dissatisfied with herself and wished she was of a purer race. She had opened up all the suspicions about her race, and made me conclude that she could be the daughter of one of George Goodin Barrett's sons, who were white Negroes and living in close proximity with her mother. These boys looked like Barretts, talked like Barretts, were brainy like Barretts, financed by Barretts, and therefore they were Barretts. They only had the name Peters as was designated to them by slavery. Did her mother tell her something that made her drop the name Moulton forever? At age twenty-one, having come of age, she did just that.

On reviewing the whole matter of interracial mix, this was the problem with many white planters. They selectively separated the good-looking mulatto girls and protected them from the other black slaves so that they could be used as mistresses of other white men coming to the West Indies to work in the place of absentee landlords. One of the reasons for doing this is when offspring are produced, most of the time when quadroons are produced, they sometimes or most of the time had the complexion of white people. These could be sent to England to be educated and brought up in England as white people born in the West Indies, and were commonly called Creoles. Many white people who worked in the hot tropical sun developed a tan reminiscent of the complexion of a mulatto. I am making these definitive statements about race because these are all my personal families. From several angles, many of my great-grandparents are Europeans.

I hope the readers will appreciate the chiastic structure of this writing. It is not a mistake. It was willfully done. I imitate old Jewish writers like Moses in the first five books of the Bible. It was written that way with the purpose of reminding readers of things of importance mentioned previously.

As I observe slavery between my black and white families, I am inclined not to be biased, but I have to be. Slavery is not my problem, but the way slaves were treated is a problem that I cannot overlook. Yes, they were forcibly taken from Africa by church people who made a fortune from them. I am not going to name the churches. That will be another book someday. If the slaves were treated like human beings, then the stigma of slavery could have been shifted from the Europeans to the tribal structures of Africa, who had to have helped the Europeans capture their brethren and had them shipped off to a strange land. When they got to this land, their names were changed to that of their captors. People should not believe that this was always the case.

Women are no different from other women except under extreme circumstances, and men are just the same. When men and women get together, multiplication will take place. In Jamaica, West Indies, there were thousands of British men working as overseers for absentee landlords. These men were without their wives on most occasions. Many women refused to leave the homeland because of one fear or another, so husbands had to leave for Jamaica alone. Many of them had housekeepers who were in fact their mistresses. When they sired children, these were not registered, but their surnames, under British tradition, was that of their mothers.

It is well known that visiting kings had children in Jamaica, but this was kept undercover. When these children grew up, they took their rightful names, especially after the abolition of slavery. Many black people in Jamaica are now complaining that they haven't got their right names because the ones they have are Europeans. Many of them have their correct names, but since they are black, they would prefer African names. Some of these complaints are correct. For example, my ancestors, the Barretts, named some of their faithful slaves after them. There were many Edward Barretts on different Barrett farms and they produced many children named Barrett who were not related to the family at all. This was the case with many other families in the West Indies. One day I was at a funeral that many of my family members attended. Some were white, and most were black or mulattoes. I was introduced to a family member I did not know by a cousin of mine who was his nephew. He had not yet heard my name when he told me that sometimes people claimed to be relatives when in fact they had only taken the name of their slave masters. I immediately told him my name and said, "We haven't got the same name, and my grandfather Peter Bonnick is much whiter than you are. And I know you have heard of him, because he is very closely related to your father." He quickly apologized and said he did not mean it that way. I then gave him a history lesson on the family, and he apologized further. We became friends when he found out that I was much more educated than he was. This story can be repeated all over Jamaica in most families.

One day, I was at the record office in Spanish Town going through the Barrett family record when I came upon dozens of Barretts born in Accompong, in the parish of St. Elizabeth. I was shocked at the discovery. And when I investigated further, I discovered that one of the Maroons in the days of slavery worked on the Barrett estate and took on the name Barrett, and from then on a host of Ashanti Barretts were produced in Accompong. You never know what you will find when researching genealogy.

Based on the make-up of the Jamaican population, no matter how dark a complexion they have, European genes are intermixed. The same goes for many white people there who think that they are so European that they cannot associate with other people. All that has to be done is a gene check, and many people will find out how black or white they are. There are many black people in the western hemisphere who are over 50 percent white genetically. This brings me to the conclusion that racism is taught and is not an innate disposition.

Elizabeth Barrett Browning could not have thought that the man who helped to heal her was a man in whom the tar brush passed nearby. Here was a man who had the blood of slaves, which she abhorred in such a way that she became almost deluded. And this man captivated her in such a way that she fled from the home of her father and siblings to go to a place she'd only heard of. There must have been some unknown supernatural force working in and out of her. The evidence available did not suggest that she knew her father had spied on him and found out that he was Negroid. Her father seemed not to have showed it to anyone except George Goodin Moulton-Barrett, his son, who was a barrister-at-law and who redrafted his will to omit Elizabeth first, then Henrietta, and lastly Alfred, all three for marrying during their father's lifetime. How her father kept this secret from so many children, I do not know. Modern-day children would have found out. The question is, had she found out who Robert was, would she still have eloped with him? Or suppose she found out, were there overriding influences from Robert that captivated her more than her hatred of the blood of slaves? These questions I cannot answer, so I will just believe that she did not know.

The name Tittle seemed to be extinct. The author knows Jamaica very well, and he has not come across that name, nor has he found anyone in the United States with this name. It was originally British Jew, but when his forbears arrived in Jamaica prior to the 1692 Port Royal earthquake, he probably looked just like another Englishman. This was Robert Browning the poet's third great-great-great-grandfather. He lived on Jew Street in Port Royal, and was apprenticed to Henry Wayte, the cordwainer of Port Royal. After its destruction, Edward Tittle moved with many of the Barretts to Liguanea, and settled in the village of Half Way Tree. A cordwainer is a person who manufactures leather goods to include books and shoes. He is not only a shoemaker. I know the exact spot on Eastwood Park Road, near the junction of Molynes Road where both Edward Tittle and Hersey Barrett did business on opposite sides of the road. Hersey had a general store, and Edward had a leather store. Little did they know that their descendants would be in the greatest elopement recorded a few hundred years later.

As I researched that coincidence, I found out that there were many similar stories, but because the people engaged in them were not rich or popular, these great stories remained unpublished. This is what I would like to do if time permits.

We have in the family of the Tittles the same kind of miscegenation that went on in the Barrett and other British families. Edward Tittle had a son by the name of John whom he had with a slave woman on his farm at Half Way Tree. This boy grew up as a house slave and carried the last name Tittle. From all inclinations, this lad could be called a white Negro. As far as my research goes, there was no birth certificate for him in Spanish Town. It was the custom for slaves born in Jamaica at that time to not be registered but recorded in a property book, such as the one Edward Barrett of Cinnamon Hill kept. This boy, whose name was John, did not grow up as a slave per se, but was tutored at home like the rest of Tittles' white children. Because of Jewish discrimination, the Tittle family grew up as Anglicans, and did not appear Jewish or practice the religion, so all other British people on the island just considered them as regular white people. As this boy John grew up, no one thought he would become famous and be the great-great-grandfather of the poet Robert Browning. John also knew and did business with the ancestors of Elizabeth Barrett, who would become Robert's wife. There are many such coincidences in the ancient Jamaican aristocracy, but few, if any, will create such an impact as Robert and Elizabeth's. It is presumed that John Tittle got a good education even though he was not in the wills of his father and his stepmother. His father died before her, and as far as they were concerned, John did not exist.

Prior to the death of his father, John was articled to the Reverend William May, the rector of Kingston, to be a clerk in holy orders. This is the training period to become an Anglican minister. This William May was not a poor man. He was one of the largest slave owners in the parishes of Clarendon and Vere, and he had a large and extensive cattle farm. It was his old property by the name of May Pen that became the capital of the new parish of Clarendon, which incorporated the parish of Vere when Sir John Peter Grant reduced the twenty-two parishes to fourteen. Chapleton was the capital of Clarendon, and Alley was the capital of Vere. There was a dispute among the representatives of both parishes regarding which of the two towns should be the new parish capital. A compromise was made and William May's property became the new capital.

John was the protégé of this very rich pastor for many years, and when he took the examination to become a pastor, he came through in excellent fashion. This young man was now a problem in Jamaica because the white plantocracy would not accept him as a minister. He was not white enough. A few years later, he got a call to go to St. Kitts where there was a vacancy. The people accepted him there for a while until the wealthy English landlords found out that the tar brush passed nearby. John, in the meantime, was acquiring properties in St. Kitts. Where he got the money, we do not know, but he became a partially wealthy man. His greatest exploit there was to capture the love of the only daughter of the wealthiest man on the island. He was Dr. George Strachan, a medical practitioner. By marrying Margaret Strachan, John began to acquire more properties, more slaves, and got into more lawsuits. Everywhere he bought lands, the white people opposed him, until he left St. Kitts with his wife and went back to Jamaica.

One of the reasons why he left was he had earned enough money to go anywhere. His father-in-law died suddenly from a heart attack shortly after Margaret married a white Negro. Dr. George Strachan and his colleagues on the island of St. Kitts had a proclivity toward hating Negroes, so when his daughter fell in love with one who had the tar brush passing nearby, he took it to heart and did not recover. His only son also did not like his sister to be married to this man. And since his father's properties were left to his two children, a separation of the properties began, and many white people began to lay claim to some of the properties that were not theirs. Many lawsuits arose, and even though John Tittle and his wife were successful, they both decided to sell the disputed ones and left for Jamaica. They had other properties they left under the care of overseers, and both became absentee landlords.

On their arrival in Jamaica, they acquired more properties, and it was there that Margaret Strachan gave birth to a baby girl whom they named Margaret Tittle. This Creole quadroon passed for white. And since she was born in a hot climate and her parents had money, no one cared about how much Negro genes were involved. They went about their business as white people owning slaves. There is no record of his brother treating him as equal or whether they had any altercation at all. They seemed to have lived as strangers. There is also no record of the Reverend John Tittle pastoring any church in Kingston or St. Andrew. What we do know is that his mentor William May had passed on.

Having not many friends in his native land, it is deemed that John migrated to England based on the fact that his teenager daughter showed up there in school, somewhere around London, where the Browning families were well established. It was in school that Margaret Tittle met a Robert Browning and got married to him. There is no record of her parents taking part in her life again, except that on a later occasion it was found out that her father's estate in St. Kitts had been left to her. We presume that John Tittle made a will and left his properties in St. Kitts to his only child. Based upon the painting of Margaret Tittle Browning that I saw, she was most beautiful and delectable to behold. She had three children, Robert, Margaret, and William. This Robert was the father of the poet Robert Browning. There were so many Roberts in the family that each will have to be identified.

It was Margaret Tittle Browning's son Robert who inherited her St. Kitts estates. He had a rude awakening there when he went on visit as an absentee landlord. According to the book by Vivienne Browning, *My Browning Family Album*, after Margaret Tittle died in 1789, Robert, the grandfather of the poet, got married again, this time to a nineteen-year-old girl named Jane Smith, and produced nine more children. He wanted Margaret's son Robert to be away in St. Kitts so that he could play around with his young wife, who was younger than his son. So he sent Robert to St. Kitts to look about his mother's slave plantations. The awakening he had was during a visit to his grandfather John Tittle's church, where he sat in the wrong seat. He was told by the white church warden that those seats belonged to white people, so he should sit at the back reserved for freed blacks and mulattoes. He went ballistic at the request and he left the church quite angry—who wouldn't? Here is an Englishman being called a mulatto. Now we know that the genes of John Tittle have passed down to his grandson.

Robert's anger was so great that when he arrived back in England the whole order of the Rosicrucians had to be brought into play before this white Negroid could be calmed. He demanded from his father who his mother was, and all his father told him was that she was a Creole from the West Indies, and she was one of the most beautiful women he had seen. Now a Creole, according to Europeans, was a European born in the Western Hemisphere. Nowhere in this definition is anything about being Negroid. Well, the story did not stop there. The properties in St. Kitts were sold, and as far as is known, no other member of the Browning family ever went to the West Indies. This is not the only famous family to have come out of the West Indies and made a great impact upon England. The Gladstone family also did, as well as some of the Spencers.

As a historian, I look back with a certain amount of pride on how these two that are the topic of this book once trod the ground with which I am very familiar. I consider how they grew up just as I did, played on the same streets I patrolled, and did everything as I did, only in a slightly different manner. They were rich and I was poor. They owned animal-drawn carriages and used kerosene lamps and candles, while I drove motor cars and had electric lights. As a boy, I rode donkeys and used kerosene lamps made of tin, while my ancient relatives who had much more wealth than me but none of the modern conveniences I had. They had all the wealth, but not more fun.

The irony of the whole situation in examining the Barretts and the Brownings who would later become one family is that Elizabeth was complaining of her dark complexion, for which I am not sure she had the evidence. While Robert, who must have had the evidence from his father, did not complain about any blood of slaves he had. He did not complain of any hard times he had as a result of having Negroid blood. What it did to him was some wealth he did not have.

Many people thought Elizabeth was poor when she left her father's house. She was not. Her uncle Samuel Barrett Moulton-Barrett left a tidy sum for her in his will. Her grandmother Elizabeth also left her a good sum. She also had an unmarried cousin, a Jamaican sugar baron named John Kenyon, who helped her out. He was also a close friend of Robert Browning the poet.

Another set of ironies seemed to have developed in Robert's father's mind. Since he was called a mulatto in St. Kitts and no one told him enough about his mother, he made sure he married a German lady named Sara Ann Wiedemann, ten years older than himself. While his father married a second wife who was aged nineteen, and twenty-six years his junior, the son married one much older. These two men did the opposite of each other, as related by Vivienne Browning. Now Robert the poet also followed his father and married Elizabeth, four years his senior. I cannot see anything wrong with these age differences because to each his own.

When both Elizabeth and Robert died, they left behind one son named Robert Wiedemann Barrett Browning, and he owned a monstrous building in the city of Asolo, Italy. A poor man could not have owned that building, and he had some difficulty with maintaining it the way he wanted, so he sold the love letters of Robert and Elizabeth for a large ransom. He died a wealthy man in Italy where he was born, and this ended the consecutive Robert Brownings because he had no recorded children. Rumor has it that he had two illegitimate girls from a Frenchwoman, but no one has heard of them since his death.

It probably never came to the mind of the poet's father that the German lady he married was a Jew. He was only concerned that people thought he was a mulatto in St. Kitts. Had he traced back his ancestors, he would have found out that his mother, Margaret Tittle Browning, apart from having Negroid blood, also had Jewish blood from her father John, whose father Edward Tittle was descended from the Jews at Jew Street in Port Royal before it was destroyed by the earthquake in 1692. Edward then left for Half Way Tree, where he set up business.

Many people are concerned over mixed blood, but all the people of the world are just that. According to the Scriptures, we are all made of one blood to dwell upon the earth. Now that genetic engineering is proving everyone the same, it is time people stopped being overly concerned about who they are and try to make the best out of life. All people become sick, and all people die.

There were, and still are, many prodigies in the family of the Barretts. The first recorded one was George Goodin Barrett, the son of Edward Barrett of Cinnamon Hill, the fifth descendant of Barretts from 1655 who took Jamaica from Spain and made it into a British colony. This boy matriculated at age fourteen at Oxford University and graduated at age eighteen, read law at the Inns of Court, and became a full-fledged barrister-at-law. I am repeating this young fellow's name because he is the one who ran his father's larger properties and slaves in a legal and systematic way to increase the wealth of the family. He is also one of those who would not get married, but he produced many sons with Elissa Peters, several of whom went to England to study under the care and protection of John Graham-Clarke at Newcastle-upon-Tyne.

George's first son was Thomas Peters, and he was a contemporary of John's first daughter, Mary Graham-Clarke. Thomas Peters was a real Barrett who passed for white even though he was a quadroon. There were four other siblings with him with the last name Peters. They were all boys. All these were produced by a prodigy. All these had the blood of slaves. All these lived in close proximity to Mary. The genes of prodigies run in a family, and since all descended from a prodigy, even if they were not themselves prodigies, any one of them could have produced prodigies. By writing all of this, I want to show a correlation with what could have happened to two white persons allegedly producing someone of dark complexion.

Elizabeth Barrett Moulton Barrett was born about nine months, twenty days after the marriage of her mother Mary Graham-Clarke to Edward Barrett Moulton-Barrett. This suggested that there was no interference from a third party. Many third parties were living at the same place simultaneously. In those days, people did the same things as they do now. We are not trickier or smarter than they were. We have no new sin on earth since the time of Noah and the flood. We cannot fool ourselves by thinking people were more decent. When it comes to adulterous relationships, those old-time people were just as smart.

Elizabeth, even though she did not go to a traditional school as the boys did, was also herself a prodigy. Most of the time, it takes a prodigy to produce another. With private tutors, she was able to produce, at age fourteen, a book of poems entitled the *Battle of Marathon*. Women were not well recognized in Europe as writers in those days, unless they were exceptional. She got hers published in her name. Even the famous French writer, a contemporary of Elizabeth, had to publish her great writings under a male pseudonym, George Sand. Many people thought that this writer was a man, so her work was published all over Europe without people knowing she was female. The publishing of this book by Elizabeth showed signs of being a genius, which was hardly present in the Moulton family, and none of her siblings ever showed such brilliance. The possibilities exist that something is funny. Of the twelve children of Edward Barrett Moulton-Barrett and Mary Graham-Clarke, only one was a prodigy and only one had dark complexion, and this was Elizabeth. The readers will have to think for themselves.

Fifty Wimpole Street is a place that will be in the minds of people forever. It was here that Elizabeth found out that she could love another of the opposite sex with a view of becoming one flesh. It was here that she considered she might have within her veins the blood of slaves. She did not believe her present father or mother had it, so who could it have been? It was here that she abandoned her beloved father as she knew him, and decided to flee with another man who had the blood of slaves. There is no evidence that she knew this, but her father had the documents that the tar brush passed nearby Robert. From the evidence we have, she still loved the father who cared for her, but there was something more than paternal love. Erotic love had to have its place, and this was suppressed by her to keep paternal love in place. When one form of love supercedes the other, the one that is dominant will take over, and this was the case with Elizabeth. She had no choice. She could no longer suppress what was dominant, so she succumbed to the greater force. We may say all that we want about her, but she did what she wanted to do.

When she arrived in Italy and decided she would make it her home, the die was cast and she would continue her profession there. And it was there that she wrote the best of her poetry. She established herself in Florence, where she met many Americans of her profession, and succeeded as well as she would have had she stayed in England. Her health improved to a point where she traveled frequently to France and other places. And in 1849, she gave birth to a son who would survive her. She had two miscarriages before, but with the help of more modern physicians, she was able to go nine months with this pregnancy. She was also able to get off the dangerous drugs and home remedies she was addicted to in England, such as morphine and heroine. These were given to her by no ordinary doctor but one who was physician to Queen Victoria. His name was Dr. William Frederick Chambers. The home remedies given to her by her father included donkey milk and a tankard of porter daily for many years.

When her son was born, she gave him the name Robert Wiedemann Barrett Browning, thus continuing the name Robert through many generations. She brought him up as English, but he took on the role of an Italian and lived that way until he died in 1912, having reached the age of sixty-two, seven years longer than his mother, who died when he was eleven. It is presumed that she told him the story of her father Edward who would not reply to any of her nine letters she wrote him from Italy asking for forgiveness for her elopement and marrying a man who was too poor to marry Mr. Barrett's daughter and had a touch of the tar brush. Since no one knew what was written in these letters, it is difficult to clearly state what was in them, but from experience, since I have similar letters in my possession written to her brother George Goodin Moulton Barrett, who was the caretaker of the shares she had in the same investment with her father, I made the deduction that the letters of forgiveness written to her brother were similar to those nine letters she wrote to her father, who gave them back to her husband Robert when he visited fifty Wimpole Street some years after the elopement.

The fame that Elizabeth got while in Florence was sufficient for the English people to recognize her work and give her some recognition. When Robert died, he was buried in Westminster Abbey, in a section called "Poets' Corner." Since Elizabeth wrote more poetry than he did, it would have been nice if the British government had removed her body and placed it beside her husband. This is believed to be a poetic mistake, and it is not late for the Society of Antiquaries to rectify this ignoble situation. The British government would make a lot of money if both writers were resting in that famous abbey. When I visited Westminster Abbey in 1989, I went to Poets' Corner and saw the lonesome tombstone of Robert Browning. I inquired of the caretaker why the British government did not request the removal of Elizabeth's remains to the Abbey beside her husband, and he said something to the effect that she had not been patriotic enough. I have often said before that patriotism is a form of arrogance, and I will be repeating this from time to time. What she was unpatriotic about was slavery. Sometimes in her writing she wrote about the evils of slavery, even though she was an absentee slave owner herself. If this is the reason, it is time that the British government set aside their simplemindedness and do the right thing. A very good gesture would be to bring her body home to England. This is the home of the Barretts historically and politically.

We have heard very little of *Pinkie*. This is the famous painting of Sir Thomas Lawrence that the Woolworth Company bought the rights to, and it became the celebrated postcard picture for more than a century. The Jamaican government should use this portrait as an advertisement for the tourist industry. The house where she was born at Cinnamon Hill overlooking the sea around Montego Bay and Rose Hall property should be a government museum, and not owned by any private person. This would be great advertisement and a marvelous tourist attraction in a wonderful tourist area. I wonder where the historians of Jamaica are and why this has not been done. These important historical facts should also be taught in the schools and colleges. Where are the marketing specialists for the tourist industry? Cinnamon Hill is a much more important place for tourism than some of the places they are trying to utilize. If the government does not own the property, then it should recommend its owners to use it as a tourist attraction.

The importance of the Barretts on the north coast should not be overlooked. Beginning with Cinnamon Hill, many Barretts of worldwide importance emerged to take their places all over the world. Even though he came from the south coast, Dutton Barrett was a governor of Barbados. People like Richard Barrett, three times speaker of the House of Assembly, was born in London but his father Samuel Goodin Barrett was born at Cinnamon Hill, and Richard returned to Jamaica to build Greenwood Great House in 1809. He was also a prodigy like his uncle George before. They all matriculated at age fourteen and became full-fledged barristers-at-law by age twenty. He was so brilliant that the slave owners selected him to represent them at the House of Commons during the debate of slavery in 1834. He represented them in such a way that the British government decided to give them over £20,000,000 as compensation for freeing the slaves. Some slave owners became wealthier as a result of the money they got to free their slaves than while owning them. The owners also sold their properties, and with these monies they went back to England and lived happily ever after. Richard was also custos of St. James simultaneous with two other Barretts from Cinnamon Hill who were the respective custodes of St. Ann and Trelawny. There had never been a time, and never has been since, when three members of one family were the custodes of three adjacent parishes at the same time. It was very unfortunate that Richard lost his life in a tavern in Montego Bay, where it seemed someone rigged his liquor. The family would not allow any postmortem, so officially no one knew how he died. He was buried at Cinnamon Hill Cemetery. It is of significant note that most Richards in the Barrett family died under tragic and suspicious circumstances. They remind me of the British royal family and the name "Charles." Charles I was beheaded, Charles II abdicated and fled the country, Bonnie Prince Charles died mysteriously, and Charles, Prince of Wales, with Princess Diana is another story in the twenty-first century.

When the Sam Sharpe Uprising took place in December 1831, by January 1832 the Colonial Church Union was formed, made up of church leaders who owned slaves, and planters whose properties were torched. The Barretts' properties were not torched. Their black *bushas* who were promoted slaves organized the slaves on their properties and would not allow the rebels to burn them. On these Barrett properties were schools and churches established to teach slaves to read and to Christianize them. Many of these slaves could read and were even deacons in their respective churches. Preachers such as Hope Waddell from Scotland and his wife were the teacher and preacher to the slaves, and were paid to do so by the Barrett family. The Church Union was specifically set up to destroy churches that taught slaves to read and qualified them to be overseers of their masters' properties. The Barretts had no problem teaching and promoting slaves, hence their properties were protected by their slaves instead of being torched. The antislavery ministers were burned out by the Church Union leaders, and these acted similarly to the United States KKK against black people. They were as aggressive as and more vicious than the KKK, and these were the leaders and ministers of churches. The only difference was they owned slaves. They linked up with the militia, and when suspected slaves in the uprising were caught, they were handed over to the Church Union, who hanged them before they were tried. From the Church Union came the judges, the jury, and the hangmen. All were active members of the slave-holding churches who every Sunday preached about Jesus Christ. This hypocrisy could not be defined by anyone except Satan himself. The same Christians who preached on Sundays were out looking for slaves on Monday to murder them.

Most of the north coast ministers who were in the antislavery movement had to flee to Kingston and other places. The Union also tried to label members of the Barrett family as rebels, but was afraid to touch them. They had too many slaves and too many Barretts to deal with, so they murmured and kept quiet. There were also too many Barretts in the militia at that time who were trained by the British to use firearms. It seemed strange that Rosehall and Palmyra were adjoining estates to many Barretts, and their two estates owned by the White Witch of Rose Hall were razed to the ground while all Barrett properties were untouched. It was the same uprising that killed the witch Annie Palmer. Many people are saying that the witch was just fiction, but they only had to read the history of the Barretts at Cinnamon Hill to find out that it was Samuel Moulton-Barrett, the former member of Parliament from England, who ordered his slaves to have her buried.

Even though there was much racism at Cinnamon Hill, there was also much integration. It was the integration members who when they died caused Edward Barrett to remove those two doors on rooms occupied by his two sons who loved to mix with mulattoes and quadroons. He concreted up the doorways but left the two windows through which one can climb up to see inside both rooms. When this author went there in 1987, he climbed up on a chair and looked inside both rooms. They were empty, and there were no doors or entrance to the outside, or anywhere for that matter. I heard this story from the family, which was passed down through many generations. So when Peter Bonnick spoke about his ancestors and acted as they did, one can look back at history and imagine one was there when these things happened.

This Church Union that took over the execution of the slaves after the 1831 uprising was not much worse than the churches in Europe, which were the headquarters of the local churches in the Caribbean. These European churches were the owners of most slaves anywhere. They ran the barricades of West Africa, and these churches sold more human beings than any other group. Even though there were other European churches such as the Quakers and Presbyterians that were against slavery, the largest churches were slave traders. The Barretts were also the greatest family of slave traders, but the younger generations of the family established ways of treating their slaves much better than other Europeans did. I personally am happy that there was some semblance of decency among my ancestors, who allowed many of their slaves to buy their freedom in those difficult times, even though a slave was still a slave. In comparison to the other slave owners, the Barrett family had nothing to be ashamed of in their treatment of slaves.

When the Church Union was finished with the execution of slaves in 1832, they began to burn down the houses of ministers who were helping the slaves to survive the most inhuman treatment ever administered to innocent human beings. These people went to church every Sunday to praise a God who said, "Love your enemies, do good to them that hate you, and pray for those who spitefully use you and persecute you, that you may be the children of you Father who is in heaven" (Matthew 5). What hypocrisy.

In closing this book on a glimpse of the Barrett family through whom Elizabeth Barrett Browning and the author came, I would be remiss not to say that this family produced some of the greatest military leaders of England, many prodigies, and many wineheads. Some of the prodigies were wineheads, and others were brilliant lawyers. It is with much difficulty that I have to mention one of Elizabeth's brothers, Septimus, who ruined the Moulton-Barretts' fortune. It was a good thing that most of them were on sound economic foundation; otherwise, the family would have been reduced to poverty. He drank so much liquor and ran up so much debt that his brother had to sell Cinnamon Hill, the beloved ancestral home, and two other properties to keep him out of debtor's jail. When he died, this brother, Charles John, was relieved of the problem. And even though he was not poor, he had to adjust his way of life because of Septimus. I had to write this because the Bonnicks from St. Elizabeth, who are descended from these Barretts, have a great percentage of wineheads in the family. All around one can see them. I am still dismayed at the number, and many younger Barretts have also joined the winehead company. The shock to me is it's not only males. The females also love their liquor. What a travesty.

I will now conclude with what made my ancestor Hersey Barrett famous. He claimed, and many others have supported him, that he was the axeman who chopped off King Charles I's head. Based upon what I have seen historically, it is possible that he did it. On record, there is no reference of him. The official hangman was there, but no eyewitness said he did it. The story I am advancing is that a hooded man other than those present came up and did the job for the hangman Richard Brandon. William Tegg, on page 112 of his book *The Trial of Charles I*, stated that there was another man there named Ralph Jones. They were all hooded, so no one knows for sure who did the execution. A man named Joyce and another called Hugh Peters were also suspected of inflicting the blow that severed the king's head. They were also present and were hooded. In her book *The Trial of Charles I*, C. V. Wedgewood said that there were many suspects who could have inflicted the final blow, and no one knows for sure who did it.

Hersey Barrett and many others said that he did it when a dispute arose among the soldiers of whom he was a lieutenant, about whether they should kill the king. They believed that he was a king by divine right and no one should kill him. It was then that he hooded himself and did the job without anyone at the time knowing. This was the reason given by him why he packed up his family and joined the expedition of Penn and Venables in 1655. He decided to settle down wherever country the British captured from the Spaniards. He had no hope of ever returning to England, because he thought Charles' son, in protective custody of Spain, would return as Charles II and take revenge upon the enemies of his father. That was exactly what happened.

We do know, however, that after the Restoration in 1660 Charles II gave Hersey Barrett crown land in Jamaica when all the known regicides were either executed or had fled the country. We also have no information of Hersey Barrett being present at the king's trial, but we know he was an officer in Cromwell's Red Coat Army. We also know that after the departure of King Charles II from the throne of England, the name Hersey Barrett appeared in history as the man who severed the king's head and no more action could be taken against him. His family should not be ashamed of this, because in a revolution, the leader of the defeated party always lost his head.

Be that as it may, the Barrett family is a very interesting one, and I hope someday to write more about this illustrious family and trace their connection back to Ensign Barrett, who came from Normandy with William the Conqueror, and to find out how French he was or how Viking he was. Since I am also descended from another French family, Montique, I would also like to know more about Barretts and their original family names from the Vikings. May someone much younger do this for me. I will be happy when this is done.

Bibliography

1. J. Marks: The Family of the Barrett
2. V. Browning: My Browning Family Album
3. Kelly & Hudson: Diary By E.B.B.
4. Landis: Letters of the Brownings to George Barrett
5. McCarthy: Elizabeth Barrett to Mr. Boyd
6. Betty Miller: Elizabeth Barrett to Miss Mitford
7. Heydon & Kelley: E.B.B. Letters to Mrs. David Ogilvy
8. Julia Markus: Dared and Done
9. Dormer Creston: Andromeda in Wimpole Street
10. Boas: Elizabeth Barrett-Browning
11. Crowell: Robert Browning
12. Betty Miller: Robert Browning

Elizabeth

Cinnamon Hill (old part of house), 1987

Cinnamon Hill (back part), 1987

Water jug, Cinnamon Hills, 1987

Author at Johnny Cash's dining table at Cinnamon Hill, 1987

New section at rear that was put on about 1868 (Cinnamon Hill).
This has two rooms without doors on the ground floor.

Printed in Great Britain
by Amazon